TRAVEL CHARME
Fürstenhaus Am Achensee

Travel Charme Pertisau GmbH
Pertisau Nr. 63
A-6213 Pertisau am Achensee
Tel.: +43 (0) 52 43 / 54 42 - 0
www.travelcharme.com

TRAVEL CHARME

„Ein Buch ist wie ein Garten,
den man in sich trägt."
arabisches Sprichwort

Danke für
den pfleglichen Umgang.
Auf dieses Buch freuen sich
auch weitere Gäste.

Ihre Gastgeber vom
Travel Charme Fürstenhaus Am Achensee
Tirol

DIPLOMATIC MOVES

To the Munros
with love
Sally
April 1995

DIPLOMATIC MOVES
Life in the Foreign Service

Sally James

The Radcliffe Press
London · New York

Published in 1995 by
The Radcliffe Press
45 Bloomsbury Square
London WC1A 2HY

175 Fifth Avenue
New York
NY 10010

In the United States of America
and Canada distributed by
St Martin's Press
175 Fifth Avenue
New York
NY 10010

A full CIP record for this book is available from the British Library

Library of Congress Catalog card number: 94–61510

A full CIP record is available from the Library of Congress

ISBN 1–85043–924–9

Copy-edited and laser-set by Selro Publishing Services, Oxford
Printed and bound in Great Britain by WBC Ltd, Bridgend, Mid Glamorgan

TO MICHAEL
WHO SHARES THE MEMORIES

Contents

Illustrations

Acronyms

B & B	bed and breakfast
BBC	British Broadcasting Corporation
BDSA	British Diplomatic Spouses' Association
BP	British Petroleum
BWIA	British West Indian Airways
CARICOM	Caribbean Community and Common Market
CARIFTA	Caribbean Free Trade Association
BOAC	British Overseas Airways Corporation
C of E	Church of England
CD	*Corps Diplomatique* (Diplomatic Corps)
CE	common entrance
Cento	Central Treaty Organization
CFA	*Communauté Financière d'Afrique* (African Financial Community)
DHC	Deputy High Commissioner
DSWA	Diplomatic Service Wives' Association
ECAFE	Economic Committee for Asia and the Far East
EEC	European Economic Community (the Common Market)
FCO	Foreign and Commonwealth Office
FO	Foreign Office
GEC	General Electric Company
GLC	Greater London Council
HMS	Her Majesty's Ship
IMF	International Monetary Fund
IRA	Irish Republican Army
IUD	inter-uterine device
IVP	intra-venous pylogram

KLM	*Koninklijke Luchtvaart Maatschappij NV* (Royal Dutch Air Lines)
MP	Member of Parliament
MRT	Mass Rapid Transport
NATO	North Atlantic Treaty Organization
NZBC	New Zealand Broadcasting Corporation
ODA	Overseas Development Administration
PM	Prime Minister
PNDC	People's National Defence Council
PPP	People's Progressive Party
RAF	Royal Air Force
RIBA	Royal Institute of British Architects
SAS	Special Air Service
SBC	Singapore Broadcasting Corporation
SLFP	Sri Lanka Freedom Party
SSC	Sinhalese Sports Club
TEFL	Teaching English as a Foreign Language
UAR	United Arab Republic
UDI	Unilateral Declaration of Independence
UK	United Kingdom
UN	United Nations
UNCTAD	United Nations Committee on Trade and Development
UNP	United National Party
USAID	United States Agency for International Development
VJ	Victory over Japan
VIP	very important person
YWCA	Young Women's Christian Association

Glossary

amah	maidservant
asantahene	chief of the Ashanti tribe
dagaba	Buddhist monument
dolmus	taxi
durbar	ceremonial occasion when chiefs receive homage from their subjects
eskijee	rag-and-bone man
jamahiriya	network of local and regional people's committees in Libya — has ideological connotations
kapici	caretaker
mahanayake	Buddhist equivalent of an archbishop
palazzo	palace
Perahera	annual festival at the Temple of the Tooth
poya	Buddhist holy day
satyagraha	civil disobedience
stupa	Indian word for *dagaba*
Thai Pongal	Hindu festival
tjanting	pen-like instrument used for making batik
wee	Indian hemp

Acknowledgements

I am very grateful to my parents, Heward and Helen Bell, for keeping these letters safely for me, to the BDSA for their help and advice and to Gun Pieris and Kaminée de Soysa who jogged my memory of our time in Sri Lanka. Also I would like to express my appreciation to Dr Lester Crook for his invaluable guidance through the publishing process and to Anthony Kirk-Greene and Selina Cohen for their suggestions and corrections.

Finally I want to thank my family and friends, notably Sir Robin Butler, for all their moral support and encouragement.

Foreword
by
Sir Robin Butler

I have no right to offer a preface to these delightful letters. I am not a member of the Diplomatic Service and I have never served the government abroad. When Sally James asked me to write a foreword, nonetheless I found myself wanting very much to agree and I justified it to myself on two grounds.

The first is long acquaintance. My friendship with Sally and her husband, Michael, stretches back over all the years covered by these letters and before. I first met Michael when I played rugby against him for the Oxford Greyhounds against the Cambridge LX Club in 1958. Michael was already known to me because he had made a century before lunch for Cambridge against the 1956 Australians, including Lindwall and Miller. I did not see this innings but I had read about it and, after Bannister's four-minute mile, I regarded it as one of the great university sporting achievements of my era.

If that had been the limits of our acquaintance I would not have forgotten it. But, after a brief spell at Cranleigh, Michael came to teach at Harrow, where I lived. We then shared a good deal of sport together — squash, golf and tennis as well as cricket and rugby. Michael was always politely uncomprehending about why I found these activities so difficult when he found them so easy — 'Why did you hit the ball into the woods,' he said to me one day at Worplesdon, 'when it's so much less trouble to hit it onto the green?'

This was the time at which he and Sally decided to take the plunge into diplomatic life, as I was joining the Home Civil Service. Michael and I next found ourselves together when he was resident clerk in the Commonwealth Relations Office and I was starting in the Treasury. We lunched every day together in the canteen and played indoor cricket in the corridor of the resident clerk's flat.

Then Michael and Sally went abroad and the period covered by these letters began. Because I only saw them when they were at home, I played no part in the events recorded in this book. Reading the letters below is for me like *Rosencrantz and Guildenstern are Dead* — what was going on when the characters were off the stage?

I only make one appearance, and that was when Margaret Thatcher paid a prime ministerial visit to Singapore in 1984 with me in tow as her private secretary. Michael, as Deputy High Commissioner, was fielding the fast balls for a High Commissioner whose relationship with the Prime Minister was not the happiest.

That brings me to my second justification for writing this foreword. Although I have never been a member of the Diplomatic Service I have visited many of our overseas posts and have been picked up, dusted down, briefed and sent into action by those serving in them. This gives me the opportunity to pay my small tribute to the diplomats and their spouses who play such a heroic role representing their country abroad, far from home and family and often in conditions far from ideal.

The letters in the pages below bring out vividly, frankly and with a complete absence of side the loyalty, the endurance, the devotion and the trials of those who serve Britain in this way.

Sally has a clear eye and a warm, lively style. Her letters tell it how it is, with a complete absence of affectation. No wonder — she was writing to her parents a plain story of the ups and downs of diplomatic life. It is one of those books which, once I took it up, I found hard to put down: I always wanted to know what happens next. I am sure that other readers will find the same.

Introduction

All places that the eye of Heaven visits
Are to a wise man ports and happy havens.
Teach thy necessity to reason thus:
There is no virtue like necessity.

(John of Gaunt, *Richard the Second*
by William Shakespeare)

A casual conversation with a babysitter one evening in 1962 when my husband, Michael, and I arrived home from the cinema transformed our lives. Our babysitter started telling us all about diplomatic life and the more he told us about it the more exciting it sounded. Michael was 27, had been a schoolmaster at Harrow for two years and was then teaching at Cranleigh, and if he wanted to take the Foreign Office and Commonwealth Relations Office exams, which had an upper age limit of 28, he had to act fast. He did, and after several months of exams and interviews was accepted by the Commonwealth Relations Office in 1963. At that time the Foreign Office and the Commonwealth Relations Office were run separately until 1965 when they were merged into the Foreign and Commonwealth Office.

From 1963 until 1989 we had seven overseas postings — in New Zealand, Ceylon or Sri Lanka, Guyana, Turkey, Ghana, Singapore and Barbados. During our first postings in New Zealand and Ceylon in the 1960s letters were our main communication with home; telephone contact with the family was a treat only on rare occasions, perhaps a Christmas Day call. This situation continued in the 1970s with postings in Guyana and Turkey and in the early 1980s, when we were in Ghana, an overloaded and broken down service meant that it was very difficult to make calls. It was only in our last two postings, in Singapore and Barbados, that telephone communications were good, but by then the letter writing habit had become deeply ingrained.

These letters have served a dual purpose in that they are also diaries, the only diaries we have. Without them we would have no written record of our diplomatic life, and memories get very blurred over the years. They cover personal and social details and my observations about the country in question, but they are subjective and I make no claims to being an expert on world affairs.

Occasionally, particularly in the earlier letters, the language I use may give the impression of a haughty *memsahib*. I hope not, but terms such as 'underdeveloped', 'third world' and 'boy' were accepted and used commonly in the 1960s and 1970s when people were less sensitive about 'political correctness'. I do not want these expressions to mislead readers about our lifestyle.

The letters I have drawn on are written to my parents, with one or two exceptions to our children. When I first looked through the cases of letters my mother had carefully stored away I had no intention of writing a book. But, with encouragement from others, I thought the letters gave an overall picture of diplomatic life which, with its pleasures, problems and wide range of experiences, was worth recording.

I also hope they throw some light on the attitude of wives towards overseas service, which has changed tremendously since we joined in 1962. In the early days wives usually expected automatically to follow their husbands wherever they went, with no queries about their own careers. Indeed being a diplomat's wife was regarded as a career in itself. They accepted almost without question that their role was to support their husband and the Embassy or High Commission, and perhaps to occupy themselves with voluntary social work. If a wife wanted to take on paid work while overseas she had to ask permission from the head of post and this was not always given.

But since the 1970s things have been changing. Wives, or spouses as they are now called to include husbands accompanying their wives, who previously felt their contributions were unappreciated by the Diplomatic Service have increasingly been making their feelings known. The DSWA (Diplomatic Service Wives' Association), which became the BDSA (British Diplomatic Spouses' Association) in 1991, is the organization through which their views are represented. There is now help for spouses who wish to work overseas. Various courses, including TEFL (Teaching English as a Foreign Language), which I took before our Singapore posting, can now be financed by the Diplomatic Administration Spouse Sponsorship Scheme. It is no longer necessary to ask the head of post's permission to work, though it is still customary to inform him of the intention. Spouses' views on forthcoming postings are, we are told, taken into account by the administration. In 1989 the administration agreed to allow spouses to claim for time and expenses incurred on official entertainment. And, about 15 years ago, the Foreign Office started to pay for three fares a year for schoolchildren.

Diplomatic life can be lonely. Other than with one's colleagues, it is difficult to be frank and open, for we have to be 'diplomatic' with the friends and acquaintances we make overseas. A lot of people meet diplomats and, knowing they are birds of passage, do not particularly want to get involved. Countries vary in friendliness and in some, however hard one tries, it is difficult to become involved in local life. And finding work can be extremely difficult.

This book is presented chronologically with a brief introduction to each country. Virtually all the information is thus contained within the letters themselves, which have been edited.

1

New Zealand

Michael had been working for an introductory five months in London in the South East Asia Department dealing with Chinese hostilities on India's northern borders when we heard with great excitement of his first posting to the British High Commission in Wellington. We were due to arrive in Wellington in May 1963.

In the 1960s it was usual to travel to posts by sea and the only accommodation we could get at such short notice was the royal suite on SS *Athenic*, which carried about 70 first class passengers. The royal suite was very luxurious and every morning a news sheet and fruit were delivered with the breakfast. When we reached the tropics and the sailors changed into tropical uniform, all the soft furnishings in the suite were also changed — from winter materials into flowery chintz.

When we left England in March Tim, our elder son, was just three years old and Andrew, our second son, was 11 months old — his first birthday party was held on board ship. I was 25 and six months pregnant. Jackie Malcomson, the cousin of a friend of ours, came with us as nanny for her gap year. The Commonwealth Office paid for her passage. Her help was invaluable on the boat and indeed throughout the year.

As third secretary in Chancery Michael was responsible for helping with political and commercial reporting, or in effect doing anything the High Commissioner thought useful. Our main political role was to persuade the New Zealand government that we were serious about joining the EEC and that while they should not continue to rely solely on the UK to sell their wool, lamb and milk products, we were not deserting them. This was proving to be a difficult task.

1

1 May 1963, SS Athenic, *Shaw Savill Line,*
Somewhere in the Pacific Ocean

Tomorrow we arrive in New Zealand and shall be very glad; five and a half weeks is a long journey with only two ports of call, at Curaçao and Panama, though we did moor alongside Pitcairn for an hour. It is a very small island, about seven miles by three, with 143 inhabitants who are all descended from nine mutineers from the *Bounty*. They were led by Fletcher Christian, who had cast adrift Captain William Bligh and the rest of the crew in a open boat, and some Tahitians who settled there in 1789. [In 1994 the population is less than 50.] They rowed out in two boats and came on board with their huge feet and sold us carved tortoises, flying fish, and fruit and grass skirts. They have wireless, but the only outsiders they see are the Shaw Savill boats which call once every two months. It is thousands of miles from anywhere, and we took four islanders on board who are going to New Zealand, one of whom is to have an appendix removed, for they have no doctor or nurse on the island.

People have been throwing pre-dinner cocktail parties all week. We seem to have been invited to them all. I suppose we are in training for diplomatic life.

Let's hope they have found somewhere for us to live.

9 May, 66 Homewood Avenue, Karori, Wellington

Several people from the High Commission met us at the docks and brought us up to 66 Homewood Avenue, which is very nice indeed, with large rooms, three bedrooms and a super modern kitchen with an automatic washing machine. The house is built of wood, with a corrugated iron roof, and is all on one floor, which is normal here because of earthquakes, which happen frequently — mostly little ones I am told. We only have the house for five months, but are hoping to extend the lease.

As we have had to bring everything with us except basic furnishings, we have been terribly busy unpacking and I am hoping we do not have to move again. Jackie is absolutely marvellous — very practical and efficient and pleasant company. She has really been a tower of strength and can cook and turn her hand to anything.

Yesterday the first secretary and his wife gave a cocktail party of 100 people for us to meet. It was all rather terrifying but everyone is very charming. Afterwards we went to Mr and Mrs Harrison's, he is the Deputy High Commissioner, for dinner. They were friendly but Mr Harrison has an old-fashioned manner and seems rather shy about meeting people; he reminded me of a classics don at a university. It was very smart, with about 20 people, and they seem to have several Indian and Chinese servants to help. I was really exhausted at the end of the evening, especially after having to work really hard to remember all the names.

The New Zealand winter weather has been beautiful since we arrived, with clear skies, sun and no wind. Wellington is most attractive. On our arrival it looked like a Mediterranean port with white houses and lovely hills all around. The boys are very well. There is a kindergarten three minutes away just down the road near the shops and we are going to try to get Timothy in, although there is a waiting list from birth. We are hoping being English and diplomatic will do the trick.

19 May 1963
Thank you for your letter. It took over a week to arrive so I suppose it must have just missed a diplomatic bag. Apparently these are taken personally all around the world to all diplomatic postings by couriers, very often retired army officers, who never let the bags out of their sight during the entire journey, and some countries only receive one a week. Therefore if letters posted to the bag room in England just miss a bag departure they can take some time to reach their destinations.

There was another cocktail party in our honour at a second secretary's house after which we had to go with the High Commissioner and his wife, the Cumming-Bruces, to a university function where he introduced us to all the bigwigs — the vice chancellor, chancellor, Mr Holyoake, the Prime Minister, and all sorts of people and it was a bit overwhelming.

Sir Francis and Lady Cumming-Bruce are absolutely charming and completely without formality; he always arrives late for everything. His full name is Sir Francis Edward Hovell-Thurlow-Cumming-Bruce and he has an aristocratic, rather unworldly manner. He is certainly not the rumbustious back-slapping New Zealand type, but the New Zealanders are apparently flattered to have such a distinguished gentleman in their midst and like him very much. His wife, Yvonne, is a painter, extremely artistic, rather vague and very friendly, and we are lucky as they live just at the end of our road and we can use their tennis court whenever we want.

Some New Zealanders whom we had met on the boat invited us to visit them for tea at their farm. We duly turned up at 4.00 p.m. and were shown around, but since nothing happened in the way of food or drinks, at 5.30 p.m. we said we must be getting back for the children's supper. They looked at us in amazement and said, 'But you have not had tea yet.' We were shown into the dining room, where there was a vast spread of food on the table, and roast lamb and vegetables were brought in to accompany the cakes and sandwiches. We now understand the New Zealanders' eating habits — tea at 5.30 p.m. and supper, sandwiches, at 9.00 p.m.

1 June 1963

The women here have rather a poor time on the whole because they all have large families, four on average, in order to benefit from the very generous family allowance scheme which is trying to increase the two million population of the country; if you can produce six children you can practically retire on the proceeds.

There is no domestic help here and New Zealand ladies are intrigued by my having brought Jackie. This is a real do-it-yourself society and women have time for very little other than their domestic chores. The men are all mad about golf, cricket and fishing and go off at the week-ends if they are not busy reroofing, relaying foundations, rebuilding or, which happens frequently, building new houses, and leave their wives stuck at home with all the children.

Most of the golf clubs are segregated, with women not being allowed to play at the same time as men. They are not even allowed to walk around with their husbands. Some of the tennis clubs do not allow children in their grounds, which again means that the wives are left at home.

The men leave work at 5.00 p.m. and rush to the pubs (again single-sexed) which close at 6.00 p.m. to drink half a dozen whiskies before going home. This is known as the 'six o'clock swill' and is considered quite normal. If beer is preferred the tankards are lined up on the bar and filled with a hosepipe.

Jackie is going to be able to do her physics at the university in the mornings. It is extremely easy to get into university here as there is no competition at all and there are places for everyone who has taken the required exam at school. I think their first year is about equivalent to our A level. On Monday there is a national holiday because of the Queen's Birthday. As all the shops are shut here on Saturday anyway, this makes three days with no shopping. I only hope I have not forgotten anything.

12 June 1963
Last week was busy and included a cocktail party at our great friends Bobby and Guy Powles. He is a lawyer, she is a very talented painter and they have a son, Timothy, the same age as ours. They have been so helpful. They have introduced us to lots of people and have generally shown me the way around. There were a lot of older people there, including the ombudsman who is her father-in-law (I don't think we have an ombudsman in England), Professor John Beaglehole who is the most famous New Zealand historian, and his son Dr Tim Beaglehole who is the same age as Michael and funnily enough used to teach him economic history at Cambridge.

I do find it exhausting standing for hours, though I have borrowed a shooting stick for these occasions. But I am fine otherwise, and have a charming gynaecologist, Dr Brian Corkill, to look after me and am safely booked into the Salvation Army Bethany Hospital for the end of June. Not long now.

At the weekend we drove up to Wanganui, which is about 135 miles from here, armed with all our food because we planned to stay in a motel. We hardly met any cars, even though we were driving on the main road north from Wellington. On the Sunday we went to visit Harry Cave, a former New Zealand test cricketer whom we had met when they were in England in 1958 when Michael had played cricket for Cambridge against them, incidentally scoring 74 runs.

He is a sheep farmer and they gave us an enormous lunch and lots of lemons and grapefruit, which they have growing in their garden, and were very kind. The gardens here are beautiful, everything grows so well.

18 June 1963
The hurdle of giving our first party is now over. Sadly no one had refused the invitation so there were over 40 people and unfortunately

the girl who was going to help got chickenpox, so we had to do all the food by ourselves, and New Zealanders expect masses to eat at cocktail parties. The party also involved getting the children to bed and out of the way very early in the afternoon. But it was a great success. Everyone commented on the marvellous food and Jackie took a photo of it in colour.

The only problem with parties here is that the men and women tend to split up, with the women at one end of the room and the men at the other, and unless you are brave enough to cross the barrier you can spend the entire evening talking only to your own sex. It was supposed to end at 8.00 p.m. but people did not leave until 9.00 p.m. We have now learned an important diplomatic lesson, which is that the only way to get people to leave parties is to stop serving drinks.

There was quite a good mixture of people — from the High Commission, from the New Zealand Foreign Office, some ordinary citizens, as well as other diplomats — and everyone seemed very merry. At the parties here nearly everyone has whisky and soda or gin and tonic so it is very easy — you just walk around with two ready mixed jugs filling glasses.

So that is our first diplomatic party dealt with — I wonder how many more we shall have to give in years to come?

26 June 1963

Mrs Harrison, wife of the Deputy High Commissioner, who is rather formal and aware of her important position, invited me around one morning to go through the *Foreign Office Protocol Book* with her. This tells you what to do and how to behave correctly on all official occasions. Most of it really seemed to be about basic good manners and common sense, though seating at tables can be rather complicated as such care has to be taken not to offend anybody.

One of the residents of Homewood Avenue invited me for morning coffee to 'meet the neighbours'. It was very kind of her indeed, but it was all so formal, with some ladies wearing hats and gloves, and I have never seen so much food. We started off with three-decker sandwiches and savouries, then went on to cakes and fruit flan. I could not eat anything else for the rest of the day. These New Zealand ladies make so much work for themselves. They start by getting up at the crack of dawn to prepare lunches for their many children to take to school (there is no such thing as school meals in this do-it-yourself society) and then seem to clean and cook and wash for the rest of the day.

When I first arrived I was trying to get hold of a fourth for tennis one Friday and I asked a friend whom I met at the shops. She seemed rather surprised and told me she could not possibly play tennis on Fridays as she was always too busy at home 'filling her tins for the weekend'. Apparently that means making cakes and biscuits.

Bobby Powles took me to have lunch with a very charming lady, Mrs Yaldwyn, whose husband is chief justice. She has a beautiful house filled with lovely pictures and books. Bobby said this is quite unusual in New Zealand, for most of the houses you visit here do not have a book in sight. I think they are all too busy to read as they are doing useful things like decorating, reroofing, repiling along with gardening, cooking and filling their tins.

11 July 1963
Nothing happened here yet — still waiting. I am afraid the gynaecologist was wrong in his 'end of June' forecast. Timothy is so happy at school and they are very pleased with him because of the lovely way he talks, but I suppose soon he will develop a New Zealand accent. I am already finding the English accent rather too refined for down under.

The New Zealand papers have been full of the moral decline of Great Britain as witnessed by the Profumo affair. [John Profumo, secretary of state for war, had to resign over a sex scandal during which he lied to the House of Commons about his affair with Christine Keeler, who had also been having an affair with the Russian naval attaché.] They are extremely critical people and yet seem very sensitive to any criticism of themselves.

25 July 1963
Bethany Salvation Army Nursing Home, Wellington
Thank you so much for your telegram and letter and card. Isn't it marvellous? We are thrilled with Lucy. She is absolutely sweet and very pretty with dark hair and very large doe-shaped eyes. She weighs 8 lb 5 ozs and is wide awake and looking all around.

They are letting me go home after nine days, usually they keep you 12, but I have a monthly nurse who has arrived and I shall be able to stay in bed. The hospital is rather old-fashioned. I am sharing a room with four others, which is just as well as I am not allowed to see Timothy or Andrew here at all, as children are not allowed in, and the company stops me being so homesick. The food is absolutely ghastly. And as it is run by the Salvation Army we have hymns sung to us each evening by the nurses, which usually makes us all cry or laugh rather hysterically. Such is the post-natal state of mind.

People have been very kind. They have come to see me every day at visiting hours, and I have had lots of flowers, cards and presents. Lady Cumming-Bruce gave me a little jacket but it has got holes in it, moths probably, though I am sure she did not notice. Sir Francis is leaving to become High Commissioner in Nigeria. It is a far bigger job, but it is very sad they are going.

3 August 1963

Having not understood what was happening since I vanished nine days ago the boys were both overwhelmed to see me when we came home from the nursing home; they literally could not speak for five minutes. When I went to the nursing home poor Timothy retired to his bed for nearly two days, sleeping and only waking up to sob. Andrew's reaction to his mother's disappearance was to shuffle firmly around on his bottom and refuse to walk at all. If I had known all this I certainly would not have stayed so long in the nursing home.

9 August 1963

Michael is enjoying his work but he finds there is an awful lot of routine mechanics to learn and he never realized quite how meticulous civil servants are in their use of words, in economy and accuracy in phrasing, so that a possibility of any misinterpretation cannot exist unless it is done deliberately. He is also mildly disappointed that he cannot leave Whitehall behind.

Nearly all the offices in the High Commission face the harbour, but his overlooks the shell of the building and security instructions say that the blinds should be perpetually drawn, so it is artificial light all day.

New Zealand politics do seem terribly parochial, and their foreign affairs debates are very boring. Their main preoccupation is with preserving their trade with us, ensuring that we allow no other country to compete over butter and mutton and beef to their detriment.

Another thing we find over and over is that they cannot bear criticism. One of our commercial people nearly had to be recalled recently because he caused a furore in the press, to which even the PM replied, by telling New Zealand to stick to what it could do, i.e. primary production, and forget about secondary production.

Enough politics. Time to feed Lucy.

6 October 1963

I have made my first diplomatic *faux pas*. We were at a formal, grand and very sticky dinner party the other day with senior distinguished guests, and we were much the youngest there. At one stage there was a gap in the conversation and out of nervousness I started talking about sheep shearing we had seen in action on a farm the other day, and how it was very clever the way the shearers managed to cut the fleece off in one piece and how it was amazing how fast this was done.

After I had recounted the story the gentleman on my left, who was an elderly New Zealand civil servant, having looked at my place card to check my name, said, 'But surely, Mrs James, this is not so unusual. You can see sheep being sheared in England.' And I replied, 'Yes, of course, but there are other things to do in England.' There followed a deathly hush; all 13 other guests stared at me and I wished I could vanish for ever under the table!

24 October 1963

There was a diplomatic reception at Government House which was really fabulous. We were all introduced to Their Excellencies, Sir Bernard and Lady Fergusson — he had been a very famous brigadier in Burma during the war — and had to curtsey and bow. I was terribly nervous, heaven knows why, for they are very sweet. The whole diplomatic corps was there — the Thais and some others in national dress and the rest of us in tails and decorations.

After being introduced at the line-up we had champagne and Their Excellencies walked around meeting people. Her Excellency's lady in waiting, whom I know, came up to me to ask if I would mind if she brought Her Excellency to talk to me. So she came and I had not a clue whether I had to curtsey again or not, so I didn't. I had read that you are not supposed to speak until spoken to, but as this makes it rather difficult for her to hold a conversation with anybody, I ignored that too. Lady Fergusson obviously had a cleft palate in her youth and still has a slight speech impediment, so I reckon she manages very well and she was very friendly. I talked to Mr Ivanov, the Russian ambassador, the South African ambassador, and all sorts of other people. The grandeur of the occasion rather went to my head and I drank masses of champagne. At the end we all stood aside and Their Excellencies walked up the length of the room, with us all bobbing and bowing, and they then stood on the dais by their thrones and the band played the national anthem. His Excellency then thanked everyone for coming, and they left, and we left soon after. It started at 9.00 p.m. and finished at 11.00 p.m. Altogether quite an experience.

Today I gave a coffee party to organize a bring-and-buy charity sale. Last week I gave a cocktail party and a large dinner party. Life is really far too busy on top of a baby and two others, but I expect I shall survive somehow.

25 November 1963
Have not heard from you for ages. Last letter received on 20 October. I am rather fed up with having no news, but I suppose a letter must have gone astray. I did not hear about Rozy's [my sister's] baby till it was three weeks old. I still only know that it was a boy, but don't know his name, weight, colour of hair and all the other fascinating things there are to know about newborn babies.

This is the time of year for winds. And what winds! Southerlies straight from the South Pole to windy Wellington. They come up through the Cook Strait and rattle around the hills in the harbour basin and we never know from which direction they will come. I nearly got blown over one day by the docks and was saved by clinging onto a convenient lamppost. There were gusts of 93 mph. The inhabitants of Wellington have permanently creased faces from battling with their environment. We have earthquakes as well, but there is surprisingly little damage as the houses are of wood and no building is above four stories, and there are no chimneys to fall off and do damage.

Wasn't it terrible about President Kennedy's assassination? We were all completely stunned by the news and still can hardly believe it. It is a real tragedy from all points of view. It has even made the headlines in the very parochial New Zealand newspapers, replacing the more typical, 'Mrs Jones has won the flower competition at Wanganui for the third year running'. Hope to hear from you very, very soon.

11 December 1963

Did I tell you we were giving a cocktail party for our High Commissioner? Well, at 3.30 in the afternoon on that day Sir Francis rang me up and said he had just heard from London that we were in court mourning for President Kennedy and was terribly sorry but we would have to cancel the party. We had wondered what was happening as we knew the Americans could go to no parties for a month and the Canadians and Australians also had to mourn for four days, but London was terribly slow to inform us of procedures. Anyway, the office phoned all our guests for us and we put all the food in a deep freeze, and the next day I had to organize the whole thing again for the following week.

But we were lucky because most of the people could come and we had a most successful party. The Cumming-Bruces lent me flowers, in fact I was picking them in their garden at Homewood, and Sir Francis came and said why didn't I take a vase from their drawing room, already arranged. So Lady C-B brought it around for me, a lovely one. We had about 30 people, mostly older than us, and everyone seemed to enjoy themselves.

On 3 December we had the Government House garden party — 2000 guests and a fight for tea and strawberries.

Happy Christmas!

2 January 1964

John Gielgud arrived to do *Ages of Man*, his solo Shakespeare anthology performance, which I had seen in London in 1959. Unfortunately Michael could not come as the High Commissioner and his wife went off to London that day and he was being a dutiful third secretary and looking after them, making arrangements for their flights, luggage and packing, telling Lady Cumming-Bruce what to wear and reminding Sir Francis of things he had forgotten to do. But they sweetly gave us a trout he had caught, a hare pie, oysters, a red umbrella and chest waders for Michael to fish in! Anyway I was able to see Gielgud, who was really wonderful and had the audience spellbound. I have not enjoyed anything so much for ages.

The next day our Deputy High Commissioner had a lunch for Gielgud and very kindly asked us, together with the Prime Minister, the mayor and distinguished people from the arts here — not very many of them I am afraid. I sat next to John Perry from the London theatrical agents, Tennents, who is keeping Gielgud company on this tour. After lunch Michael and I drove him and Sir John all around Wellington and they came back for tea. Gielgud was really pleasant and quite natural; he thoroughly enjoyed himself. I am to go and see John Perry when we get back and get seats for all the Tennent productions in London.

They are off to Auckland today for three days, then to New York where he is going to direct Richard Burton in *Hamlet*.

13 January 1964

My great friend here, Jane Haddock, and her two sons sailed for South Africa this week, and we saw them off very sadly. They are in Overseas Shell and will be abroad most of the time. Heaven knows where or when we will meet again.

Our best man, Michael Oatley, has now been sent to our Embassy in Lomé which is in Togo between Nigeria and Ghana. Have you ever heard of it? [We were later to visit this country regularly during our posting to Ghana.]

28 January 1964

Delighted there are so many replies to the nanny advertisement — but how very difficult to choose! If only Jackie could stay another year. I agree that £6 is more reasonable than seven guineas, which is really rather too much. Norlands is where all the really wealthy get their nannies. [Jackie's year was up and she was leaving and my mother was finding a replacement for us.]

A buffet supper here last week for 16 was a great success with very charming people — university professors, New Zealanders from their Foreign Office and American diplomats. Yesterday 45 for cocktails, also successful. A waiter did the drinks and caterers the food so it was relatively easy, except remembering who everyone is and who to introduce to whom.

19 March 1964

I think diplomatic wives should get a dress allowance. My cocktail dress situation is bad. I seem to have only three dresses that are nice — the others are old and holey or too big. And two of my older ones are too small. Three babies in three years does make the dress situation more complicated. Anyway an Australian friend has been home to

Sydney and has brought me back the most fabulous gold cocktail suit on approval, which is really lovely, fits perfectly and is terribly smart. Jackie and Michael think it is heavenly. But we have got no money and it costs £20. Do you think you could possibly lend me £20? If you could I will have the dress, otherwise I will have to send it back.

The recent Plowden Report, which is a review headed by Lord Plowden on the workings of the Foreign Office, is very good. At last someone seems to understand the problems of having to move from post to post while trying to give children a settled education. We shall get £365 per annum for each child at boarding school and £89 per annum for each child's uniform.

13 April 1964

Am now involved with the New Zealand Broadcasting Corporation. I went for an audition and have been selected, as one of 12 out of 150 applicants, for their broadcasting drama course. I am sure the Central School helped. We, that is diplomatic wives, are not allowed by the Commonwealth Relations Office, or the Foreign Office, to take up paid employment overseas without requesting permission from our head of post. Luckily we have a very nice new High Commissioner, Sir Ian Maclennan who has a very friendly wife Peggy, who does not mind at all. Not everyone is so lucky. [Heads of posts were known to refuse to allow wives to work.]

29 April 1964

Have just had the busiest two weeks ever — we were out to cocktails or dinner every night and had Andrew's second birthday party thrown in.

The Alfred Deller Consort are touring Australia and New Zealand and gave a concert here. We went, I admit, with trepidation as a counter-tenor is inclined to make me laugh. But they were wonderful. There were six of them and they sang sitting around a large table. They sang Byrds Mass, which is really beautiful. Then Desmond Dupne played the lute and they sang madrigals and folk songs, and it was lovely. Afterwards we went to the High Commissioner's as they were giving a party for them. They were all sweet and Deller himself quite normal in spite of his voice. He has a beard and a son who is a counter-tenor too. There was a gorgeous baritone, Christopher Keyte, who was at Cambridge at the same time as Michael and who knows John Alldis

13

very well — you remember the organist at our wedding? — and says his choir, the John Alldis Choir, is making an excellent name for itself.

Last night we stayed in. Amazing.

1 June 1964

Cherry Engholm [Jackie's replacement] has now arrived safely. She is extremely helpful, we get on very well and the children took to her straight away. It is marvellous having a proper trained nanny. Perhaps she learnt her efficiency from her father, Sir Basil Engholm, who is in the civil service in the Ministry of Agriculture and Fisheries. She rushes the kids out for walks, brushes their shoes, automatically tidies up their clothes and toys and consequently the house is always spick and span.

Timothy is very grown up now and I am pleased as I have managed to get him into an excellent school starting in September. He has really come out of his shell lately — he is lively, talkative, gregarious and dying to go to school.

12 June 1964

Since Jackie left last week Timothy has been full of how he also wants to go back to England to see Granny. He has just told me to tell you to meet him at the airport tomorrow as he will fly to England on his own. I asked him if he is going to see Grandpa while he is there and he said yes, he would have a look at him too.

25 June 1964

The Swedish ambassador invited us to a very nice cocktail party. His wife is a sweet friend of mine, with grown-up children, and we play tennis and do pottery together. Afterwards we were invited to dinner by the Australian trade commissioner, Des McSweeney. He is older than us but great fun and terribly fit and plays squash with Michael. They took us to a super restaurant. There are only about six decent restaurants in Wellington, and only four of those have licences. We had to take our own wine, and the waiters decanted it into orangeade bottles in case the police came.

We have really got so many friends here now that I wish in some ways we had a second two-year posting lined up; it is going to be so difficult to say goodbye.

But it is still not absolutely definite, and we have now been waiting for six months for a reply from the Personnel Department about our postings.

16 July 1964

Michael Macliammoir, the Irish actor, was here doing *The Importance of Being Oscar*, which was an excellent solo performance based on Wilde's life, again arranged by the British Council — what would we do without them?

4 August 1964

Last night we went and heard John Ogdon, the pianist. He is marvellous. He played Beethoven, Liszt, Busoni, Scriabin and Debussy. We went with friends and drank red wine and ate paté before and after.

My broadcasting course is going well now and I am learning a lot and enjoying it — roll on the work. By the way, your letters do not seem as frequent as they used to be. The last one I had was the only one in over three weeks.

2 September 1964

Life has been so hectic recently, I am really quite exhausted. We have had about two nights at home since 17 August, and have given two large cocktail parties here. Still, it has been fun.

Cambridge Circus, a Footlights revue, which has been having a great success in London and is going on to Broadway, came to Wellington, and we discovered that the producer was Humphrey Barclay, who was head boy when Michael was teaching at Harrow.

Also another of the cast was at St John's with Michael, David Hatch. Anyway, it is a terribly funny show, really excellent. Humphrey, Jo Kendall and a chap called Tim Brooke-Taylor came to lunch and after the show we had a party for everyone at the house and we talked and drank till about 2.00 a.m.

It was really fun — we all had mutual friends to talk about, and they were all sweet. Let's hope they have a good success on Broadway. [They did.]

13 September 1964

Timothy has had his tonsils and adenoids out. They are so old-fashioned here that we were not allowed to see him until two days after the operation. So we are relieved it is all over and all being well he will start his new school on Monday.

14 October 1964

Michael and I had a gorgeous holiday in South Island, which is really heavenly. The west coast, where we spent two days, is very deserted and rugged. Gold mining took place there until the late nineteenth century, but now it is very poor. The roads are terrible and often unmade but our Morris 1100 coped very well and we made good times the whole way.

We saw mountains, lakes, glaciers, forests, sea, rivers and very few other cars. We also played golf and climbed a very high hill to get a view of Fox Glacier. The glaciers, Fox and Frank Josef, are disappointing as they are receding rapidly — two miles in the last eight years — and are not all that spectacular.

29 October 1964

Ameena Ahuja, who is the wife of the Indian High Commissioner here, is translating some Chekhov short stories, which have not previously been translated. He wrote hundreds and returned to them for solace whenever his plays were unsuccessful. How he managed to write so much as well as spending his life as a doctor in the countryside, travelling long distances in terrible conditions to see his patients, is a mystery. But he said that medicine was his lawful wife and literature his mistress and when he tired of one he spent the night with the other — I am not sure where his wife, the actress Olga Knipper, fitted in. Ameena speaks Russian, and interpreted for Khrushchev and Nehru when posted in Moscow, but her English is rather Indianized and she needs my help. I am thoroughly enjoying it, particularly as she is also a professional artist and is giving me a lovely painting in return. She gives me, or her Indian servant does, a fabulous Indian curry for lunch each day — so tomorrow Michael is going to join us.

After a dinner of trout caught in Lake Taupo by friends we really had a night on the town and visited the nearest Wellington has to offer in the way of night clubs (there is really no choice), which we discovered to be a poky dive with a rather bad Beatles-type group where you twist with a predominantly Maori gathering. Quite mad, but fun. Dunedin, at the south of South Island, sounds like the end of the world. We heard all about it from an English friend who has emigrated there, an unusual occurrence as it is the only town in New Zealand with a decreasing population. This is not surprising as it is cold, bleak, Scottish in atmosphere, with grey buildings made with granite imported from Scotland, and there are not many jobs around.

16 November 1964

Timothy and I watched Michael play cricket at the weekend for the university in the local league. He is doing terribly well this year and making lots of runs, and might be chosen to represent Wellington in the Plunket Shield. This is like our county cricket only they play all the matches in three weeks in January. Michael would like to play, but does not want to use up three weeks of holiday to do so. But he might play in half the matches, or the office might consider it good diplomacy and let him have the time off.

30 November 1964

Still no definite news about coming home. But it seems that we will be coming home in May for good, or for three months leave, most likely the former. I must say I hope so. Much as I enjoy it here, New Zealand has its limitations — though my broadcasting is going well now.

21 December 1964

Busy as usual including a 'gay young things' party, which meant standing around, dancing or stomping, and we felt really old and left at midnight — I am going to be 27 in three days time! Michael has got into the Wellington Plunket Shield side and he starts playing on Boxing Day. Now I must put the tree up. A Very Happy Christmas. We will all be thinking of you!

11 January 1965

Had a very pleasant three days in Christchurch where Michael played in the Plunket Shield Wellington v Christchurch which was a good match, and met all the Wellington team. Sunday was our sixth wedding anniversary and we had a heavenly childless day on the beach with a Dutch bachelor friend of ours who has a gorgeous house on a hill with a view over Christchurch and the sea. The hillside was covered with pine trees and smelt like the Costa Brava.

The new Deputy High Commissioner and his wife, Barry and Sheila Smallman, are coming to lunch in an effort to cheer themselves up as their two eldest children, who are only ten and eleven, have just flown home to boarding school and they will not see them again for six months. They are very friendly and we play tennis with them. He is extremely tall. They are Baptists and I think they are wonderful as they are always cheerful and talkative at parties without any help from alcohol! We also had our information officer, who needed cheering up because his wife has had to fly to England with their 19-year-old daughter who has just had a nervous breakdown and no one trusts the psychiatrists here.

20 January 1965
It is sweltering. It has been hot and gorgeous since Christmas. Wellington has not had weather like this for 28 years or more. The Maori carvings have their tongues out as this is a symbol of defiance.

27 January 1965
Had planned to go to the races at the weekend but could not go because we are in mourning for Churchill. Michael was asked by a friend of his on New Zealand radio to read a speech of Churchill's as his English voice would be more appropriate than a local one. Yesterday I gave a farewell party for Bobby and Guy Powles who are off to Samoa where he is going to work as a magistrate. We shall miss them a lot. [Bobby Powles tragically died of cancer shortly afterwards.]

11 February 1965
There is now definite news of our homecoming: we shall be leaving in July. There has been a worry over the house as our lease is due to expire on 19 May and the solicitors have airmailed our landlord, who is in England, to see if we can have the house for the extra weeks.

When we get home we have two months' leave, then Michael is to go on some administrative course for three months and will probably have a job in Whitehall for a while. So please could you try to get Timothy into a school near at hand for September? We should love to stay with you on arrival, then we shall have to find somewhere else. Of course all this would be easier to plan if we could know how long exactly we shall be home for, but heaven knows when we shall know that.

8 March 1965

Our holiday was lovely up in the Bay of Islands in the very north of North Island. We went big-game fishing, swam, sunbathed, ate oysters off the rocks and cockles from the beach and fished from the wharf. Timothy just adored it. Especially as he caught three fish, nearly, by himself.

Have now decided to fly home as the long ship journey with no help with the children — Cherry is not coming back with us — would mean spending most of our time in the dining room as the children have to eat at separate times to the adults.

24 March 1965

There is a large ECAFE (the UN Economic Committee for Asia and the Far East) conference in Wellington and Michael has the honour of being on the UK delegation of distinguished chaps, including the Minister for Overseas Development. It is very interesting meeting delegates from all over the world; there are 30 countries represented. Michael has been working a 15-hour day looking after our delegation, who are either senior FO people or Ministry of Overseas Service people (now ODA). They have spent two or three evenings with us and I have also had them to lunch twice.

There are some fascinating Iranians, Afghans, Laotians and Vietnamese and it has made us realize how important French is in this job as not many speak English.

Over the last three weeks I have painted my second portrait, which I love doing. Mrs Holyoake paints in the same class as me. She is a very ordinary and homely little woman for a Prime Minister's wife, very friendly with no airs and graces at all, and she discusses important political things like what to eat for tea in the evening and the problems of getting the weekly washing dried.

6 April 1965

Last week I did a lot of broadcasting in my biggest part for the NZBC so far. I loved it and, as I get paid £2.10.0 an hour, it is quite lucrative. They are very good productions and mostly professional English actors and actresses, and I think if we were staying longer it would develop into frequent work. Still …

Have now heard that we shall probably be posted again next spring after Michael's course. This is really rather good as at this stage we are so much better off abroad than at home. But I hope you will be able to come and visit us on our next posting and that it will not be so far away.

After two years in New Zealand one is pining for a real city. I am longing to see London again.

Must stop and cook as Michael is bringing some official chap home for lunch and we are also giving a dinner for eight tonight. We are living on mushrooms which we picked from a friend's farm on Sunday.

22 April 1965

The kids really enjoyed the weekend we have just spent at Wairakei which is north of Wellington. They loved the hot thermal pool and were fascinated by the bubbling mud, boiling volcanic lake and geysers which were all around us. All in all, except for the six-hour journey each way, it made a lovely break.

My NZBC parts are really getting larger now. This one is a loud blonde in her late twenties.

Now we are starting to work through lists of people we should invite to the house before we leave. At the moment the lists seem endless and time seems to be moving far too quickly.

Please could you keep an eye on the *Surrey Advertiser* for houses to rent?

2 June 1965

Nearly finished giving our farewells now; two more cocktails and that is the lot. Several people are giving us parties, including a wine and cheese party by the chap who is head of NZBC News. Sadly I have had no broadcasting for two weeks. Perhaps because I am leaving?

The High Commission is organizing a stall for a YWCA fête, along with the other embassies here, and it is very hard work making stuffed toys and collecting things together, but Lady Maclennan is very good and imaginative.

28 June 1965

The children were delighted with their Good Journey cards which arrived today and are longing to come and stay with you. Thank you so much. We are all so excited.

Only a week or so more in this house and leaving New Zealand for ever two weeks on Wednesday. I can hardly believe it. I have had a terrible back which seized up on the squash court, and gave my last cocktail party lying flat on my back with visitors coming to say goodbye to me in the bedroom.

21 July 1965
24 Brahms Street, Vanderbijlpark, Transvaal
It was very sad saying goodbye to all our friends, and they all came to the airport to wave us off, and really after the hectic packing and farewell time we were pretty worn out.

We stopped at Mauritius which is a delightful isle — 60 per cent Indian population, plus Creoles, Chinese, French and English. We had a fascinating morning being shown around a sugar plantation and factory managed by a French family who live in the most incredible style with nannies and uniformed servants everywhere. I found the most impressive scene was a newborn baby in a large nursery in a very elaborate cot with three nannies in attendance. I meanwhile was trying to keep my three in order all by myself. We were also shown all around the island being driven by smartly uniformed Creole chauffeurs. It was a real glimpse of luxury! Now in Johannesburg and are staying with Michael's cousin Brian Edwards and his South African wife Yvonne. We try to avoid discussing the subject of apartheid with them as we know we can never agree on that, but they do try to put their case forward continuously, particularly as South Africa has just been thrown out of the Commonwealth, and no one we meet seems to want to talk about anything else. To prove to us how well the Africans are treated they arranged for us to visit a township, Soweto. We were taken around by the superintendent and it was all very embarrassing as he took us into a couple of houses, or shacks, without even knocking on the door, and with the family sitting around just marched us through to the kitchen to show us how well equipped they were, and then we walked out again without talking to the family at all.

He wanted to show us more but we said we had seen enough. Soweto is like a prison camp with barbed wire all around and security lights. But we were shown very smart cars which were owned by Africans, and were taken to a pub where they could all buy beer, and shown shops and schools, and the Afrikaners tried very hard to convince us that the Africans had a very good life. To try to argue against apartheid with South Africans is a hopeless battle and it is really impossible to have a relaxed holiday here. But the children are bearing up marvellously, and knowing nothing of apartheid or the Commonwealth and loving the swimming and sunshine are really enjoying themselves. See you very soon now!

2
Ceylon (Sri Lanka)

When we got back to England we rented a house near Guildford, which was where my parents lived and where I had been brought up. Tim went to the local primary school. Michael was sent on a training course, mainly in economic and commercial work, at the Civil Service College in Regent's Park.

After four months we heard that we had been posted to Ceylon, where Michael was to work as first secretary with particular responsibility for reporting on Ceylon's domestic politics and social problems. This was to prove a fascinating job as Ceylonese are great gossips and very indiscreet and we had marvellous connections which we were able to build up following our close friendship with Ian and Gun Pieris whom we had known at Cambridge.

This time we flew out and arrived in Ceylon in March 1966. Ceylon had received independence from Britain in 1948. Solomon West Ridgeway Dias Bandaranaike of the SLFP (Sri Lanka Freedom Party) had defeated Sir John Kothalawala of the UNP (United National Party) in 1956 by a large majority and was in office until September 1959, when he was assassinated by a Buddhist monk because the Buddhists wanted more power in the country. The death penalty had been abolished but was brought back; the monk was hanged and the monk behind the assassination, Buddharakitha, was gaoled and died in prison.

After an interim period the UNP, with Dudley Senanayake as Minister of State, was elected in March 1960 with a small majority but was defeated in Parliament later in the year and Solomon Bandaranaike's widow was swept into power on a wave of public sympathy. Five years later, in 1965, Dudley Senanayake was re-elected as Prime Minister with J. R. Jayawardene as his deputy. The years from 1965 to 1970, when Mrs Bandaranaike was re-elected, were considered by many to have been the calmest Ceylon had known since independence. This was also the time of the Green Revolution and an increase in food production.

7 March 1966
The flight went well and we have all arrived safely in Ceylon, but it is all very strange and unreal and hot.

The drive into Colombo from Katunayake airport takes an hour, but would be a lot quicker if there were not so much happening all around — cyclists, buffalo carts, rickshaws, children, merchants, animals, the streets are alive with colour and action, plus of course the little tin-roofed houses, the sheds, the shacks and the poverty. It is all so strange and different and there is so much to see that it is impossible to absorb, and of course lack of sleep and jet lag do not help.

We were driven straight to our house at number 31, Torrington Avenue, Colombo 7 — which is obviously a smart, residential area of the city — and it is lovely, vast, a palatial mansion with enormous rooms, quite nicely furnished and very comfortable. It is built in the old colonial style with wide verandas all around and it has very high ceilings with enormous ceiling fans, which make it cool. [It is now the Iraqi Embassy.] On the veranda lined up to greet us were five servants. A head boy, Masanam, who is a Tamil from southern India, a second boy, Supardi, a cook, a nanny and a gardener who are Sinhalese. The servants are all called 'boy' here, and it takes a lot of getting used to, especially when they are much older than I am. I think I shall use their names.

It seemed as though we were acting in a film as we duly shook hands with them all, but I am beginning to come to grips with the servant situation, and think I shall adapt to it quickly, as in this blazing heat life without help would be quite impossible.

Masanam is very helpful indeed and extremely smart with a turban and he changes his uniform into a very smart one with brass buttons all over it in the evenings. The nanny has got good references, is rather old and has very bandy legs, but the children seem to like her though I feel they will play her up a fair amount. The cook is very good too, and all our meals are served with great style.

The first morning I was taught by Masanam that after breakfast each day the cook will emerge from the kitchen area (which I have not yet visited but think is very basic as he apparently sleeps there) and ask for the menus for the day. I then take my big bunch of keys and in real chatelaine style go to the storeroom and deal out the daily rations of rice, sugar, tea and cigarettes for the servants and any items required for the day's menus, as everything has to be kept under lock and key.

After that I do not have to worry about meals for the rest of the day, which is wonderful; they appear regularly and the cook bicycles each day to the market for fruit, vegetables, meat and fish, though I sometimes have to do some shopping at the grocers. Oh, yes, my other morning duty is to inspect his accounts of the previous day's marketing and dole out the necessary rupees.

So far we have been having English food. You can buy imported lamb and bacon, at a price, and most things are available, but terribly expensive. We will be glad when our food supplies arrive on the boat.

One of the very first things we had to do was join a swimming club to cope with the sweltering heat, not so much the temperature which is around 81 degrees but the horrible humidity. Sadly, after joining, we found that it was very much a Europeans only club, so have now also joined, through the Pieris's help, the local Sinhalese club and Michael is playing cricket this weekend for them and will be the only white man in the team. Having Ian and Gun here is a godsend, they are introducing us to lots of Ceylonese and lots of useful contacts. [Ian Pieris is a Sinhalese who was with Michael at Cambridge and got a cricket blue for two years. He later captained the Ceylon cricket team and was chairman of the selectors. He runs a family rubber business and plantations and is married to a Norwegian, Gun, whom he met while in England and who has wholeheartedly adapted to life in Ceylon.]

Instead of the Overseas School, which is the international school here, we have managed to enter Timothy for the St Thomas's Preparatory School, which has a high standard and is a local C of E fee-paying school attached to the leading boys' school in Ceylon. Ceylonese schools split up their classes into three streams according to race — Sinhalese, Tamil or Burgher (Ceylonese of Dutch origin or mixed race). Timothy is in a Burgher class; in fact there are very few white children at St Thomas's at present. The streams only ever mix on the games fields. It seems a certain way to encourage Sinhalese–Tamil problems as children are made aware from an early age of their racial differences and in the playground at the age of six are already inclined to stick together with their own kind. [As has been proved since.]

Gun has also been my guide around Colombo. There are areas of the city that are terrible (dirty, overcrowded and poverty stricken), which only vast sums of money would improve. But she has taken me all over, and we have visited unusual places in search of things we need, areas which I would never have gone to on my own. But you never feel threatened in any way.

The amount of washing and ironing in a tropical house is never-ending and luckily for me it is done by the washing *amah* who comes daily, washes everything, by hand until our washing machine arrives, lays it out on the lawn to dry, irons it and then goes home.

Another of my onerous duties is to go out each morning into our lovely garden, having spoken to the cook, to speak to the gardener and give him his instructions for the day. As I know nothing about tropical gardens I rely on Gun for this information. Today I ordered the replanting of three orchids and manuring. The flowers here are superb with bougainvillaea and hibiscus in profusion.

4 March 1966

Timothy is enjoying his school and Andrew and Lucy have started at a Montessori kindergarten down the road, again mostly Ceylonese children, and attached to a large girls' Catholic school. If successful Lucy can stay there for the three years of our tour, and Andrew can join Timothy at St Thomas's next year. The Pieris' are a real blessing and Gun is continuing to show me the ins and outs of Colombo life. The Ceylonese we have met are charming and friendly and we are trying to arrange Sinhalese lessons; this will be a great asset if we can learn it reasonably well, but as it has a different alphabet I am rather doubtful. Luckily most Ceylonese speak English in Colombo, certainly the educated ones. But this will not continue as in the Sinhalese and Tamil streams at the schools the children are now taught English as a second language, not as a first language which was the previous practice. This again seems very short-sighted, as who outside Ceylon speaks Sinhalese?

Sundays here do not exist and instead the Buddhist *poya* days are celebrated. These are holy days which do not come around regularly each week like Sundays as they are based on the movements of the moon and this causes lots of complications; for example, as there are ten days between the last *poya* and the next which will be on Monday, today, Thursday, is a half holiday. It is all very involved and a new system introduced by the Prime Minister, Dudley Senanayake. Let's hope they abandon it.

5 April 1966

Bad tummies are very common here and I have just recovered from three days in bed. The doctor came and I had to have a specimen analysed to see if I had amoebas. Luckily I have not. The water has to be filtered and boiled for safety.

5 April 1966

The monsoon is starting in earnest now with tremendous storms, almighty crashes of thunder, violent lightning and rainfall, which floods the kitchen even though they, our Ministry of Works from the High Commission, have tried to repair the roof several times to no avail.

But we are getting far more acclimatized to life here and not finding the heat so tiring. We have played a lot of tennis, and must lose pounds of weight with the sweat literally pouring down us. Andrew had a lovely fourth birthday. He was thrilled to bits with his train; thank heavens we brought it with us as there is literally nothing in the shops here.

Our first dinner party is over, and everything went well, though we had to borrow china, glass, saucepans and everything else as our luggage has not yet arrived; the docks are very slow here, and we are dependent on the rather scanty office float. It is all such a change from Wellington. We were playing tennis, got home at 7.00 p.m., nanny put the kids to bed, we had showers and changed and came downstairs at 7.55 p.m. in time to receive our guests. We had the Pieris', the Brazilian ambassador and his wife (he is a very lively dapper ambassador), a Sinhalese lawyer and his wife and some office colleagues. I did not do a thing except order the food and a bit of shopping. We really have a super cook; Masanam knows exactly what to do and looks so distinguished dressed up in his evening suit with the shiny brass buttons.

On 1 May, the workers' revolutionary day, Mrs Bandaranaike and her opposition party have a rally at the end of our garden: we live next

27

door to a small park containing the independence memorial. Last year they went wild and threw stones and rioted and there was a lot of violence. I hope they do not attack us this time. The police have forbidden processions, but this probably does not make much difference. Ceylon is still in a state of emergency following an abortive coup in February. At the moment the newspapers are full of suspects and communist infiltrators and detainees committing suicide, far more exciting than life in New Zealand.

9 May 1966

Up-country is beautiful. We have just come back from a tea estate where the English planters have a lovely house, pool, tennis court, and of course a garden with a fantastic riot of colour and endless tea estate workers to look after it. There was wonderful country all around, hills, paddy fields and tea bushes everywhere. We enjoyed ourselves very much. Enclosed is the invitation to a Muslim wedding we went to last night. As you can see they were two sets of first cousins marrying. It was a fantastic, colourful affair held in a large hotel and there were over 2000 guests.

It all started with a ceremony with the two grooms, but not a bride in sight, sitting at a table with some priests and mumbling and chanting went on for some minutes, about dowries apparently, but we could not understand the lingo. Then the fathers, who are brothers, put several gold chains around the two grooms' necks.

We then filed into the ballroom and what a sight! The two brides with diamond tiaras and the most over-elaborate dresses were arranged in two tableaux surrounded by overdressed maids and pages. There were two backcloths; one had moving clouds projected and the other had shimmering water effects. It looked rather like the finale of a musical comedy.

The grooms joined them and they all sat with very serious faces for another hour or so. The guests of honour were the Governor General, Sir William Gopallawa, the Minister of State, J. R. Jayawardene, several cabinet ministers and leader of the opposition, Mrs Bandaranaike, whose hand I had the dubious honour of shaking.

So there we sat, drinking insipid orange juice and watching the lovely tableaux which were very strongly spotlighted. We were positively dazzled. The band played a variety of music, jazzed up Ava Maria included, and we all wondered what would come next. Then in came the dancing girls, a flurry of red feathers, bikinis and belly dancing, followed by a performance of the limbo.

After that we went into a specially built pavilion, all 2000 of us, and sat down to curry and Muslim sweetmeats and fireworks. We then went home. Quite an experience.

10 May 1966

There is a family planning clinic near to us and I turned up on spec to see if I could help. I was asked if I would fill in various forms while the doctors examined the patients who had their legs strapped up in the air in a most inelegant position having their IUDs (inter-uterine devices) fitted; these are a fairly new form of birth control in Ceylon.

There is an extremely nice local lady gynaecologist who weighs about 16 stone and laughs all the time, and she told me that the Ceylonese are not very keen on being present in the room when these devices are fitted and if I did not mind it would be very helpful, and as I do not speak the language and the majority of patients do not speak English I cannot do interviews. It was interesting and hard work, with two doctors side by side and me filling in two forms with all the details simultaneously. They deal with different types of birth control on different days of the week.

The IUD is not 100 per cent successful by any means. There were two pathetic girls, both under 30 with six or seven children each, and they were told that they were pregnant even though they had had their devices inserted and they had not fallen out, which they seem to do quite often. The poor things were desperately upset. It really seems so unfair that after having made the brave move to attend the clinic and have the weird devices inserted that they still got pregnant.

Pottery has also started and is great fun. There is an excellent teacher and only two other pupils who are both very good; I am much the worst. It is harder than in New Zealand as we have to knead our own clay in good underdeveloped country fashion and this takes time and is tiring. In New Zealand this was done by machine. All the equipment is old, battered and basic and we work outdoors under a shady tree. I really feel part of Ceylon working like this with no other Europeans around, particularly as no one there speaks much English, and they do have wonderful potters in this country.

29

30 May 1966

The bulk of our luggage has now arrived in a vast lift van, so I have been busy unpacking. Most of the stuff I have not seen since last May in New Zealand.

It was ghastly as the whole lot was riddled with cockroaches. They must have got in on the boat and laid millions of eggs. They were everywhere and made me feel quite sick. Every glass or cup had little ones squirming at the bottom. They have made holes in the blankets and done other damage, including eating the strings of all the tennis rackets.

We had to take all the wrapping paper out into the garden as fast as we unwrapped to burn it all. Several times since I have woken up at night with nightmares about cockroaches crawling all over me.

Filaria is a big problem in Ceylon. We had a dinner party the other night and one of the guests was Dr Neville Rajapaksa, who is a world expert on the subject.

Apparently we all have to have filaria tests every six months and the children have to be kept up late as they have to take place at night. It is a disease, like malaria, which is carried by mosquitoes and if it is not diagnosed early enough worms block the lymphatic gland. This causes elephantiasis when different parts of the body, usually the legs, swell to a huge size. We have seen quite a lot of cases of this around.

6 June 1966

Have you seen the recent *Vogue* with pictures of Ceylon? There has been a terrible fuss here about the article as the models were all photographed outside the temples, which are very sacred, and the Buddhists have been very offended.

Questions have been asked in Parliament, and the editor of *Vogue* has to apologize. They talk about 'scantily dressed' models, though they are all wearing long dresses and trousers.

Actually it is a good article, and would encourage tourists — which is what they want. But there is very little hotel accommodation here, only the Galle Face Hotel, Mount Lavinia and the Taprobane in Colombo, and out of Colombo the resthouses are small and often very basic. [The situation is very different now.]

PS. Please could you send me some fluoride tablets which are unobtainable here? The water is terrible and everyone has decayed teeth.

13 June 1966

Last night we gave our first cocktail party for 80 people. It started at 7.00 p.m. and finished at 10.30 p.m. — successful? What heaven just to order what I want, leave everything, and just do the flowers. I quite enjoyed the party and I usually loathe my own.

Our High Commissioner, Sir Stanley Tomlinson, duly received his knighthood in the birthday honours, so the Queen's Birthday party had added interest. Sir Stanley is a very friendly man with a great interest in wine and hobbies of trout fishing and reading poetry and fiction. He has also managed to learn Sinhalese to add to his French, German, Spanish and Japanese. [In the first part of his retirement he rewrote Sir Marcus Cheke's book, *Diplomatic Procedures: Code of Etiquette*, which tells us all how to behave, what we should do, how and when!] They had 700 people, all in the High Commissioner's garden, which was floodlit. Thank heavens it did not rain.

This is our first evening in for a week. We are meeting more and more people. The Ceylonese are such fun and so friendly and the diplomats here are a more interesting lot than in New Zealand.

Went to dinner with our Deputy High Commissioner, Jim Dutton, a man who never stops working. He and his wife are very religious — they are fundamentalists and believe everything in the Bible — at least the wife does. It was embarrassing at dinner; there were 14 of us including the American ambassador and wife, who is a relation of the Kennedy's, four Buddhist Ceylonese, the Jewish chargé d'affaires and a few Europeans. We all duly sat down to dinner at our allotted places, then our host asked us all to stand up again and he said a very long grace in front of a large picture of Jesus with the caption, 'Christ is the silent listener at every conversation' — just the thing to get a diplomatic party going! I overheard the hostess saying to Ramati, the Jew, she hoped he did not mind.

20 June 1966

There was a large, interesting dinner with the Indian trade commissioner where the guests included Colonel Derek de Saram. He is a very well-known pale-skinned Ceylonese cricketer who before the war scored 100 for Oxford against the Australian touring team which is a bond with Michael as he also scored 100 against the Australians as a freshman at Cambridge in 1956. He is also a politician and a soldier

31

and has recently been released from four years in prison for heading a coup against Mrs Bandaranaike. He is the second politician we have met who has just emerged from prison. [He was also a low-handicap golfer and was later to manage the Royal Colombo Golf Club.]

The rest of our luggage has now arrived and our washing machine is working. Marvellous. I do all the washing now it is so easy. I just put soap and clothes in and leave it.

The nanny sat spellbound watching the cycle from beginning to end. She had never seen anything like it.

30 June 1966

Do hope the presents for Lucy's birthday arrive OK. There is nothing in the shops and they have now also made it impossible to buy materials without coupons — and you only have coupons if you have a rice ration book — which we and lots of others do not — so no materials.

Ceylon has a national bank strike next week and various other strikes on tea estates around the country. There is also lots of talk of devaluation following India. The government here is in a fair old mess.

Last week we gave a very pleasant dinner party. Amongst the guests were Sathi and Padmini Coomaraswamy, he is a businessman who is also a distinguished Ceylonese cricketer, Antonio de Rocha de Ferera, the Brazilian ambassador, George Seymour and his wife Marie Claire, the Canadian first secretary [whom we saw again later as Canadian High Commissioner in Singapore], Siva Chinnatamby, the country's leading gynaecologist who is always off on family planning conferences all over the world, and a brilliant young lawyer, Lalith Athulathmudali, who was president of the Oxford Union. [He later became Minister of Security during the Tamil troubles in the 1980s and formed his own party in the early 1990s. He was assassinated in April 1993.] An interesting collection.

Michael now plays golf quite regularly before breakfast with the Prime Minister, Dudley Senanayake, whom we had met at breakfast at the Pieris' shortly after our arrival and who is very pleasant indeed. A Ceylonese custom is to go out to breakfast to eat string hoppers which are made of rice flour and curry and which my tummy finds a bit difficult to cope with so early in the morning.

As he is a fanatic about cricket he was interested in Michael's record, and when they got on to golf he asked Michael if he would like to play with him early one morning. Michael enjoyed it very much, and although they did not talk much politics other diplomats and senior Ceylonese all know about this special connection and seem to think that Michael might know all sorts of interesting inside information.

11 July 1966
The labour adviser from the British High Commission in India, Alan Read, has been staying with us for a few days as Michael is in charge of labour affairs in the office, which is quite a job as there are more unions in Ceylon than in England and France together. We have just come back from the Simpsons' upcountry tea estate where we spent two days. They laid on a party of planters with whom Alan could discuss labour problems as lots of the tea estate workers are on strike now. They are stateless Tamils from south India who are doing very well compared with the life they would lead back in India, but badly in comparison with the average worker here. But overall they are not too badly treated and we hear from all sides how much better their conditions are now than they were a few years ago. Schools and hospitals have been organized, and the 'lines' they live in, which are rows of one-storey huts, are in better condition. Poverty is very comparative.

21 July 1966
We all went for the day to a beach house at Bentota, which is about one hour from here. Several firms have houses there for their staff to use. It is a lovely spot and we ate lots of curry, and swam very carefully, for it is extremely dangerous in the monsoon and frequent drownings occur down the coast. The bungalows are on a spit of land with sea one side and river the other — so you can always swim in the river and water-ski. [This area has now been totally developed with hotels.]

6 August 1966
Drove up to Kandy, which is in the centre of Ceylon, for the state funeral of the *mahanayake* of the area — he is the Buddhist equivalent of an archbishop. We went officially on behalf of the British government to lay a wreath as no one else from the office could go. It was quite an occasion.

We drove up in a cavalcade of official cars with sirens and police clearing the way and scattering children, animals, hens and all the paraphernalia of village life to all sides. We were with the Australian High Commissioner and his wife, George and Elizabeth Upton, who are very friendly and unassuming. [He later became Australian High Commissioner in London.]

When we arrived we were ushered into the temple to see the deceased lying in state. He was uncovered and had been dead for seven days. We all walked around the body, which I found quite a shock as I had never seen a dead person before. We then had a service in the open air with hundreds of people in the blazing sun in front of the funeral pyre, which was enormous. There were lots of speeches in Sinhala, including ones by the Prime Minister and Governor General, which were rather boring as we did not understand a word. Then Buddhist monks in saffron robes climbed to the top of the bonfire to deposit the body. They then came down and set it alight. The whole thing shot up in flames and was very spectacular.

The strange thing was that no one was very sad or moved, and people talked and joked throughout the proceedings. But I suppose for Buddhists death is not sad at all, merely a moving on to the next stage. It was a colourful occasion too with all the national dress and the Kandyan princes in all their glory. But it was very hot, and we all wished we had brought sunshades with us.

14 August 1966

Ian and Angela Beer are staying with us. Ian is headmaster of Ellesmere School in Shropshire who used to play back row forward for England and he has been invited by the Ceylon Rugby Association to coach for three weeks. [He was later to become headmaster of Harrow School and president of the English Rugby Union.]

Yesterday the clerk of the House of Representatives, Sam Wije-singhe, whose wife Mukta runs the Girl Guides here, invited us all to hear the debate on the budget and have lunch in his rooms. Sam is a beautifully old-fashioned gentleman with impeccable manners who cherishes British institutions and Mukta is a very energetic, outgoing, impressive lady.

He said he had asked two other ex-rugger playing MPs as well. Guess who they were? J. R. Jayawardene, the Minister of State and power behind Senanayake, who never wears Western clothes but always looks very elegant in traditional Ceylonese dress, and Pieter Keunemann,

34

leader of the Communist Party and ex-president of the Cambridge Union. It was an amazing mixture. JR, as he is commonly known, is a formal, awe-inspiring figure but he is very friendly to us as we know his brother. He is always remembered for a speech he made in San Francisco advocating a League of Nations.

JR and Pieter seem to get on well, but it was too awkward to discuss politics so we stuck to games. Keunemann spoke after lunch. He is a terribly handsome man in his fifties, aligned to the Moscow party, whom I often see doing his daily swim at the SSC Swimming Club. He looked up to the speaker's gallery after he had made a joke to see if we were laughing, and then was very critical of JR. All very amusing, and Ian was thrilled.

21 August 1966

This afternoon we are off with the Pieris' to the jungle at Yala, which is in the south east of the island. We are staying for five nights and it is quite a palaver getting ready for we have to take everything with us as our bungalow is in the middle of nowhere. Apart from all the food for ten people we have to take all the water. We have got a Land-Rover so we will be able to see more of the jungle. Also there is a drought in Yala, where it has not rained for four months, so it should be good for seeing animals. There is a drought here too and unless it rains soon we shall have water rationing. And this is supposed to be the wettest season.

At the moment we can buy no butter, no dried milk and fresh milk is strictly rationed, nail files, washing powder, tissues, prickly heat powder, or potatoes. But crabs and prawns are lovely!

1 September 1966

Yala was lovely though parched. Luckily our drinking water (which we took with us in large containers) lasted out, but we had to rely on the river, not very clean, and the sea for washing for five days. So the children never washed, only swam and loved it.

There are only three bungalows in the game parks and they have to be booked months in advance. Hotels have not been invented in the jungles of Ceylon. [They have now.] There was a cook provided; we lived on curry and rice and I have put on pounds. All nine of us went off twice a day, early morning and early evening, with a tracker. We saw a lot of elephants — really exciting to see them wild — and one charged us, which was *too* exciting! And crocodiles, monkeys, buffalo, deer, pig and lovely birds — including hundreds of peacocks, some of which danced with their tails up, which was an impressive sight. Unfortunately we saw no leopard or bear, I think because of the drought.

We wore sarongs nearly all the time and it was lovely to live wild for a while with no other signs of civilization. We didn't even have a radio with us.

Yesterday we took Timothy and Andrew up to Kandy to see the annual *Perahera*, a Buddhist festival. Kandy is attractively set out around a lake and has a lot of charm, and the Temple of the Tooth is old and fascinating. It was built to house the tooth of Buddha which was brought into Ceylon around AD 313. You cannot see the tooth as it is hidden in several gold caskets shaped like *dagaba*s. *Dagaba*s are called *stupa*s in India and are mounds of earth built over relics which are developed into large pagoda-like structures, which are representative of Buddha's mind. These gold caskets only emerge once a year at the *Perahera* ceremony when they are paraded through the streets on the back of a white, very large tusker elephant. According to someone who has actually seen the tooth it is enormous and if it really had been the Buddha's he must have been a giant. In 1915 there were famous *Perahera* riots, which were a serious outbreak of Sinhalese–Tamil communal violence, but happily it is normally an occasion of celebration and rejoicing. It takes place at night and is very exciting, and very long, in front of large crowds, many of whom wait patiently for 12 hours or more.

There were 100 elephants in fantastic illuminated costumes, flaming torchbearers on both sides of the column, whip-crackers with four-yard-long whips, marvellous drummers, pipers, cymbal players and dancers of all varieties and ages. We were all quite entranced. I reckon it is something Timothy and Andrew will remember for a long time — we certainly shall.

17 September 1966

Now I am on the Charity Committee of our High Commission and we went to visit a Cheshire Home which was opened last year in Colombo by Group Captain Cheshire, with crippled, mongol [Down's syndrome] and paralysed kids, which was very sad. I now have to try to organize some help there on a regular basis as it seems to be run on a rather chaotic basis as regards nurses and general care.

24 September 1966

We met Jeremy Thorpe, the Liberal MP, here the other day. He was on a brief holiday to stay with his Ceylonese barrister friend, Tissa Wijey-eratne, whom he appears to visit here regularly. [Michael met Jeremy Thorpe 12 years later in Whitehall and said, 'You may not remember me, we met in Sri Lanka,' and Jeremy Thorpe replied, 'Of course I do. You were wearing a deliciously light blue suit!']

Tissa is a rather notorious communist, but delightfully witty and sophisticated, and has spent 14 years overseas — in London — as well as Peking, Moscow and Hungary. At present he is defending General Udugama who is on trial for an attempted coup in February. He sees this as a political chance for Mrs Bandaranaike's opposition party, of which he is a member, as he thinks that people will not like this persecution of General Udugama who is the first Buddhist Sinhalese general, and that this is going to cause anti-government feeling.

At the moment Dudley's party is going through a bad time and people think that if there were an election Mrs Bandaranaike would walk it — if the army did not revolt again meanwhile.

We have a new cook, Cruz, who suggests food to eat when I cannot think what to have, or cannot get what I want to have, which happens frequently, and is a great help. He is a very big, jolly man and his speciality is tricks for children — the favourite is producing eggs from their ears! Timothy and Andrew are always asking when they will see you again and when can they go back to England because they like England more than Ceylon as they can toboggan there.

4 October 1966

The rain has been terrible for ten days and there are dreadful floods now with thousands homeless. It is dreadful to see all the flooded little shacks with people living on their roofs and on bridges and in trees. It does seem to be stopping now, though we are still getting very heavy downpours.

The Cheshire Home is so depressing. There are 12 children there, the house is leaking everywhere and the beds are all soaking wet. No doctors seem to visit or help the children. They appear to be just dumped with a kindly matron who has no chance to do very much. We are going to see another Cheshire Home, there are two in Ceylon, then decide what we can do best to help. I think if the group captain saw the state the home is in after a year he might think twice about opening it without efficient follow-up checks. He has left it in charge of a committee of Ceylonese who really are not always the most efficient people, and have masses of problems of their own to cope with.

18 October 1966

Trincomalee is wonderful for a holiday. We went with Bunchy and Ghoolbai Gunasekera; he is Sinhalese and runs a trading house in Colombo and she is Indian, a very sweet couple with a four-year-old daughter. It takes four and a half hours to drive to Trincomalee, which is on the north-east coast (in the dry zone) and populated mostly by Tamils. [Since the violent flare-up of Tamil–Sinhalese troubles in the 1980s this has become one of the Tamil areas of Ceylon that is uninhabited by Sinhalese and unvisited by tourists.] It is a quiet place now, a naval base for Ceylon's *very* few boats and air force base for their *very* few planes. During the war the whole of the Far Eastern Fleet was based there. It is a magnificent natural harbour.

The highlight of the holiday for me was on one of our boat trips around the harbour when we saw a mother and father elephant and two baby elephants all swimming in line from one island to another with their trunks up in the air.

Yesterday we came home via Polonnaruwa to see the magnificent remains of what used to be the capital of the Sinhalese kings around AD 700. It is not by any means all excavated — it used to have a population of one and a half million — but there are vast *dagaba*s, temples and wonderful statues of the Buddha, lovely carvings and frescoes.

We would like to have stayed there longer, but it rained so hard that we had to go back to the resthouse for lunch. This is on the banks of a huge tank; these are the man-made irrigation lakes which abound in Ceylon, primarily for the growing of rice, which is the country's principal food. The Sinhalese were so excellent in irrigation that by the eighth century, so it is said, the King of Kashmir sent to Ceylon for the loan of irrigation engineers.

Ceylon abounds in history and there are many other places we must

38

visit. In particular there is another large ruined city at Anuradhapura which is earlier than Polonnaruwa and was constructed around 300 BC and used to have five million living there. In fact Polonnaruwa was constructed by Sinhalese who had to abandon Anuradhapura to the Tamils who looted and demolished their city. I am afraid the Tamil and Sinhalese troubles have been around for a long time.

26 October 1966

I have had quite a success with three polio children at the Colombo Cheshire Home. Having had no medical treatment one has now had a much needed operation, and the other two are having physio and sticks and learning to walk. Up to now they have all been crawling around on all fours, no one knows their exact age, but they are round about eight years old. It has required quite a lot of pestering various medical contacts we have, and I have to get wives to help with transporting them to and from the hospital, but it is really worth it. Two of the children should be able to lead reasonable lives after this, although the third will always be very crippled. The next thing is to tackle their education: at the moment they receive virtually none and all three are bright and lively.

8 November 1966

We have been to two dances. The one on UN Day was with a rather stuffy party, half the men would not dance; the other was the New Zealand/Australia/Ceylon dance where we sat with the New Zealand and Australian High Commissioners and a distinguished party, including Sir John Kothalawala, an ex-Prime Minister of 75. He is a very rich, flamboyant character who has a farm in Kent with a heated swimming pool [this was quite something in 1966], a house in London and a farm with a small zoo near the airport in Ceylon. He danced once, with me, the first time I have danced with an ex-Prime Minister.

The UNP, the party in power, is in a bad way, having just lost three seats at by-elections. Dudley is not well — Michael has not seen him on the golf course at 6.00 a.m. for ages. There is a large mercantile strike on at the moment which is having bad effects on the economy. No government yet has run its full term; the way things are going Mrs Bandaranaike may well be back before too long. All rather depressing for most of our friends, nearly all of whom are UNP supporters.

Yesterday we gave a good dinner party. The chief guests were Judge Abeysundere and his wife, Mrs Abeysundere, who is an astrologist and used to advise all the ministers in the last government about their horoscopes. No doubt this government has a different astrologer. It is amazing how much notice they take of this sort of thing when running the country. The judge himself is a marvellous talker and rather a mystic.

We had the Australian High Commissioner and his wife, the secretary of the Employers' Federation — he is very involved with the strike but told the Minister of Labour he could not have a meeting that night as he was busy.

Also we had Conrad Dias who is Ceylonese with an English wife, Eileen, who are good friends of ours and he is the head of the Chamber of Commerce here, and Frank and Joan Sargeant, he is our new first secretary and they are both great fun and a welcome addition to the High Commission. Our cook excelled himself and we had a marvellous evening and the guest of honour did not leave till 12.30 a.m.

15 November 1966
At the moment I am ill in bed aching all over with mosquito-borne dengue fever. Last night we went to a dreary cocktail party but tonight we have been able to cancel one thanks to dengue.

1 December 1966
Here it is really hot, though supposedly the cool time of the year. I have got over my dengue, though it leaves you rather washed out. The diplomatic wives organized a dinner dance in aid of flood victims and we all provided food. There are 27 countries represented in Ceylon. The Governor General and PM came and it was all very successful.

7 December 1966
All sorts of people have been having charity sales to which unfortunately I have to go. And cocktail parties are far too frequent. Things are so busy now, thank heavens for siestas.

Enclosed is a list of things which please could you send as soon as possible and give me the account. The economic situation in Ceylon is really bad now and they are cutting down on all imports — and stopping all so-called 'luxury' goods. Some of the things might get through in the diplomatic air bag in thick envelopes with luck. A very happy

Xmas to you all! We will be drinking your health upcountry on Xmas day where we shall be with the Simpsons on their tea estate.

2 January 1967
Christmas on the Simpsons' tea estate, elevation 4300 feet, was wonderful. It is a lovely bungalow with incredible views of the tea country all around, and the garden, tended by countless Tamil workers, is out of this world, with tropical frangipani, hibiscus and bougainvillaea mixed with very English roses and delphiniums and all growing happily together. Christmas Day was quiet with a tree, turkey, stockings, a lovely wood fire and the Queen's speech on the World Service, just like home.

Our stay was tranquil except for our ascent of Adam's Peak. It is 7200 feet high and one of the holiest mountains in the world for Buddhists, Muslims, Hindus and Christians and thousands of pilgrims climb it every year. At the top is a footprint of five feet seven inches by two feet seven inches, but this is merely a carving and the real print is supposedly on a huge sapphire underneath. For the Sinhalese it is of course the footprint of the Buddha, for the Arabs and later for the Chinese it is the footprint of the first man, for the Hindus it is either the footprint of Siva or Saman, and for the Christians the footprint of Adam or perhaps St Thomas. But all the pilgrims meet in amity on the summit where there are temples and outhouses for priests and curators of all faiths.

The climb was through the night as the idea is to reach the summit at dawn and see the shadow cast by the peak at sunrise. It was slightly out of the pilgrim season and as it was wet and misty we climbed the safe way, up many thousands of steps instead of walking up through the jungle. It was most tiring and required concentration as the steps were of varying heights and steepness and many were broken, but thankfully it was lit by electric light. The climb took us two and a half hours each way but sadly when we reached the summit it was cloudy and we missed the famous shadow and the magnificent view of the sea and the lights of Colombo. Nevertheless we have now acquired 'merit' but this feeling soon evaporates and we can now hardly move for sore calves and knees.

18 January 1967
The poor old Ceylon government, the UNP, is depressed. It has lost its

third recent by-election, the economy is stagnating, foreign aid is not coming in the quantities expected, and now there is a world rice shortage and they have had to cut the rice ration by half. To compensate for this toughness, however, they now give the rice ration (2 lb per week) away free and this is the only country, welfare state or not, in the world to do anything like this. All who can afford it have been exhorted not to claim their ration in the patriotic interest.

Whatever the government says and despite the shortage of goods in the shops, we certainly do not get the impression that we are living under a state of emergency, which in fact we have been, with a ten-day break, since 8 January last year. The government purports to fear outbreaks of racial violence between the Tamils and Sinhalese if it does not censor the press and control public meetings. This is quite understandable as the opposition Marxist and communist parties, including those influenced by Moscow and China, blatantly incite the people to strike, commit *satyagraha*, civil disobedience, and anything else to embarrass and possibly topple the government.

Last *poya* day 25 of us went to Ryle and Kaminee de Soysa's family estate. The de Soysas are cousins of Ian Pieris' and seem to know or be related to everyone in Colombo, his brother is the Bishop of Colombo, and they have become very good friends of ours. Ryle is a small cherubic man who was educated at Oxford, which he enjoyed, and he has many business and estate interests in Ceylon.

There are 700 acres of coconuts, and a lovely old house which is uninhabited but kept up for the occasional family visit. We walked, talked, drank, had a lovely curry lunch, then played 'cricket' under the coconuts much to Timothy and Andrew's delight.

23 January 1967

Just spent three pleasant days watching the West Indies play Ceylon. It was great fun to see. Ceylon made 400 runs, Ian Pieris and Neil Chamnugan had a thrilling ninth wicket stand of 70 runs in 50 minutes against Wes Hall and Charlie Griffith. The West Indies were then 549 declared, with three centuries including Sobers. It was the first test match of Clive Lloyd from Guyana. The match ended as a draw with Ceylon not out in the second innings. Lots of good batting and bowling. [Neil Chamnugan was later to knock Michael out in the final of the single wicket competition.]

27 January 1967
I have given up pottery now. They never got around to baking the pots, so it was all rather pointless.

5 February 1967
Andrew today started at St Thomas's Preparatory School. He went off very happily and pleased with himself in his smart uniform and I hope he continues this way when he is made to work hard. Thank you very much for Timothy's present, which has arrived in time for his birthday. Sadly the big gun had snapped in two on the journey but the screaming bazooka part still works!

Perhaps because we started off with caviar and vodka cocktails a dinner party we gave for our new DHC, Jim Dutton, was very successful. Two of the guests, Judge Abeysundere and his wife, are very friendly now and I frequently get sent gifts of her home-made pickles and curries, which are all very hot and delicious.

The other day the judge arranged for me to spend a morning at court watching a murder trial — there is a very high murder rate in Ceylon, especially in the hot weather — and then an appeal by an MP who has been removed from his seat because of his bribery and intimidation during the election. He had been found guilty and was appealing to the chief justice and two other judges. The MP's lawyer is a left-wing character, so is the MP who is a very clever chap and equally as good at rabble rousing as charming judges. There have been a lot of these election cases, and if the chap is found guilty he is not allowed to stand for Parliament for seven years and they have a by-election. All court work is in English with translators as necessary.

Aelian Kannangara, a leading barrister and also Derek de Saram's lawyer, had a fabulous party the other day. He has a vast house and it was a sit-down dinner for 100 with dancing to two bands until 5.00 a.m. — we left at 1.00 a.m. [Aelian Kannangara was later appointed ambassador but was unable to take up the post due to a change of government.] Dudley Senanayake, the Prime Minister, was there and I sat and had a long talk to him. He is really sweet and he loves his food, but the poor chap has not really much grip on the present chaos here. He loves talking about golf and cricket and sat solidly and watched the West Indies versus Ceylon for three days. There is going to be an Oxford and Cambridge golf match soon. The Cambridge team consists of the PM, his brother Robert, his cousin R. G. Senanayake, who is in the opposition party and a leftist, and Michael.

Now I have started painting classes. There is quite an interesting teacher but I do not think I will enjoy it much as all the women spend half the time discussing cooking and it is hard to concentrate. But the Colombo College of Art is no better as there they all speak Sinhalese and I cannot understand anything.

12 February 1967

You know I mentioned a party where I had sat with the Prime Minister? Some new left-wing paper printed a slanderous article about Dudley at a dissolute Western-style party saying that he stayed all night, danced lasciviously, drank, carved a sucking pig which had been cooked alive after being beaten with rods, and had also been fed with beef. All terrible things for Buddhists. The host, Aelian Kannangara, denied this in the newspaper, but the police raided the newspaper office and the paper was banned, the editors prosecuted and parliamentary questions asked. Dudley did in fact drink brandy, and there was a roast sucking pig to eat, but he did not dance, and never does.

There are often incidents of this type here. Ceylon is full of endless gossip, intrigue and rumours.

Now I must go to our wives sewing group. I loathe it, but bring a few things home to do on the machine. As I am on our Charity Committee, and one of the senior wives, don't laugh, I have to seem keen to encourage the junior ones. I would far rather visit the Cheshire Home or the family planning clinic more often.

26 February 1967

Our labour adviser from Delhi and his wife, Alan and Dorothy Read, are staying with us. We had a large party for 60 trade unionists and some benign employers — not so many of them. The unionists are all left-wing — Marxist, Marxist Revolutionary, Independent, so they say, Peking Communist and Moscow Communist. The last two categories did not turn up, rather to our relief. Dress informal produced open-necked shirt, shirt and tie, spruce suit, national dress and a type of bed jacket with a white sarong.

The main trade union leaders are almost more dignified than high commissioners. They are chauffeur driven and are accompanied by their staff, secretaries, stooges and bodyguards. These people watch their masters, and then copy them. They all smiled happily when the big boss took a whisky and not fruit juice. Some 60 people drank nine large bottles of whisky, six bottles of gin and six of brandy.

There were no unseemly incidents, though we were slightly worried when the three policemen guarding the cars came in for a quick noggin at the end rather drunk already — brotherly comradeship. I am not sure how much good a labour adviser does, but Michael finds he helps him to meet people he would never have an excuse to talk to otherwise. This is important because the government is indecisive and feeble and the unionists are taking great advantage of this and having a desperate effect on the economy.

There has been a three-week general bank strike with no sign of an early end. The public sector, which has not had a pay increase for 15 years, the plantation workers and dockers are all threatening strike action. Ceylon as usual is in a state of emergency, but we have been under such a state for all but 19 of our days here now and it means little. It just gives the government useful reserve powers. They have so far only been exercised to ban some processions, large-scale protest meetings and press criticism. Now I feel an expert on the labour scene here. There is masses of anti-British and anti-West feeling, all discussed in mostly good humoured fashion.

15 March 1967
St Joseph's Nursing Home, Colombo
I expect you have now heard from Michael that I am in the above nursing home having had my appendix removed very suddenly. This happened eight days ago. I felt ghastly for two days after, but since then have quite enjoyed my stay with lots of visitors, lots of flowers, a very comfy nursing home (for Europeans only) and I am going home this evening.

The only drawback is that Dr Noel Bartholemew, one of the leading Ceylonese surgeons who always has an orchid in his buttonhole, did a laperotomy, which was a much larger operation than necessary and I shall have a very big scar. But there we are. Anyway I am quite pleased to take it easy for a while as parties in this hot weather are quite exhausting as you stand with sweat pouring down your legs, and I now have a wonderful excuse not to do anything.

24 March 1967
Malwatte Bungalows, Aislaby Estates, Bandarawela

Having had a week in Colombo convalescing, we are now at the above address 4000 feet up having a lovely few days in a planter's bungalow with some American friends, Jack and Maria Eaves, from the United States Embassy. It is so hot in Colombo now that it is heavenly to be up here.

The children are having a wonderful time; the boys playing cricket with our friends' son who is quite good for an American and the girls running around the lovely garden and playing with their dolls. The children all read a lot. Lucy reads upside down; perhaps a result of her New Zealand birth? There is golf, tennis and bridge in the evenings. The days are hot and sunny and the nights cold with log fires, a perfect climate. We would all like to stay up here for a month.

17 April 1967

Back yesterday from an east coast holiday with the de Soysas, which was most successful. I feel I have seen a lot of the island now. We stayed the first four nights in a rather rough bungalow near Batticaloa, which was very small and cramped as there were 11 of us in all. Batticaloa is a dull place, described as the 'muddy lagoon', though it has an attractive fort, and its population is mainly Tamil. But we drove daily for three-quarters of an hour to a heavenly beach, which was calm, shallow and deserted.

Then we went on to stay two nights at the resthouse in Galoya, which is again fairly basic but in a lovely setting. This is an area of the dry zone that used to be jungle, but which is now being cultivated and colonized. For the last 20 years they have been constructing dams for irrigation, clearing jungle and building roads. The main Galoya water scheme collects water from 700 square miles, the area of Surrey, its water surface covers 35 square miles, and its volume is greater than all the other tanks in Ceylon put together.

We were taken to visit some Veddhas. These are a dying tribe of a completely uncivilized people of great antiquity — one of the primitive types of mankind. They are more primitive than the Aborigines, with a far simpler, utterly basic lifestyle. We saw a group of four families. They were very short (the average height of the men is just over five feet and of the women four feet nine inches) but sturdy, a blackish brown colour, with wavy hair and rather vacant expressions. They live in primitive huts in the middle of the unhealthy dense jungle and are scantily clothed. They looked very wild — we must have been among the very few white people they have seen — never smiled or made any expression at all. They stared at us and we stared at them. Then one chap posed with a bow and arrow and did a warlike dance!

After two nights in the resthouse we drove on to Ratnapura in the south-west area of the island, at the centre of the Ceylon gem-mining industry. We stayed at the manager's bungalow at a rice growing estate belonging to the de Soysas. It was paddy planting time, and Ryle de Soysa had to be there at dawn for the ceremonies that go with new cultivation of his land with garlands, lamps, firecrackers, dancing and local delicacies. We all joined in the planting and waded knee deep in the paddy mud planting seed. It was a very biblical scene, side by side with the nearly naked paddy workers with Adam's Peak in the background.

And now we are back in hot, steamy Colombo. Today we have had a great storm and rain, so perhaps the monsoon is starting. I hope so.

17 May 1967
The government is cutting down on imports more than ever and we shall have to bring lots of food back with us from leave, so we are saving hard. There are constant shortages now of butter, sugar, dried milk (fresh is never available), cheese, bacon — the list is endless. Apparently next year will be worse.

1 June 1967
No letter since I last wrote to you, the bag seems to have been delayed this week. I am longing to hear from you. What I am really enjoying is learning how to do batik. I am taught by a lady who trained in Indonesia, which is where the craft originally developed. I sit on a little stool besides a little stove with bubbling wax on top and draw with a *tjanting*, a little pen-like instrument, and paint the wax on with brushes. Ten for dinner tonight. It is so difficult to think of varied menus, indeed any menus at all, as half the ingredients are unobtainable.

9 July 1967
Went to the opening of Parliament and the Governor General, Sir

William Gopallawa, read the throne speech. All pomp and ceremony and very interesting — apart from a slight drawback. We had to listen to the speech three times, first in Sinhalese, 36 minutes, second in Tamil, 32 minutes and finally in English, 19 minutes. This showed us what a splendid, concise language English is and how mad they are not to use it all the time and unite their country instead of the hotchpotch and muddle there is now.

19 July 1967
Lucy had a lovely fourth birthday even though your present parcel had sadly not arrived. She talks with such a broad Ceylonese accent now it is very difficult sometimes to understand her.

The Eaves, our American Embassy friends, have now left, which is very sad; we finally saw them off at the airport. The UAR ambassador was also there seeing someone off and we all deliberately and diplomatically ignored each other. [This was post-Suez.] Timothy was most upset as his friend Bryan was leaving. Poor Timothy, his three best friends have all left Ceylon in the last three months. These perpetual goodbyes are very depressing for all of us.

Masanam has now retired to Tamil Nadu in south India; it is very sad and I would have been lost without him. Timothy will miss his daily nonstop bowling practice! [Masanam was keen on cricket and they would play together for hours.] But we have Govindan to replace him who is also a Tamil from India and he is doing fine; he works very quickly and managed to cope with a cocktail party followed by a dinner party that we had to give last week.

Masanam, who had worked in Ceylon for 30 years, and had kept his savings in a box under his bed for all that time, had great difficulty getting permission to take his money out of the country. The authorities refused to accept that he could have saved so much money legally and were only going to give him permission to take a quarter out.

Thank heavens the situation was saved out of the blue when I raised the matter with Thondeman, a millionaire trade unionist responsible for the tea estate workers, whom we know well, and who looks after stateless Tamils on his own tea estates. He nodded and said he would mention the problem to a friend. A week later Masanam was officially notified that he could remit all his life's savings to India and that there had been a misunderstanding. [I kept in touch with Masanam until he

48

died in 1992. His retirement in Tamil Nadu, with endless problems of drought and getting enough to eat, had not been peaceful.]

24 July 1967

The main news is my great success at the Cheshire Home in arranging for the three polio children, for whom I had organized medical treatment last year, to go to school. I think I mentioned that they were getting no proper education. I approached the headmaster of a primary school very close to the home and asked him if he would take the children, and was at first met with a firm 'no'.

When I asked him the reasons he said their disabilities would make it impossible, and when I asked him why he said that there were steps which they would not be able to climb when entering the school. This conversation went on for a while, but gradually he softened, and admitted that they probably would be able to cope, and finally accepted them. I shall never forget the happiness on the boys' faces when I told them that they were going to be able to go to school.

Gave a curry lunch for 20 on pre-*poya* day and that evening we went to a party for Ryle de Soysa's fiftieth birthday. I spent most of the evening sitting with his brother, the Bishop of Colombo, J. R. Jayawardene, who is the real brain of the government and at present acting Prime Minister, and Ian Pieris's uncle, the Chief Justice, Hugh Fernando. He and his wife Doris are very friendly and we see a lot of them. Hugh is only 5ft. 2in. and a very slight build; he is particularly sweet with children and Lucy loves sitting on his knee. Dr Gamani Corea, who is the chief in the Ministry of Economic Planning, was also there, and is another of Ian Pieris's relations! He gets all the good jobs here as he is an enormously articulate academic theoretician, but apparently sees too many alternative points of view to make decisions. Michael met him on a trip to Nuwara Eliya, which is upcountry in the centre of the tea-growing area, when visiting unionists and seeing labour conditions with Alan Read our labour adviser, and Gamani pointed out that he would get more insight into Ceylon's economy and industrial conditions by keeping him company on the golf course for two days. So they played 72 holes of golf and in the evenings I joined them drinking beer in his family bungalow. [He later became governor of the Central Bank and Secretary General of UNCTAD, the United Nations Committee on Trade and Development.]

The de Soysas very kindly had us to stay on their rubber estate at Ratnapura overnight as we had to be at the official opening of a new dam two and a half hours away from Colombo at 5.46 a.m., which was the auspicious hour. We had to get up at 2.30 a.m. It was fascinating driving around the irrigation area, and then we came home around the south coast — 16 hours in a Land-Rover.

Excellent you raising £28 at your coffee party. On the 26th I am doing exactly the same thing. We have raffles of things they cannot get here, which is easy enough as that means most things. Nescafe and asparagus tins are particularly popular. I have 60 people coming — ghastly, I dread it.

We really feel ready for leave now. I have got to the stage of not being able to think of anything to say to people and am longing to watch television again.

30 November 1967

All now happily settled back in Ceylon and the kids have returned to school. Timothy and Andrew have got way behind in maths after their weeks at Holy Trinity Primary School [the local primary school in Guildford] and Timothy, to his disgust, is having some extra lessons to teach him about division as his class has been doing it all term and he has no clue at all. But they are very happy to be back in spite of academic problems.

And now I have to prepare lots of figures of expenses and costs of one year living in Colombo as we are having the dreaded inspectors here in January on a periodical review of the post. Working out the figures for all the entertainment we do is an awful job, and whatever happens they always seem to end up cutting down on the staff and our expense allowances. On the 28th the wives are having a sale of work; luckily I have missed the work.

Looking forward very much to seeing you on 8 December and hope you have a good flight.

7 January 1968

The 15th was the *Thai Pongal* holiday. This is a Hindu festival rather like our harvest festival and we had two get-togethers with Hindu friends to celebrate, one at 10.30 a.m. and the other at 6.30 p.m. We passed a Hindu procession in which there was a man hanging from three butcher-type hooks in his back and lots of people with sticks through their cheeks. I was very sorry you were not there with your cine camera — it was all very nasty and the children were agog.

Had some good tennis yesterday with Michael, Noel Costa and Prince Arunachalam. He is commonly known as Aru, and is not really a prince, though he comes from a very distinguished high-caste Tamil family who had great wealth, most of which Aru has been through. His grandfather was appointed the first black judge in the British Empire. He is a close friend of the Maharajahs of Baroda and Jaipur and frequently goes there to stay. But when you see him at the golf club he plays with one club, barefooted, without a caddie, does all his newspaper reading there to save on subscriptions, and they have had to have the club telephone padlocked because of him.

10 February 1968
Have you heard of Arthur C. Clarke? He is an Englishman who writes lots of science fiction books and lives in Colombo just opposite the Pieris'. At present he is making a film with Stanley Kubrick called *2001: A Space Odyssey* which is costing ten million US dollars. We met him the other day when the High Commissioner had cocktails for a delegation of space scientists who have been here on a Commonwealth conference. He had brought his giant telescope to the party and we all looked at the moon and he showed me what a satellite looked like. Apparently his great hobby is table tennis. [In 1995 he still lives in the same house in Colombo and from time to time has had huge telescopes, giant dishes and even mini-hovercraft in his garden. At one time he dabbled in solar powered cars. He runs a business, Underwater Safaris Ltd, with a Sri Lankan who, with his wife and three children, shares his house with him, but is now rather deaf and fairly infirm due to a muscular disease.]

The weather is getting hotter. No rain since you left; the lawn is looking brown and dry and we may get no more rain until May. There are problems with the house as all our pipes are getting blocked and our water supplies are getting more spasmodic and inefficient, but the landlord refuses to do anything so we are not going to pay any rent.

23 February 1968
Our water supply has been getting worse and worse, but at last the

landlords have agreed to do the pipes for 3000 rupees, and they have started today, thank God. A proper water supply will make life much easier all around.

14 March 1968

Have given several parties recently and all went off well, including another trade union party where we had the three top trade unionists and two permanent secretaries and about 40 people in all who had lots in common and lots to talk about, so there were no problems there.

There has been an international cricket team out here for ten days. It beat Ceylon easily. I am very glad as there has been a lot of politics coming into the selection, it always does, and neither Ian Pieris nor Neil Chamnugan were chosen because of their English-speaking backgrounds and they both should have been. And an awful doctor, H. I. K. Fernando, who is one of the selectors, made himself captain instead of Michael Tissera, who is the best player here and has been an excellent captain for two years. Gamini Goonesena was on the tour and it was fun to see him again as we had not seen him since Cambridge. [He is a Ceylonese who had captained Cambridge, played for Nottinghamshire and emigrated to Australia, where he played for New South Wales. He was one of the best leg-spin bowlers in the world. He eventually came back to live in Sri Lanka and had problems settling in as he had become too Westernized and did not speak Sinhalese.]

Micky Stewart and the other cricketers were very sweet to Timothy when we all went for the day to the Bostocks' beach house at Bentota and played cricket on the beach with him for an hour or so. [Micky Stewart had been captain of Surrey and played for England. He was the first professional manager of the English cricket team in a not very successful period. His son, Alec, has also played for England.] Timothy bowled four of them out — two England players and two county ones, including Denis Amiss, Derek Underwood and Keith Fletcher, and he caught another one out and made 11 runs!

Mark and Lif Bostock are an extremely popular and hospitable English couple here and are friendly with everyone. Mark is a larger than life character with a booming voice who likes to go to cocktail parties wearing slippers and sitting on his shooting stick. He is an influential businessman and very involved and caring in the development of Ceylon. He owns Bandarawela tea estate.

23 March 1968

It is hot and sticky and we are far too busy, but we managed to escape with Timothy on another archaeological tour of Ceylon. This time we started at Mihintale, which is magnificently set in the centre of Ceylon on a hill of several peaks, three of which have *dagaba*s on them. It is very important historically because it was here that Buddhism first arrived in Ceylon from India around 250 BC. This was at the request of King Tissa of Ceylon, who sent his nephew as an envoy to King Asoka (a Buddhist who ruled most of India) with a gift of rare shells, which were considered as valuable as gold for Indian temples. In response Asoka sent his son, Mahinda, as a missionary and, according to legend, he arrived at Mihintale by air.

It was a good climb up a wide, gentle stairway with a magnificent view over forests and hills. The Anuradhapura *dagaba*s were in the distance to the west and the whole area had a feeling of holiness about it. In fact you are not allowed to photograph the site without prior permission from the Archaeological Department in Colombo and there is a stipulation that people must not feature in photographs unless in a respectful attitude.

From Mihintale we went and stayed overnight in a resthouse at Anuradhapura. We were following Tissa's footsteps, as after his conversion to Buddhism he and Mahinda went on to Anuradhapura to convert the people. At that time it had been the capital for over a century and is much older than Polonnaruwa, 300–400 BC, and larger: they say it was 50 miles in circumference, not counting the suburbs, with 50 miles of ramparts. After converting the city, Tissa imported a branch of the tree from Bodh-Gaya under which the Buddha had received his enlightenment and planted it at Anuradhapura, and there it stands, more than 2250 years old, the oldest tree in the world.

Next morning we drove south to Sygiria and climbed the famous rock. Michael did not dare come to the top as it is very steep and very high with rather a wobbly iron railing for support and he gets vertigo, but Timothy and I made it. Fantastic engineering to have built a complete city in approximately AD 300 on top of a 2000-foot hill.

Sadly we were unable to see the famous Sygiria frescoes even though we had a permit from the authorities in Colombo. They were defaced recently and are being renovated and are closed to the public. We were also told that it was the wrong permit.

After a curry lunch at the resthouse we drove west to Dambulla. Another climb, more gentle this time, to see some ancient rock temples built in caves — fascinating, spooky, filled with statues of the Buddha, incense, monks, all pitch dark and reeking of history and originally built by a Buddhist king in hiding from Tamil invaders. The walls and ceilings are covered all over with paintings.

20 April 1968

Had a lovely holiday in Yala in the south east of the island with the Pieris' and all the children. We stayed at the game reserve in a bungalow by the sea; we could swim morning and evening which was perfect. We were a large party so you can imagine the organization of taking everything, including water, for five days. We saw four leopards, and lots of elephants. We all slept out on the veranda in a row at nights, and one night an elephant came right up to the bungalow.

Unfortunately I had oyster poisoning the day we left. I had not been quite right the whole holiday, so when we came back I saw the doctor, had a test, and I now have roundworm. No wonder I was getting thin. Anyway I was quite shocked, but she dosed me, and all the family, so I should be OK now.

I think I shall start playing golf here when the weather cools down a bit as, with caddies and cheap lessons and lots of little boys to look for balls, it seems an ideal place to learn. The caddies take bets on the players and with their bare feet they are very good at discreetly putting balls in strategic positions to make sure that their player wins.

2 May 1968

Yesterday was the opposition's May Day parade. It went past our house for two hours and then there were speeches next door in Independence Square until 10.00 p.m. I felt quite nervous seeing these thousands of red shirted, banner waving, shouting Ceylonese passing 50 yards in front of me. But it all passed off quietly with no stone throwing this year.

5 May 1968

Today there is another rally in Independence Square, this time for the government, with thousands of children and farmers, which Dudley, the Prime Minister, has arranged to thank them all for their Grow More

Food Campaign efforts. Already there is a terrible noise outside and hundreds of people are there at 10.00 a.m., and it does not start until 3.00 p.m. I only hope it does not rain; it is very overcast.

18 May 1968
The Ceylon cricket tour to the UK is finally cancelled due to some impossible behaviour by two of the selectors — Dr Fernando, whom I mentioned earlier and who is no cricketer, has made himself captain and wicket keeper, and another selector, Dhanasiri Weerasinghe, who is not much good either, has also got himself selected. [Problems with Ceylon cricket continued for years. There was a takeover of cricket management in the country by politicians, including the president of the board, Tyrone Fernando, who was MP for Moratuwa and Minister of Prisons and Prison Reforms. He had never played cricket apart from fielding for one over during a match of his constituency team in Moratuwa; to qualify for president of the Board of Control you are supposed to have played first class cricket.]

Went to a birthday dinner at the Milroy Pauls. He is a surgeon. It was very pleasant and all family except for us. They are Tamils and Wakeley, their son, is emigrating to the USA with his wife Sandra. He is a lawyer in the civil service and the future of Tamils in government service is doubtful; a lot of pressure is put on them, not least that they must be fluent in Sinhalese, which Wakeley is not, and he is not prepared to learn, so he is off.

30 May 1968
The temperature is in the nineties and the humidity is in the nineties and everyone is dripping the whole time and it is unbearable. We have given a cocktail party for 120 for the newly arrived head of Chancery, Peter Maxey, and his American wife Joyce. We had hoped that it would not be so large but sadly hardly anyone refused. But it went very well and included several ambassadors and high commissioners and cabinet ministers and even Pieter Keuneman, leader of the communists, Moscow wing, turned up. It was quite a feat to get him as he does not frequent capitalist haunts; it must be because we meet on our daily swim. Anyway he was able to chat with our new arrivals who have just come from Moscow and Joyce said that he is far the most attractive and presentable communist she has ever met. He is very handsome.

My batiks caused great talk. I have done another abstract one now — 'The Creation'. I have now made my first sale and have another commission.

Now I am involved with talking books for the blind. This means reading books for hour after hour to be recorded. They make 28 copies simultaneously, which are then sent to blind students. I am supposed to be editing a sort of magazine for them too. But the whole thing is very time consuming. Anyway I am roping in as many friends as possible to help.

It is certainly worthwhile. The equipment cost thousands of pounds. They got it last year, but the lady organizing it has been ill for seven months and so not much has been done. They are therefore very behind with the whole project.

1 June 1968
Thank heavens the monsoon has now broken and it is much cooler, with lots of rain, so no swimming or tennis, but what a relief not to be dripping all day long.

12 June 1968
I think you will be seeing us all sooner than expected. It is all in the air yet but the office has had a letter from London saying that the inspector recommended that due to various office changes Michael should leave this year instead of the originally planned September 1969.

Though they had said in London we might be recalled early, we never thought it would be a year early. I do hope it is all confirmed soon as we have to arrange what to do about schools for the children.

Really life in the Diplomatic Service is chaotic. Some colleagues, a first secretary and his wife, heard suddenly that they are to go for three years to Bangkok in September. They were supposed to stay here until next June and then be posted to London. They are very thankful they left their youngest son at school in the UK last year or they would not have known what to do with him.

The Maxeys from Moscow packed all their stuff in January in Moscow — it has suffered all sorts of trouble and is still sitting in London waiting for a boat to Ceylon. They have been living out of a suitcase for six months now, and still no signs of anything, which is extremely frustrating.

Another first secretary and his wife were all set to go to Kuala Lumpur, and had sent their luggage off. At the very last moment they were transferred to Delhi. They are now trying vainly to get their luggage back from Kuala Lumpur.

And of course the Sargeants sadly did not even have 18 months here before they were sent off to Lumbumbashi! And where shall we live when we come back? There is no doubt that the only thing is to get the children to boarding school as soon as possible, then at least *they* are settled. If we come home this year there is no telling for how long; it could be six months or it could be three years.

Anyway, that is enough of all our complications. Let us hope we will know where we go and when before too long.

23 June 1968
Many thanks for letters — the post and diplomatic bags are chaotic due to the BOAC strike — so your letters came surprisingly quickly. Also your parcels posted months and months ago have finally arrived with lovely things — matchbox toys, material, swimming costumes, clothes and food.

It looks very likely now that we will be coming home in December so we are trying to make a provisional booking on a boat on 30 December. We think now we will put the children back in Holy Trinity School in Guildford when we arrive home, and we will write to the headmaster to see if he can have them as soon as our plans are definite. It seems unfair for Timothy and Andrew to start a new school in mid-term. Then we will write to Edgeborough [a prep school] to see if they can start in the summer term.

Am very busy doing batik and have been commissioned to do two for the VIP lounge of the new international airport at Katunayake. A fabulous airport built by Canadians and opening in August.

28 July 1968
We have decided to remove Timothy and Andrew from St Thomas's and send them to the Overseas School for their last term. Timothy has not been happy there recently — he is now the only white boy in his class — and there is bullying, which the headmaster does not seem able to stop. St Thomas's standard is high, but it really concentrates too much on the three Rs to the exclusion of all else. There is a new head-

master (a good friend of ours) at the Overseas School now and he says that they both seem well ahead with their work; he was particularly impressed with Andrew's reading.

We had 20 people to a buffet supper and to see the film *Billy Liar* with Tom Courtenay, which was greatly appreciated. We had a formal dinner for 12 three days later to say goodbye to a second secretary who, poor thing, has been posted to Georgetown, Guyana. [Little did we know that we would be posted there four years later.]

10 August 1968

Max Adrian is doing his one-man Shaw performance arranged by the British Council, anything like this is such a treat in Ceylon.

17 August 1968

The Wijesinghes, Sam and Mukta, invited us to dinner and I found myself sitting between J. R. Jayawardene, Minister of State and effectively Prime Minister, and Maitrapala Senanayake, acting leader of the opposition when Mrs Bandaranaike is away. I found it hard work, though they seem to get on fairly well and no one wanted to discuss politics.

There was a very posh Hindu wedding at the Mount Lavinia Hotel with 2000 guests, including the Prime Minister and Governor General and anyone else you can think of. It was an amazingly colourful ceremony with priests covered with paint and ashes, the groom in a fantastic costume, all white, a throne made of millions of jasmine flowers and drums, dancing and singing.

The ceremony is all in Sanskrit, so half way through, that is after one and a half hours of not understanding a word that was going on, the High Commissioners of Pakistan and Canada, the ambassador of the Philippines and assorted friends, including us, retired to the hotel nightclub and emerged two hours later in time to line up and shake hands for the reception. An unusual evening. The bride was the daughter of a senator who is also the Minister of Local Government.

10 September 1968

I have been asked to play Adela in *Passage to India*, a dramatized version of E. M. Forster's book, and have said yes even though it will take a lot of rehearsing and run for ten days. It should be good as they have some excellent Ceylonese for the Indian parts, and three people who trained at the Central School — the producer, the actress for Mrs Moore and me. It is a long part and I just hope I shall learn it OK as I am so out of practice. I am looking forward to it very much, and it gives me a bona fide excuse to miss cocktail parties as they rehearse from 5.30 to 8.30 p.m., but I can go to dinners if I want. It finishes in early December and I shall then have three weeks to immerse myself in packing and farewells until we leave.

My batiks are going well. All sorts of people want to buy them, and I could make quite a lot of money, but I just have not got enough time with everything else, unpaid, that I have to do — family planning, Cheshire Home, books for the blind, entertainment, and lots of work for the ghastly sale we have to organize in November (for which I am knitting ducks and stuffing them) and children. The two batiks at the new airport look super.

25 September 1968

They have had great difficulty casting the smaller English parts in *Passage to India* and a lot of the English people here think it is a terrible play — 'Who is E. M. Forster?' — and have refused to have anything to do with it, let alone play the parts, which in lots of cases are too true to life, although the play was written in 1924. Colonial attitudes still abound here even though Ceylon became independent in 1948 — over 20 years ago. But it has been done in Delhi and Calcutta and was a great success, and I think it will go down very well.

A rugger tour is here from India, among them Stephen Smith, a Cambridge blue and English international, whom Michael played with at Cambridge and who was also a colleague at Harrow where he taught for six years. He is a missionary in a school 20 miles out of Calcutta. There is no English spoken and he and his wife both have learnt Bengali. They have three kids, no running water, no leave for five years and no financial help with education. Really grim and total dedication. [Tragedy later befell the Smiths when one of their children drowned in an open drain at the bottom of their garden in India.]

7 October 1968

Still awaiting a definite OK for our departure. It is a bit much, as we probably leave in two months, to have no definite notification. So I think I shall definitely come, plus kids and luggage and car, on the December boat even if Michael has to fly later. I could not face having no luggage for six months or so, which is what happens if it goes unaccompanied.

Kids all well. Timothy and Andrew very happy at Overseas School and doing ridiculously easy work. The headmaster thinks that they both have 'scholarly' minds. Thank you St Thomas's! But still no reply from Trinity in Guildford; I suppose he will be able to take them in for half the term, if and when we get back.

25 October 1968

I was hoping we would have some news from London re our departure date in the bag that came today. But no luck.

The Maharajah of Baroda is staying in Ceylon with a friend of ours, Aru, and we were invited to meet him. He is very short, has a funny wispy beard, is chubby, looks slightly spivvy, but was very pleasant indeed. He had a diamond ring the size of a small egg on one finger and a retinue of two tough bodyguards, otherwise you would never know he is one of the richest men in the world. It was a very small party, and we talked to him a lot. He is the president of the Board of Control for India of cricket, and Michael had met him briefly when playing against the Indian test team for the Minor Counties. He asked us out in the evening, but sadly we could not go.

Rehearsals are going well, though the production is causing controversy! I do not know why Colombo's attitudes are so behind the times. As I said, the play has been a great success in both Delhi and Calcutta, and as it was written 46 years ago, and is not even *about* Ceylon, people's outdated views amaze me. In fact the people who have asked me, 'Is it a good idea to put a play like this on?' have all admitted to having never read the book. They have just been 'told' the story. Anyway I should think we will get good houses as a result.

Lots of parties and dinners including three farewells for friends in Lever Bros who are off to Ghana, poor things! [We did not know what was in store for us.] And we have been sailing and managed to break our mast.

5 November 1968

Today we heard that we are going to leave next month. It is a great relief to know what is happening and we are very pleased. Also Michael has been assigned to a department so we shall definitely be in the UK for two to three years.

We really have had a fabulous time here and it is going to be dreadful saying goodbye. But the children are longing to go back to England, and the boys are longing to go to Edgeborough in the summer. Poor little things — I hope they will like boarding school as much as they think they will.

But I am dreading telling Govindan, Supiah, Cruz, Rita and Rangasamy that we are going. So far I have found jobs for two of them and hope I shall be able to fix them all up.

Today I had a letter from the Maharajah of Baroda from India saying how sorry he was not to have seen us again and if we come to India we must let him know and he will look forward to seeing us at his home. So kind of him and if we were staying longer I think we would nip over to Bombay and accept his invitation; apparently his palace there covers several acres. He comes to England each summer so I will write and send him our address and you might find a maharajah on the tennis court next summer. [We did.]

The Prime Minister was at the golf course this morning and I told him we were going. He said he was very sorry, but he would be in London as well in January at the Commonwealth Prime Ministers' Conference, so I explained we would not be back in time to see him. He was rather disappointed; I expect he thought he could escape with Michael and play golf one day. He really is a charming man, so friendly and natural, you would never know he was Prime Minister.

I am getting thinner all the time — I must have a test and see if I have 'parasites' again.

22 November 1968

The play opens in two days but there is a crisis over the sets, which are not finished yet, so today they have the army in to help. For the first night, in view of the subject matter, we have invited the Indian, Pakistani and British High Commissioners, who will all be sitting together in the front row. [The play was a great success, with full houses every night.]

Alan Read from Delhi is staying again. The post is so dreadful there that half the time he cannot get in touch with his children at all. And I have written twice to Mr Brown at Trinity about the children arriving in the middle of next term and have had no reply. But I suppose it will be OK.

20 December 1968

It was lovely to hear you on the phone and an amazingly clear line. I think this will be my last letter from Ceylon. Time is passing so quickly I have no time to think.

Fantastic farewell parties are being given for us which started on 5 December, when the play finished, until 30 December, our last night in Ceylon. The High Commissioner and Deputy High Commissioners are both giving large cocktail parties, and our next-door-neighbour colleagues, Ed Wynne and his wife, are giving an enormous one for 250. I have a lovely sari which I shall wear. A friend will wrap the six yards of material around me in the correct fashion. The Pieris, Butlers (Australian High Commission), Seymours (Canadian High Commission), Purcells and Maxeys (British High Commission) are giving large buffets with dancing, the Sinais (Indian High Commission), Coomaraswamys, Pereras, Fonsekas, Werasinghes, Dan Piachaud and Gunasekeras (Ceylonese) are giving large dinners. One lady is giving me a hens' sherry-type party for 50 ladies. We also have a few lunches thrown in. I do not think anyone has ever had so many farewells!

4 January 1969, SS Chitral

We were completely exhausted when we got on board on New Year's Eve. It was terribly sad leaving and we were very depressed. Everyone was amazingly kind, and all sorts of people gave us farewell presents. The large party given by our neighbouring colleagues two nights before we left was a great success. I wore my sari, which was much admired, and we had lots of photos taken, which have most of our friends in them — a lovely souvenir. Ian and Gun gave a very informal dancing party on our last night and I ended up at 3.30 a.m. swimming in their pond in their drawing room!

The servants were very sad, particularly Govindan, and we felt really awful as he had sent us a beautiful arrangement of flowers to our cabin which must have cost him half a week's wages. He was terribly upset. But we have got him another job which is a relief. [In 1995 we are still in touch with Govindan who has retired to India.]

There was a lively party on board on New Year's Eve, but I felt so sad at midnight and was missing all our friends in Colombo so much that we went to bed at five past twelve thoroughly depressed! We shall arrive in England on Timothy's ninth birthday. We land at Tilbury and can drive off in our car. See you on 7 February — How exciting!

In 1970 Mrs Bandaranaike was re-elected as Prime Minister. She remained in office until 1977. In 1972 Ceylon became a republic, the Governor General became president and the country was renamed Sri Lanka. The 1977 elections returned the UNP to power with a huge majority. By this time Dudley Senanayake had died and, as Prime Minister and leader of the ruling party, J. R. Jayawardene became the first executive president under the new constitution.

In October 1982 he was elected president for a second term. In December that year he held a referendum instead of a general election, which kept him in power. When Jayawardene resigned in December 1988, Premadasa took over and was elected president. Two months later a general election was held and this was again won by the UNP. After four and a half years in power, Premadasa was assassinated on 1 May 1993, one week after the assassination of Lalith Athulathmudali. To this day neither the assassins nor the reasons for the assassinations have been found.

Prime Minister D. B. Wijetunge (a peaceful man nicknamed 'Dearly Beloved') became acting president. Parliament then conferred the presidency on him until the end of Premadasa's term. This should have been in December 1994, but after consulting an astrologist Wijeratne called for early elections in August 1994. These were won with a slender parliamentary majority by Chandrika Bandaranaike Kumaratunga of the SLFP, whose mother took over as Prime Minister after her father was gunned down in 1959. Her husband, a film actor turned politician, had been shot dead by Sinhalese extremists in 1988. This was the first time in 17 years that the SLFP had been in power.

Presidential elections were called for November 1994. In October, during the election campaign, Gamini Dissanayake, the opposition UNP candidate and 51 others, including several leading opposition figures, were killed in a suicide bomb attack thought to be by the Tamil

Tigers. Three weeks later Chandrika Kumaratunga was swept into victory by almost two million votes.

We arrived home in February 1969. We knew we were to be in England for two or three years and needed somewhere to live. My parents suggested that we convert their house, Warwicks Mount in Guildford, into two houses, for it was getting too large for them. This was done successfully and we lived there very happily. It was to prove a great bonus as far as the children were concerned, for when we were overseas Warwicks Mount, with Granny and Grandpa, was a secure base for them.

The children all started at Holy Trinity Primary School, which was down the road.

Michael had two interesting jobs in Whitehall, first in the Defence Department, dealing with joint projects ranging from ships to aeroplanes to tanks and requiring frequent meetings with other Whitehall departments, and then in the Commodities Department, involving international negotiations about agricultural products and overseas travel.

3
Guyana

I n the spring of 1971 we heard that we were being posted to
Guyana, with Michael as Deputy High Commissioner. Although
this sounded important we were not quite sure where Guyana was
and had to get the atlas out. We had been told it was in the West Indies,
though it is in fact on the continent of South America. Its main crop is
sugar; its population is predominantly African and Indian; it is a former
British colony and it has produced many West Indian cricketers.

The African Guyanese were originally brought in as slaves to work
on the sugar plantations, but when slavery ended in 1833 they mostly
moved into the towns. Indian indentured labourers were then brought in
to replace them. The Indian Guyanese, who outnumber the Africans,
still tend to work on the sugar estates. The Afro-Guyanese have apparently always considered themselves superior to the Indian Guyanese
and the country has a long history of racial troubles.

At the time of our arrival an extremely powerful Afro-Guyanese,
Forbes Burnham, had been Prime Minister since 1964. He had replaced
the Indian, Cheddi Jagan, whom the USA and UK had manipulated out
of office because of his open support for communism. Burnham, in
practice, was to prove just as radical. Guyana gained its independence
from Britain in 1966.

The children came with us on a banana boat to Trinidad in July 1971
and we flew from there to Georgetown. At this stage Tim had been
boarding at Edgeborough Prep School for a year and Andrew had just
had one term there. We hoped that we would find a suitable school for
Lucy in Georgetown.

30 July 1971

Well, here we are, in the Co-operative Republic of Guyana, settled into our very pleasant house which backs on to a swampy, low lying area of the botanical gardens, where there are opossums, mongoose, monkeys, parrots, humming birds and all types of tropical flora and fauna. And just out of sight — hidden in a thicket — a statue of Queen Victoria is lying on its back.

Georgetown, which is on the mouth of the Demerara River, is very attractive, with white wooden houses, which were built by the Dutch — a lot are built on stilts to cope with the massive rainfalls they have here — and wide tree-lined avenues. The cathedral is said to be the largest wooden building in the world; it is white and most impressive.

Our area is new with concrete houses, but attractive and the streets are safe for the kids to play around in as there is no through traffic. We have joined three clubs; one is within walking distance and the kids can go there on foot to swim and play tennis. But sadly the sea is brown and unswimmable in with mud brought up the coast from the Amazon, with the Guyana rivers — the Essequibo, Demerara, Berbice, Mazaruni and Cuyuni — adding to the problems. And most of the country is covered by tropical rainforest.

The town is very clean, far better than Colombo, and as the streets are all laid out at right angles I am beginning to find my way around in the car, but shopping is slightly alarming. There are a lot of 'choke and rob' gangs around. They come up and grab you around the neck with one arm, holding a cutlass in the other hand, and take whatever they can. And the police take no notice at all.

So we go out without our watches, jewellery, bags or money (or a little tucked away), and buy everything on account or by cheque and hope for the best. If we cannot park right outside the shop we wish to visit we go home again, but as there is virtually nothing in the shops this is no hardship. We do not walk around more than is absolutely necessary and avoid some areas altogether; it was all a bit scary at first. We are already getting into the habit of looking behind us all the time.

There is one very nice walk which is quite safe in daylight, right along the sea wall from the Pegasus, which is a British Airways hotel, to the lighthouse. As the town is below sea level this fortification built by the Dutch is vital to Georgetown's survival. There are views over a vast expanse of muddy sea and people fly kites there at the weekends.

At nights we have a guard and all the houses around are well illuminated with security lights, so it feels fairly safe.

Our diplomatic life here started in great style. On our second night we had dinner at Guyana House, ex-Government House, at a farewell dinner for Michael's predecessor. It was given by the acting president, E. V. Luckhoo. He is a barrister who comes from a brilliant and very distinguished Indian family. He has beautiful old-fashioned manners, is extremely considerate and kind and was very welcoming to us. It is a beautiful, large white wooden traditional Guyanese house and it was a very merry West Indian evening indeed, with everyone on first name terms from the beginning — which is so much easier than having to remember two names. The Guyanese are so friendly and cheerful and full of fun; we really were made to feel at home.

3 August 1971

Great News. Our luggage arrived at 3.00 p.m. today on a battered old cart pulled by oxen. It is now 10.00 p.m. and we have been unpacking ever since. It is still only half done but there are no cockroaches this time.

We have two maids who come daily — a cook, Irene, from 10 a.m. to 6.30 p.m., and a maid, Aleetha, from 7.00 a.m. to 2.00 p.m., who will sleep in when we want a baby sitter. We also have a part-time gardener for the small but pretty garden, with just room for a cricket net.

7 August 1971

Sadly there are no letters from anyone in today's bag.

The rainy season is not quite over. The annual rainfall here is 200 inches a year. Last Monday was a bank holiday and it poured all day long, just like home, except there is very little to do here when it rains. Films, theatres, television, art galleries, shops, restaurants — what are they? It is not even easy to find a book to read.

16 August 1971

It has been very difficult getting Lucy into school as there is tremendous pressure on places in the few good schools here. But luckily we have got her into the convent where she can take Michael's predecessor's daughter's place. We had to take her along with her books. The nuns were very impressed with the stories she has been writing at home and with the work books she has completed, but she got her place on the strengths of these as, after two years in an English primary school, her maths is well below the standard here. A great relief.

I enclose a letter from her.

> Dear Granny and Grampa,
>   I hope you are well. I am very well. In Guyana It is very hot and swetty And i drip with perspration. There are lots of Bulls and Cows.
>   Love from Lucy.

27 August 1971

Last week we made an official visit to Skeldon Sugar Estate run by Bookers (the British company that owns about 90 per cent of Guyana's sugar estates) on the Guyana/Surinam border. Surinam was originally called Dutch Guyana and Guyana was originally known as Demerara, which became synonymous with sugar. At the moment there are threats to nationalize the Demerara Sugar Company, which is owned by Oliver Jessel, so Bookers is slightly nervous about its future. [Bookers was in fact nationalized but its personnel were later invited back into Guyana as advisers.]

We were flown up in a little one-engined 5-seater plane. It was rather frightening, but fascinating as we flew very low and got a really good idea of the coastal region of the country, which is flat with sugar, rice, coconut palms, swamps, water conservation areas, bauxite factories, and lots of muddy rivers, mangrove swamps and brown sea. Some 85 per cent of the population lives within 15 miles of the sea in the coastal belt and the vast interiors can be reached only by air or river.

There was a bumpy ride around the cane fields in a Land-Rover, a lunch, and official visits to the mayor and council, as well as to the Rice Marketing Board, whose new offices Michael opened. Then we returned to look around the sugar factory. *En route* we were offered a wide variety of drinks from coconut milk to rum. It was all very interesting and informative, but terribly hot.

Dinner with the High Commissioner, Bill Bates, to meet law president Arthur Chung and his wife on their return from a state visit to England. He is a tiny Chinese man, who was born into great poverty and spent his youth working in paddy fields, but made his way up through Chinese application. He originally hoped to become a doctor, could not afford that, but saved up enough money to become a lawyer. He then became a judge and then president. His wife comes from a similar background and she is very pretty, charming and chatty. She could not get over the gold scissors to cut the grapes at Buckingham Palace when they dined with the Queen.

Race problems are terrible here. The population is 40 per cent African, who are employed mainly in the towns, government, military and police; 50 per cent Indian, who work mostly on the sugar estates; and 5–10 per cent mixed, including Chinese, Portuguese and English. And none of them really like each other.

1 October 1971
I am very envious of you seeing the boys. They left three weeks ago today, and although the time flies by it still seems about ten weeks since I saw them and we have only had one letter from each of them.

4 October 1971
Although we meet Guyanese all the time and they are very friendly, unlike the Ceylonese they do not invite us to their houses, but I suppose this is a matter of time. At the moment the parties here are at the houses of diplomats, the English and other foreigners.

We had our first buffet dinner party for 20 people. The Guyanese are apt not to turn up, or to turn up with one or two extra members of their family or friends. A formal dinner is therefore risky — there can either be gaps at the table or a squash, and last minute re-laying is frequently required. The party seemed a success and Irene, though incredibly slow and rather unsmiling, cooks well, but needs constant encouragement and organization while we toil away together in the extremely hot kitchen.

Lucy is settling down rather slowly at school, but she luckily likes the girls there very much. One girl from her form lives up the road, an Indian girl whose father is a very successful shopkeeper. She has also made friends with Amanda Ramphal, whose father is Sony Ramphal the Foreign Minister and Attorney General and her mother, Lois, is English and they are extremely friendly and live just around the corner.

[Sony Ramphal was to become Secretary General of the Commonwealth Secretariat for ten years.] Here is another letter from her:

> Dear granny and grampa,
>   I hope you are well. In guyana it is very Hot. I go to a catholic school with nuns in which you have got to keep very Quite in classes. I am enjoying school expect I dont Like the homework. I supose they give you home work because you only have half A day at School.
>
> Love from Lucy

It seems quite healthy here. There seems to be very little dysentery around compared to Colombo, and it is all much cleaner. You can drink the water, eat lettuce without first washing it in permanganate and Georgetown itself is well looked after — apart from the fact that it is not safe to walk around in. I am converting one room for batik production and am slowly getting going.

9 October 1971

Many thanks for your letter about the boys. We were delighted to have news of them and thank you for giving them such a lovely weekend out. It is now four weeks since we saw them, another nine to go. It really is ghastly never seeing them, especially when I think that if I were home today we would be over there watching their matches.
Here's another letter from Lucy:

> Dear Granny and Grampa,
>   I hope you are well I am very well. We got a new puppy on Saturday and when we got it it cried a little at first but it soon got used to us. Its name is Tripsy and is very cuddly and nice it is a watch-dog and has to stay outside. All my freinds love it and are always coming in to see it.
>
> Love from Lucy

She is thrilled with our new puppy. At last she seems to be settling down, but we have had so many complaints of headaches and tummy aches that I was on the point of taking her to the doctor. She hardly eats anything and is getting rather too thin. I suppose she will eat again soon; meanwhile she takes vitamins.

The school is really old fashioned. For example, in England she used to write long, long stories at school and home for pleasure. The other day she wrote four pages on Romulus and Remus, got B plus, but was made to write the whole thing out again for homework to correct the mistakes.

This took her ages so now when she has to write anything, she refuses to write more than half a page in case she is made to copy it out again. The teacher writes, 'You can do better than this Lucy.' Lucy knows very well she can but is not going to be had again.

15 October 1971
We have had a cheerful letter from Tim — full of judo, football, sailing and singing — but a very pathetic letter from Andrew.

> Dear mummy, daddy and Lucy,
>
> I hope you are well, I do not feel very well. I feel home-sick and I've got two habits.
>
> One of my habits makes me bad at anything at any time and the other habit makes me bad when I'm mostly out of doors but I sometimes do it when Im in of doors too.
>
> I add up words and letters in my mind and I try to get them into twelve by adding comers, full stops, semi coulons or things like that and when I do that I say it goes into sixty, even though it may not.
>
> The other habit I've got is I keep on bending over and touching the ground. These habits may not seem as bad as they are.
>
> Please can I give up Latin I'm no good and I believe people when they say 'Latin is a dead subject, as dead as dead can be, first it killed the Romans and now it's killing me.'
>
> Or even better can you try and find a school for me in Guyana because I hate Edgeborough there are so many rough boys. The only two or three boys whom I like best are Shepherd mi, Shepherd ma, and Timothy, even thouggh they're rough too.
>
> We had an under ten match on Saturday and I was centre forward when I'm only good at back. We lost 4–0 to them, I didn't score a goal becuase of my habits.
>
> Love from Andrew James

Altogether a very upsetting letter, which he will have written last Sunday, but you will have seen him since then, thank heavens. I console myself that it was written when he was feeling low and cannot believe he is as bad as that the whole time. Anyway, please keep an eye on him. But I wish I could afford to come home and see him.

18 October 1971

I have paid my first visit to the Mahaica Leper Colony with Lois Ramphal. It is a fair distance away and seems in the middle of nowhere, completely isolated from the world. It reminded me of how it must have been in medieval Europe when strict isolation was imposed on patients because they had discovered that leprosy was passed on through contact. Then lepers were isolated in one of Europe's 19,000 lazarettos, a funeral service was said for them and, as far as society was concerned, they were dead. If they ever did emerge it was carrying a bell to warn people to keep away, and if they ever went into a shop they had to reach for the goods with a stick so as not to come too close to the shopkeeper. But English lepers were luckier than the French ones, who in the fourteenth century were ordered by Philip the Fair to be burnt to death.

In Guyana in 1971 there are a large amount of wooden huts offering dormitory-type accommodation in a clearing in the jungle. We only visited the part where the disease is not active and all the patients are fairly old. Now there is treatment which, if given in time and regularly, can rid the body of 99 per cent of the disease. But the problems of regular attendance at clinics and monitoring the medicine dosage seem impossible to solve here and the disease therefore continues to spread.

It was very sad. Nearly all the patients we saw were blind, with missing legs, arms and fingers and their faces were very deformed with noses missing. But some were really cheerful, and they obviously love visits and look forward to them a lot. In medieval fashion they are usually neglected completely by their families because of the stigma, and just left there till they die. I suppose I will get used to it, but I really felt quite physically sick at the end of it all, and as soon as I got back had to shower and wash my hair, and try to erase the images from my mind.

There was a nice formal dinner at Harry and Sheila Glovers. He is the technical director of the enormous Bookers Group here. We find that at sit-down dos we are often guests of honour and put on the right of the host and hostess. We were on this occasion, although the chairman of Bookers, Lord Jock Campbell of Eskan, was there too. He is a very distinguished older man and when you are the youngest it feels a bit odd. Still it *is* all in the protocol book. It also means we have to leave the party first as no one can go before us, and it is always difficult to know when.

20 October 1971

I nearly sent you a page on politics in my last letter, but could not as it was going by ordinary mail. So here it is in the bag.

The Indian–African racial intolerance scene is hotting up a bit unfortunately. The week before last Dr Ransammy, an Indian university lecturer who is a critic of the government, was gunned down in broad daylight in the middle of Georgetown. He is now recovering in hospital where his brother, a doctor attending him there, has been told that there is no need to cure him as they will do it again, and next time get him too. At first it seemed it might have been a *crime passionnel*, but now it seems almost definitely political, with sinister rumours going around that it was arranged by the government, which is getting very averse to any criticism.

Forbes Burnham, an Afro-Guyanese, has been Prime Minister since 1964 and it was he, as leader of the predominantly black PNC, who led the country into independence in 1966. Last year Burnham declared Guyana a Co-operative Republic and it has really become a one-party state. We are now all called 'Comrade'.

Burnham, who is a very powerful man with a physical presence to match, is developing a strong personality cult around himself. If he feels like talking he summons people to him at 4.00 a.m. He has a marvellous feel for language and (though a non-believer) reads the Bible and Shakespeare for the joy of the writing. He really seems too powerful for such a small country as Guyana. Before going into politics he read law at London University and was called to the Bar in 1948. [He declared himself president in 1980 with near-absolute powers and remained in power until he died in 1985.]

Also, the 'choke and rob' attacks are getting more frequent. Last week the Brazilian ambassador's wife had her bracelet snatched whilst with her husband in the centre of Georgetown. Luckily the ambassador had a gun on him and fired it to frighten him away. It is not a question of just white people being attacked, it is Guyanese as well, or anyone who looks as if they have something on them. There just do not seem to be any police anywhere, and if they are there they do nothing at all.

So it is all rather worrying. I drive around in the mini with its doors locked and windows shut, never walk, shop only if I can park nearby, otherwise go home again, wear no jewellery, do not carry a bag and hope for the best. Thank heavens we live where we do; it really is a comparatively safe area with no through traffic, and no strange people wandering around. And thank heavens for the relative security of the sea wall and the golf course and the Pegasus Hotel swimming pool for exercise.

All the goings on make it very interesting politically, but what is going to happen is anybody's guess. Some say it was like this before the troubles in the 1960s (when hundreds of people were killed in widespread racial riots) and will go the same way, others that those troubles were too recent and people remember them too well to let it happen again. But we will wait and see.

22 October 1971
Another pathetic letter from Andrew; if only I could see him.

> Dear mummy, daddy and Lucy,
>
> I hope you are having a nice time in Georgetown. I am Just as homesick as I ever was if not worse.
>
> My habits are getting worse especially the one which I keep touching the ground. Please may I give up Latin I just cant do anything in it. I know it teaches us some languages but I'd rather prefer learning different languages In that languages lessons like French and English.
>
> We went to Chichester Cathedral on Saturday the practice wasn't very good but the real thing was great. I don't like anybody except Timothy.
>
> > Love from Andrew James

25 October 1971
We had 40 to a buffet dinner. They help themselves, then try to find a chair. Next week we have another 30 coming — 70 to dinner in ten

days. We are trying to do lots of entertaining before the boys arrive, as we do not want to be lumbered with it all when they are here.

Michael is now the Guyanese national tennis champion! This is rather like Wimbledon with match coverage on the radio and lots of people watching. It was very exciting tennis and he played brilliantly before a large crowd who got very involved with the match and cheered, clapped, waved their arms or booed each point as was appropriate.

That evening at 10.00 p.m., when we were ready for bed, we had to go to a 'jump up' at Michael's secretary's. These are the traditional Guyanese parties with a steel band playing heavy rhythm music, expressive dancing and lots of Guyanese rum. But we found this one rather an effort, with lots of very young people whom we did not know, and managed to be the first to leave at 1.00 a.m.

The previous weekend we went with some Guyanese Indian friends of ours to the Deepvali Fair at the Mahatma Gandhi Institution. We arrived and were seated as guests of honour and then had to listen to two and a half hours of singers in a competition which consisted of singing the same long, monotonous Indian religious song over and over again.

We thought we would never get through it. At midnight the singing stopped, and we had half an hour of very good Indian dancing. All this on hard chairs with one glass of beer the entire evening. When we left our Indian host had had acid thrown at his car and the paint was peeling off all over; this in an official car park with the police turning a blind eye as usual and sadly indicative of the racial problems here.

30 October 1971
Andrew's letter today seems perhaps a little more cheerful

Dear Mummy and Daddy,

I hope you are well, My habits are about the same by average, my bending down one's going and the maths coming.

It will be half term when this letter reaches you I think. I am still feeling home-sick. At half term I'm going to choose for a Christmas present a thing called Explorers Kit with binocoulars and cameras and a compass and things like that it would be good for Guyana. We had our injections and got six smarties each but they didn't have my favourite colour blue.

On Saturday we had a first eleven match and we won because Timothy was in it. In my matches we lost on Monday and lost on Tuesday.

Love from Andrew James

What a pity we are not nearer and I could afford to come home. It seems as if they have been away for months and months — it is really terrible.

18 November 1971

Thank heavens we have had quite cheerful letters from the boys, with no more complaints from Andrew. Tim seems to be doing marvellously at everything and I really do not mind how Andrew does at the moment as long as he is happy. And in three and a half weeks they will be here; we cannot wait.

We had a few days holiday in Grenada, which is really beautiful — rather like a small Ceylon — hilly, lush and green and it was awful coming back to the brown seas of Guyana, especially as things are so hectic now with the High Commissioner away. It really is my favourite island so far, though politically it is all rather dicey with Eric Gairy, the Prime Minister, a little dictator and everywhere you go politics is the favoured subject of conversation.

Michael played tennis with Gairy at 6.30 a.m. He is a strange, twitchy man and he never stopped moving on the tennis court — picking up balls, bouncing up and down and swaying to strange rhythmical music only he could hear. Unfortunately there was a Commonwealth Parliamentary Conference on and Gairy asked us to his reception for the delegates. We did not want to go as we go away to get away from this kind of boring thing. But we dutifully went and left early, only to hear later that the Governor General had arrived after we left — what very bad protocol on our part.

I met some English people in Grenada who are starting a picture gallery and she has asked me to send her some batiks as she says the Americans are always looking for something original. So I am sending her some I have already done and am madly trying to get a few more done quickly as the tourist season starts there in December.

21 November 1971

One of our wives was buying vegetables at the stall where I get mine, when someone came up behind her, scratched her hand with a razor, grabbed the purse she was holding, ran to a waiting bike and got away. She has been here three years and says she is lucky it has not happened before.

Security is getting worse, though recently the police seem to have been making a bit more effort and prosecuting more. A new superintendent has just been appointed and apparently 200 extra policemen have been employed, but it is likely to be bad over Xmas when they all need money. And the police force is all African, which does not help Afro-Indian racial problems.

The unemployment situation is getting worse too with 500 more soon to be unemployed because a timber works run by the Commonwealth Development Corporation is to be phased out.

Also, we await to see the effects of America stopping its aid to Guyana. This is the result of the entry of China into the UN and the banning of Taiwan, which has produced these reactions in the American Senate. The USA is becoming more and more isolationist.

The Americans have been doing a lot of work here and only three weeks ago we went with their USAID [United States Agency for International Development] chap around a large rice handling depot to which they are contributing vast sums with the Guyana Rice Development Corporation. Heaven knows if they will finish this project before they stop the aid. We do hope they will at least finish the schemes they have started.

25 November 1971

There is a lot going on with Rhodesia declaring UDI [Unilateral Declaration of Independence]. The Guyanese think that Smith and the white Rhodesians twist us around their little fingers — though they put it less politely.

So we are just hoping there will not be any real unpleasantness here after the announcement of the settlement, or sell out. But there quite likely will be and the High Commission has been practising emergency exits from the office this week. Anyway we hope for the best, especially as Michael is in charge.

Now I am sending batiks over to Grenada, where hopefully they will be sold to rich Americans. I have just finished two large ones, though it's such a rush as everything is so busy here now and there is far too much entertaining to do. But our overdraft is getting rather too large as the allowances are so poor here; I only wish I had time to earn some more money. The main problem is paying for the kids' air fares [at that time only two holidays a year were paid for].

Enclosed is a letter from Lucy. Note the 'man', pure West Indian, and wait till you hear her accent!

Dear Granny and Grampa,

I hope you are well. I want to tell you that I would love to have an advent calender and thank you very much for offering, because there are none in George-town. Tripsy is a good watchdog and he bites hard man.

We are having exams next week and I don't feel like them at all but of course we have to have them.

Love from Lucy

6 December 1971

Touch wood the local reaction to the Rhodesia proposed settlement has been hostile, but not physically so. There was enormous work involved, with papers to read and to offer the local press and government in an attempt to cool their reactions. Forbes Burnham threatened to leave the Commonwealth over arms for South Africa earlier this year and we feared he might react as rigorously this time. There is still time for him to do so, but the likelihood recedes as each day passes.

The only trouble we have had was when the walls of the High Commission office were sprayed with the words 'BRITISH GET OUT'. Michael got up early and unwisely went down with his driver and started to paint them over. He was caught by press photographers and pictures appeared in all the papers. The High Commissioner's Residence was picketed, but he is out of the country, and we were left in peace at our house because we took the flag down and they never discovered where we lived.

The Surinam tennis team, which is rather good, has been over and at the end of the matches, played in front of the president and a big crowd, Michael had to join in a men's doubles exhibition match. The Surinamese had such fantastic serves he hardly managed to hit one back, and altogether he and his partner, Ian MacDonald — a white West Indian director of Bookers, an ex-Wimbledon player and a poet and broadcaster — were really outclassed. After the first set they swapped partners, each playing with a Surinamese, for a more even match. [In 1995 Ian MacDonald is still with Bookers, now Guysuco, Guyana Sugar Corporation, and his *The Humming Bird Tree*, which is a set book in West Indian schools, was recently dramatized on British television.]

Another trip to the leper colony. It is so depressing asking if they have anyone they want to send Christmas cards to, and lots have no one outside the hospital to contact at all — 'I haven't heard from my sons for two years,' is a typical remark. It is really pathetic, but they do seem so pleased to see us that I suppose we help a bit.

Our defence adviser, who is based in Trinidad, has been staying with us, on the strength of which we went on a wonderful flight to the interior of the country provided by the army. We flew over the Kaiteur Falls — 800 feet high and the highest waterfall in the world — in a very little plane, and it was really spectacular and terrifying at the same time. We landed nearby on a small strip of cleared land and were able to walk to the edge of the falls and look down, and realize the power of water. Then we flew on over the Orinduik Falls on the Brazilian border, but sadly we did not have time to stop as we had to get back to the army headquarters for lunch at the mess. The country is so vast here. You seem to fly for ever and ever over never-ending rainforests with very occasional small clearings. These are the homes of the Amerindians, who are still living very primitive lives in the jungle or perhaps where there are isolated gold and diamond prospectors at work. There have been border disputes with the Brazilians for years — they think half Guyana is theirs.

10 December 1971
Here is a happier letter from Andrew.

Dear Mummy and daddy,
    I hope you are well. I am getting very excited for the end of Term, And I wish you could come to the Carol Service. We had a Conjuror on Saturday and Timothy was one of the ten boys who came up onto the stage to help him he did about eight tricks

but i'm afraid I won't be able to tell you about them because I havent got much time as I've got to write to Granny too.

I missed the merit half holiday for being cheeky to Mr McGinn and getting two stripes.

Wolfe, the dormitory which I am in, received one star for being the most tidy dormitory in the school.

Exams are on Friday and Saturday.

Please can you send a note saying that I do not have to have food like Kippers, any kind of eggs or tomatoes.

Love from Andrew James

13 December 1971

A recent dinner at the Canadian High Commissioner's was made for me by having an hour's talk with the notorious East Indian, Dr Cheddi Jagan. He has rather faded out of the scene now, and is not doing much as leader of the opposition, but he is a real charmer, and it is quite an experience to talk to a real dedicated Moscow communist.

Jagan, the son of a labourer, was born on a sugar plantation. He founded the predominantly Indian PPP (People's Progressive Party) in 1950 and has been its leader ever since; and he served as Chief Minister twice when Guyana was a British colony. But he did not get on too well with the British, who disliked his fiery Marxist rhetoric, and he spent six months in prison in 1954.

We have met him before, but never quite so intimately and he is really impressive. His wife, Janet, who is more ruthless than him, is an American communist; I didn't like her much.

[In 1992 Cheddi Jagan, by then a much mellowed Marxist after all the years in the wilderness as leader of the opposition, won the presidential elections, which were supervised by the former US president, Jimmy Carter.]

There was an extraordinary diplomatic wives tea party given by the wife of the new Venezuelan ambassador who speaks only Spanish. We arrived at 4.30 p.m., talked till 5.00 p.m., then the most fantastic spread of tea I have ever seen appeared.

Then at 6.00 p.m., when we were all thinking we must go and start the evening social round, she announced games.

And we all sat around solemnly playing a sort of pass the parcel with cards game. Really a giggle. Then home, change, and on to two cocktail parties.

17 December 1971
The boys arrived in very good form and the plane was only three quarters of an hour late. They do not seem to have changed at all, and it is as if they have never been away, which is as it should be.

30 December 1971
They all said Georgetown goes wild at Xmas, and it certainly does. There have been so many dinners, parties and dances that I cannot enumerate them all. Real West Indian fervour.

Here's a letter for you.

> Dear Granny and Grampa,
>   Thank you for the puppet and paint by numbers. They were lovely. There are lots of cars in Guyana and you should see the way they drive man its terrible.
>   Love from Lucy

We had a multinational party for the kids, with 25 children of all colours, shapes and sizes, which was a great success. All three are in excellent form and Andrew seems very cheerful indeed, far more relaxed. Happy New Year from us all!

9 January 1972
Tonight we see the boys off and perhaps go on to a party if we have the energy and do not feel too depressed and the plane is not too late. I do hope there are no delays for you meeting them at Gatwick and in the case are three thank-you pineapples.

Lucy went off to her new school today where we are hoping she will be a lot happier; she never settled at the convent. This headmistress, Mrs Hunter, is sweet, with good ideas, and some of the teachers trained recently in the UK and are hopefully better than the old nuns with their antiquated methods.

Had two lovely days boating up the muddy, vast Essequibo River. It was very hot and very sticky, and there were mosquitoes, mangrove swamps and piranha (the blood-loving cannibal fish which swim around in shoals waiting for any blood they can find) all around us so we could not swim. But we were with a Guyanese party and the rum flowed and we all enjoyed ourselves, and it certainly made a change from the Pegasus Hotel for weekend activity.

The government has announced a 12 million dollar cut in imports and everyone is very worried and stocking up on food. Hopefully it will not get quite as bad as Ceylon as they will be able to import from CARIFTA, this is the Caribbean Free Trade Association in the West Indies. But it obviously will mean quite a lot more items will become unobtainable.

17 January 1972

Thanks to Bookers we had a wonderful flight over Guyana in a six-seater plane accompanying two of their visiting UK directors. We were right up in the interior and it was really the most fantastic two days we have ever spent. The country is vast [very easy to conceal Jonestown, the site of the later massacre in 1978 when Revd Jim Jones and 912 people died]. I don't think anyone else in the office here has ever seen the parts we saw — very few people do, as it is so expensive to go privately and there are no commercial flights. So we have been very lucky to have been invited.

The highlight of the trip was our visit to Karanambo up in the Rupununi. No matter what other country we visit or whoever else we meet in our diplomatic life I am sure this is an experience we shall never forget.

Our plane landed on an airstrip which seemed to be in the middle of nowhere on the vast, featureless Rupununi savannah towards the Brazilian border in the south-west of Guyana beyond the seemingly never-ending jungle. We walked through the scrubland and found a clearing with a group of thatched, mud huts.

This was the home of the legendary Tiny McTurk, a Scot, who has spent all his adult life in the interior of Guyana hunting, looking for diamonds and gold, and cattle ranching. When he first arrived in Guyana the only way to civilization from the interior was by boat via the Rupununi River, which joins the Essequibo, and this journey would take him several weeks and involve coping with several rapids *en route*. When they are ready for marketing the cattle from the savannah are still brought down to the coast in this fashion. He had always meant to modernize his hut, but had never quite got round to it. He had not even finished the walls, as two were non-existent. He was very proud that his home had been built without a nail.

Inside his hut was a mixture of the old and new, from bows and arrows, blowpipes and all manner of hunting equipment, which he uses regularly, to radio equipment with which he keeps contact with civilization. The furniture consisted of colourful Brazilian hammocks and a vast table, probably 15ft long, served by packing cases for chairs. The table was laid with beautiful silver, shining and polished, and sparkling crystal glass. We sat on our packing cases and, with humming birds and parrots flying in and out of the hut for crumbs, were served a delicious three-course lunch of fish from the Rupununi River, duck shot by Tiny and local fruit (mangoes and guavas) grown around his clearing.

After lunch we were taken in his dugout canoe with an outboard motor up the river and Tiny told us fascinating stories of his life, ranging from contretemps with Brazilian bandits, coping with and employing Amerindians and witch doctors, to the never-ending wonders of tropical nature. The whole visit had an air of unreality about it.

21 January 1972
In nine days you will be here and I really cannot believe it. Have just finished some more batiks and a friend took them over to Grenada this week, and I have several more orders. So am urgently in need of the new dyes I asked you for.

Lucy is terribly excited to see you. She is enjoying her new school much more than the other, thank heavens. Very cheery letters from the boys. Don't forget your tennis things.

29 March 1972
The New Zealand test team arrives tomorrow and we shall then be very involved with cricket as will the entire population of Guyana. The boys have timed their holiday well and have now been made associates of the Guyana Cricket Club, which means they can watch from the pavilion with Michael. There will also be nets for the children at the club three times a week. Enjoyment of cricket is a prerequisite for enjoyment of Guyana and the West Indies.

There are no Easter eggs here at all — imported chocolate is on the forbidden list.

5 April 1972

The whole country stops work and thinks and talks nothing else but cricket during the test matches. The Guyanese bicycle around holding their radios to their ears, concentrating on nothing else but the test progress and making the roads more hazardous than ever. The match v Guyana was a draw. The wicket is a batsman's paradise, lots of centuries, not many wickets, but very pleasant to watch.

The amazing thing about cricket here is that Guyanese women are dead keen and we have to fight for seats in the ladies' pavilion. The boys are much enjoying their privileged associate membership in the men's pavilion. Tim won't miss a ball — and the last match was five days. Andrew comes and goes on his bike when he feels like it.

There was a jump-up with all the cricketers at the Canadian High Commissioner's, which was great fun. There is a chap here whom we knew at Cambridge, Henry Blofeld. He is reporting on the tour for six newspapers and also doing radio commentaries. We have seen a lot of him; it is so nice to see old friends. There has been an unfortunate contretemps between Henry and Glen Turner, the New Zealand batsman, whom he suggested had batted boringly for too long giving no one else in his team a chance to practise.

The New Zealand v West Indies test match starts tomorrow and the boys are really excited, especially as they are meeting the cricketers. Alvin Kallicharan, who plays in the Georgetown Cricket Club in the same team as Michael, which incidentally also includes six other test players, current and past, gave Andrew a teddy bear the other day! [The Georgetown Cricket Club was captained by Steve Camacho, who is a white Guyanese and the last white man to play for the West Indies. Now, in 1995, he is secretary of the West Indian Cricket Board.]

Easter was lovely with sunshine, swimming and cricket. We all tried to fly our kites along the sea wall, which is the great thing to do on Easter Monday — a colourful sight with thousands of kites flying over the sea and all the happy, laughing Guyanese dressed in their best clothes for the occasion.

21 April 1972

It is Andrew's tenth birthday today and he has nine boys of all nationalities coming to his party. They have had a really lovely holiday. The cricket was super.

Our party for the New Zealanders went well and included West Indian cricketers like Lance Gibbs, Clive Lloyd, Kallicharan and Steve Camacho.

Lots of the New Zealanders, like Bev Congdon the captain, had known Michael when he played Plunket Shield cricket in New Zealand. They were very polite and friendly and not at all arrogant or demanding as some touring cricket teams can be.

But the party was rather difficult to organize as we did not know exactly how many would come, and how many would bring girls. So we invited about 15 extra single girls, didn't know many of them, and they all arrived between 8.30 and 9.00 p.m., but the cricketers came in dribs and drabs — and the last ones not until 10.30 p.m. So it was an awful strain wondering who would turn up. It got going eventually — until 3.00 a.m.

Kallicharan made a century in his first test match here v New Zealand and yesterday made another in the final test in Trinidad. He plays county cricket in the UK in the summer. He is a very sweet Indian, young and small, and comes from Port Mourant on a sugar estate from a very humble background. In Guyana all little boys play cricket and wherever you go they are out hitting whatever they can find with sticks, and if they then get noticed in club cricket, which is very competitive and very serious here, they can reach the top.

5 June 1972

It has done nothing but rain here. Terrible flooding everywhere. Everything in the house is going green with mould — shoes, books, pictures. I caught a cold, which turned into bronchial asthma; I'm wheezing and coughing like an old woman. Dr Kerry is giving me blood tests as it is taking ages to clear; apparently there is some tropical parasitical condition that can produce these symptoms. Anyway it is all depressing and boring in the rain and I have been reduced to playing bridge — a ladies four on Tuesday mornings.

The Duke of Windsor's death plunged us into court mourning for a week. We had to wear black or white, which are the mourning colours for Africa and the West Indies, whenever we went out of the house. This entailed a quick rush to Miss Olympe, the dressmaker, who made me a black dress overnight, which I wore nonstop. As the weather is so foul I think I may come home a week before the boys break up.

11 June 1972

Still awaiting a letter — have not heard a word for weeks. I hope a letter has not gone astray. The weather is still awful and damp. In fact someone has just looked at our gramophone, which was new when we arrived here 11 months ago, and parts are all corroding already. We are also having trouble with the cars. My brakes failed completely the other day, and Michael's did yesterday, both due to perishing pipes.

16 June 1972

At last I am feeling better; I still have a cough, but the wheezing has stopped. But the weather is still foul, so no swimming, tennis, cricket, golf or anything. And there is not even any TV and very rarely any decent films to see. I long to see telly again. It is so maddening here — the film *Hospital* was on, which is supposed to be good, so we duly went to the drive-in cinema and could not hear half of what was said as the loudspeaker system had broken down.

Also I am trying to get some batik orders finished and it is very difficult with no decent drying weather; if they stay damp for some time the wax deteriorates before the next coat.

We are going to put in a strong bid for only one more tour here. It is just too small, restricted and frustrating for three years and it really gets tedious.

There are just not enough kindred spirits; several of the nicer foreigners have left and the Guyanese themselves are beginning to get out fast because of the worsening economic and political conditions. In general the Guyanese are not as hospitable as the Ceylonese. They love coming here, but we do not get very many invitations back. So you never really get involved with the place and seem to live on the outside very much, which is not very satisfactory, but I suppose a typical situation for a diplomatic family in very many countries.

But Lucy is really happy here now with friends all over the place. She had an excellent half-term report, and has a gang of nine children living around of all nationalities and races (African, Indian, Chinese, Guyanese, Trinidadian) and loves bossing them all around.

Michael's new secretary *en route* from Washington is very young and I don't know how she will manage here. Girls just cannot go around anywhere on their own.

Still looking forward to a letter.

26 June 1972

I really cannot wait to come home on leave now in July, except for having to leave poor Michael behind for several weeks. But he is going to be extremely busy as in August there is a Non-Aligned Conference here with hundreds of Foreign Ministers from all over the world. Also lots of black power militants coming to spread their gospel — Angela Davies too [the American black activist] I wouldn't be surprised.

As soon as that shindig is over, there is Carifesta with hundreds of artistes from the Caribbean and South America in plays, dances and art exhibitions. There are some excellent Caribbean writers, including V. S. Naipaul, and poets too, particularly Derek Walcott, who was born in St Lucia [and later won the Nobel prize for his poem, *Omeros*]. In a way I am sorry I shall miss that, but it is all going to be fairly chaotic I think.

There are real food shortages now due to the floods. Beef is very scarce, vegetables and fruit are short and so expensive. They have forbidden so many imports, heaven knows what all these visitors will eat.

In celebration of the first worldwide non-aligned countries meeting to be held here they are erecting four monuments to great figures of the Non-Aligned Movement — guess who? Nehru, Tito — and, wait for it, Nkrumah and Nasser. Unbelievable waste of money, but quite likely there will be another great figure slipped in too — our great leader himself. In spite of all the forthcoming celebrations there is tremendous discontent at the moment here — everyone is complaining, and lots are leaving whilst they can.

30 June 1972

The weather here is still foul. Torrential rain again today. I am sitting in my bra and pants in the bedroom, the air conditioner has broken down again, I have just had a cold shower and I am just pouring with sweat — it is incredibly humid.

Next week I have to give a large coffee morning for expatriate and diplomatic wives — a get together to try to cheer people up — and a formal dinner for our High Commissioner in Barbados who is over on a visit. Also I have to fit in Lucy's birthday party before I leave. I must say I could do with the next two weeks passing without having to go through them.

Will be home on 17 July and am longing to see you.

Finally arrived home at 4.15 a.m. on Monday morning from the USA. I felt completely flaked for two days. It is *so* hot and *humid*! The USA was fantastic. I hope our next posting is New York. We loved it. We stayed with arty Jewish writer friends, Bill and Tana Ross, whom we had met on the beach in Grenada. I think their main claim to fame is that he wrote *Sesame Street* [a children's television programme]. They were very kind and immensely hospitable.

On our last evening we went over to New Jersey, on the other side of the river, to Fort Lee, where our host's brother, Burt Ross, is the mayor. He was elected a year ago and is the first Democratic mayor there for 40 years and, at only 28, is the youngest mayor in the USA. We went into a council meeting with the public attending — about 300 people. We walked in and sat quietly at the back. Burt then stood up and announced that they had some very distinguished visitors from Britain — Deputy High Commissioner etc. etc. and laying it on like mad — and that Fort Lee, New Jersey was honoured to give us the keys of the city. We then walked up on to the platform and were given a very large key, all suitably engraved. Then followed speeches (Michael sounded so English and they all loved it), photos and interviews. It was quite hilarious and we all then went out to dinner.

There are lots of new arrivals in the office and I am going to a meeting of the DSWA tomorrow to meet all the wives. This is the FCO wives' organization, which exists to look after the interests of wives and families. It is run from London with representatives in all overseas posts and puts pressure on the FCO in matters like paying children's air fares for holidays, looking after people flown home in emergencies, and trying to ensure that qualified wives are sent to posts where they will be able to work.

8 December 1972

I have now been asked to send some batiks to another shop in Barbados, and also have another order from someone here — so that is good. Also a nice cheque from Grenada where they have sold some more. And a friend from New Zealand has asked me to send some to her as there is a shop in Wellington which sells only batiks. So that is all going well.

Don't laugh, but I have now started to play mah-jong as well as bridge! It will be a great asset when it rains nonstop here. I really feel like an old colonial *memsahib* and we have a Chinese friend who is teaching us the complicated system. But the only thing to do here to keep sane is to keep busy.

And we are dutifully having lunches for all the new arrivals in the office and generally helping them settle in. There is quite a lot of work involved in helping them find houses to rent (the High Commission does not own many), introducing them, showing them the way around Georgetown, helping them get their children into schools, and lending them equipment until their luggage arrives, which can take forever. And some wives cope better than others. The men are in a much easier position, for they go off to the office where they immediately meet people and fall into a routine, but the wives have to create their own routine and find their own pattern for living in a strange country, and for making friends and generally sorting everything out.

A Very Happy Christmas!

15 January 1973
No letter from you or the boys for three weeks now so I presume a bag has gone astray. I just hope the boys arrived back OK. It was awful seeing them go, and it seems very empty without them.

23 January 1973
The Chinese Embassy, which has recently been established here, held a reception. There was a large picture of Mao at the end of the huge sparsely furnished rather bleak room. All the men were dressed identically, and the women too, in white shirts and black trousers, all proudly wearing their little Mao badges. Few of them speak English and the ambassador has to be spoken to through an interpreter, which is hard work — conversations take ages, but it does pass the time. There was a funny mixture of drinks — rather potent, horrible rice-type liquor, sweet Chinese wine or beer. I plumped for the latter. But there were tasty Chinese eats.

The Embassy staff mostly live all together in this large house, but gradually more and more are seeping out into the country — for trade purposes, or so they say. They were all very cheerful and full of smiles, and as there was very little verbal communication between us we just smiled happily at each other. It was quite amusing for the first one and a half hours, but then the joss sticks they were burning began to make my eyes smart and, just as we were thinking we might politely leave, a film show was announced.

We were paraded through into another vast room, with a large screen and rows and rows of uncomfortable seats. The doors were firmly closed behind us, we were plunged into darkness and had to sit through very long films about a Chinese circus and Chinese ballet with no possible way of escape.

We have just had a scandal with a couple in the office to cope with. West Indian morality is very easy-going, marriage is not an important factor of life here, and living together, usually the man with one or two women on the go, is very normal. The UK chap in the office had an affair with a local Guyanese member of staff and someone took photos — consequently he was vulnerable to blackmail. He has now been sent back to London and has had to leave the FO. I had to help the wife a lot who was, needless to say, in a dreadful state.

2 February 1973

It's Timothy's thirteenth birthday on Wednesday. I cannot believe he is now a teenager; if only we could be there. Michael Halstead, the British Council representative, is very keen for me to do a batik exhibition for the Council later this year. It will mean a lot of work but I will see what I can do.

9 February 1973

Had a fabulous adventurous weekend with Sony and Lois Ramphal. We drove for one and a half hours out of Georgetown, then got into their large powerful boat and travelled a further one and a quarter hours up the river.

There were several stops, once to shoot at a very large alligator. The Ramphals' house is surprisingly comfortable despite being in the middle of nowhere. It has running water though no electricity, but we managed very well with oil and gas lamps. We brought everything we would need with us in ice boxes and Sony mixed fantastic drinks all weekend. We went shooting Muscovy duck lying on our tummies in the rice fields, fishing, shooting alligator at night, and speeding up and down the river visiting some of the farmers on the river banks, who were extremely friendly and gave us coconut water to drink.

Guyana

23 February 1973

You may have heard from Michael about my mysterious tropical illness? I had London flu, which was going the rounds here, and the local doctor, an Indian, Dr Kerry, gave me some penicillin, and some linctus with antihistamine and it cleared up in a week. And then the day after I stopped the tablets I woke up covered with blotches and swellings and I could not swallow properly. Dr Kerry gave me some more antihistamine saying it was a reaction to the penicillin and would clear up.

But it got worse and the next day Dr Kumar, an Indian specialist trained in Canada and the leading light in a little Indian opposition party, everyone seems to be involved in politics here, said I would have to have steroid treatment and he would rather have me under observation — by this time I literally could not walk as my feet were so swollen and could not move my hands at all and felt sick and really ghastly.

So in I went to Dr Prashad's funny little Indian hospital. Actually, although basic, it was fairly clean and I had an airconditioned room to myself. It all seems to have stemmed from the penicillin, which I must never take again, and with the steroid treatment the swelling went down quickly and I gradually felt better.

6 April 1973

The boys arrived in excellent order, both on marvellous form and very cheerful indeed, and the whole of Guyana is in a ferment with cricket.

We had Australia v Guyana last week, which was a very exciting match with the usual West Indian crowds and atmosphere. Today the fourth test starts so we are all off for the day. It is really super with the atmosphere at the cricket here. We have seen a lot of all the cricketers at various functions and tonight we are showing *A Taste of Honey* after a spaghetti supper, and several of the Australians and Guyanese are coming. Jim Swanton, the grand old man of cricket writers, came to lunch with us; I think he must know more cricket stories than anyone else.

22 April 1973

Timothy had an exciting trip to Kaiteur, the 800ft waterfall, with some SAS men who, on a training exercise, were parachuted from high in the sky deep into the interior and then had to find their way through the dense jungle down to the coast. And we went with all the children for the day to Linden looking at bauxite mining and spent another morning looking round a sugar factory and fields.

Of course two weeks of the boys' holiday were taken up with cricket. The crowd got very upset at one test match at what they thought was an unfair decision against the Guyanese test players, Lloyd and Kallicharan. They threw bottles onto the pitch, let off fire crackers and a few managed to get onto the pitch, but not many, for as a result of some bad riots a few years ago, the crowd is mainly imprisoned behind ten-foot barricades. The Australians then walked off and refused to play until all had calmed down, which took quite some time.

The Aussies were a very pleasant, friendly bunch. We particularly liked a chap called Ian Redpath, who has been an Australian test cricketer for years and in his non-cricket time runs an antique shop.

PS. Andrew will be bringing all his birthday money back home with him as there is absolutely nothing for him to buy here in the empty shops.

3 May 1973

Yesterday was my regular trip to Mahaica Leper Colony. I seem to be getting used to it now, and it does not upset me so much. I suppose we get used to anything after a while. Human beings are certainly adaptable. Even the lepers living their miserable and neglected existence in the middle of nowhere seem really quite cheerful, and their joy at receiving visitors and sweets and other little gifts makes me feel very small by comparison.

10 May 1973

Still no letter from you. Also we have had no letters from the boys so I hope they are all right.

Shopping is getting more like Ceylon every day, more and more import restrictions, and food gets really boring when you cannot have any variety. At the moment we can buy no onions, garlic, potatoes, salt, white sugar or tomato paste. Guyana has to export all the sugar it produces.

Michael's cricket for Georgetown Cricket Club has been very successful. On the first occasion he got 74 with three sixes in succession and the next highest scores were 28 by Rohan Kanhai and 12 by Kallicharan, both West Indian test players.

14 May 1973

We are having serious thoughts about Lucy's education here. There are several points, the main academic one being that she has to take the Downe House common entrance in December this year or January 1974, but she is also being affected by the racial problems. [Downe House in Berkshire was the boarding school in England to which we were planning to send her in January 1975 when she would be 11½, the youngest age for admission.]

At the moment her English is getting rather poor, slangy and Guyanese. Her social life now revolves mainly around two little Indian girls who have come to live in the area. They are very sweet, but their father owns a humble store and their grandmother from over the river is illiterate. Lucy spent the night there recently and in true Indian fashion shared a bed with the mother.

Her other great friend is an African girl, whose father is Forbes Burnham's lawyer. But the problem is that Lucy, the African girl and the Indians are now being ostracized by the rest of the kids in the area, mainly as the white Guyanese in the road do not approve of the shopkeeper Indian family, and Lucy is becoming very aware of the racial tensions. The other problem is that at her school the pressure is now on for the Guyanese 11-plus exam, and she is doing nothing but maths and spelling. No history, geography, scripture, art — or anything. Really very restrictive indeed. Her grammar is dreadful now, and she will never pass an exam in England at this rate.

If we do leave in November we are thinking that the best thing will be for me to bring Lucy back when I come home in September and send her to Holy Trinity Primary School, and she could stay with you for a few weeks to re-anglicize herself. If you could possibly very kindly manage?

18 May 1973

No letters from you for weeks now.

Our news. First, have spent all this week prostrate with appalling shellfish poisoning. Michael and I went to a Chinese restaurant on Sunday night and ate quite a lot of prawns. That night we had all the usual symptoms and they were really bad. It is now Friday and I have eaten nothing solid since then and am feeling extremely weak and have lost half a stone. Michael's symptoms are not quite as severe, but he has felt low, has no appetite, and has a red rash all over his chest and stomach. So for me the whole week has been wasted, though I felt just well enough to stagger dutifully to the airport to meet Bill Bates, the returning High Commissioner, and then got home and was ill again all night.

Secondly, very good news. We are definitely, repeat definitely, not coming back after this tour! They are working on a commercial job for Michael, which he wants, in Western Europe, preferably Paris. So it really sounds promising. Four years in Europe and near enough to come back for the kids' half terms — sounds really fantastic. [This was not to be.]

In view of this we definitely want Lucy to have a term at Trinity in September. We are hoping she gets her CE so that she can come abroad with us for two or three terms before starting at Downe House. At all Western European capital cities they have international schools. It is all very complicated, and I only wish Downe would take them at ten and a half.

The water situation here is the worst for years — rice failing, sugar failing. We are lucky if we get a shower as the pressure is so bad. And this is normally the rainy season. If these rains fail completely Guyana is really in a bad way.

21 May 1973

Just a brief note to let you know that your letters have finally arrived. One by bag and the other air mail, both delayed weeks, so both methods of communication have been hopeless.

Michael and my salmonella poisoning, for that is what they think it was, are now nearly OK. I still feel nauseous from time to time, and have lost my appetite and nearly a stone.

And next week I have to give a reception for 150 for a visit of, wait for it, the Hull City Football Team!

1 June 1973

The football party was fine. The manager was Terry Neil, who is also manager of Ireland [and later managed Arsenal] and he was helped by Don Howe [his assistant at Arsenal] and both are very nice. The last guest went at midnight, and it was supposed to end at 8.30 p.m.

Giving a party when you do not know half the guests is quite a strain and I spent lots of time introducing people and making sure people were not left out. Lucy caused a great stir at the party. She and her friends helped pass food round, and each time I saw her she was surrounded by footballers, most of whom were only about 18 or 19, and holding court and looking extremely attractive and I was told more than once how Guyanese she is now.

Last Saturday the president of the Co-operative Republic of Guyana held the investiture ceremony and the seventh independence anniversary celebrations. They have now announced the date of the next election, 16 July, and we hope all stays peaceful.

12 June 1973
Darling Timothy and Andrew,

I had an interesting and busy trip with the Hull City Football Team. They were going by chartered plane down to Surinam, capital of Dutch Guyana, and Cayenne, capital of French Guyana, and there were a few spare seats, so I thought it would be a good idea to go for the free trip!

Some of them were quite pleasant, the manager Terry Neil is a famous footballer who played for Ireland. We flew in a DC3, which wasn't too comfortable, and as we left too late the first day to get to Cayenne we had to overnight in Surinam and fly on next day. This meant lots of extra hanging around for planes and transport to and from airports. Also the hotel we were put in was not very nice, and some of the team began to get difficult and say they refused to play and wanted to get home. It is quite amazing how much money these professional footballers get paid and how spoilt they all are. They had no interest in the countries they were visiting; they just sat around and looked at comics most of the time.

Next day we got to Cayenne and things were well organized there with a good hotel and super French food and they all cheered up. Cayenne is a tiny little town. French Guyana used to be famous for Devil's Island, which was a French penal colony where they sent all their most dangerous prisoners and which closed in 1946. But they now have a very large rocket base at Kuru about 50 miles from Cayenne with several thousand French people working there. All the buildings are wooden in Cayenne, and it has a remarkably French atmosphere. We went into a little restaurant in the main street of this funny little town, and the moment we went in it was just like being in France, with the smells of French cooking and cigarettes and the atmosphere. Everyone speaks French there, though I couldn't understand much as they have a very strong dialect.

At Paramaribo we had two nights in a really grand hotel. But the players were getting very homesick by this time and started saying they wished to cancel the last match; the managers had to talk late into the night to persuade the players' spokesman that since they had come such a long way they really had to play and couldn't just go home. And he explained that there were very few planes from the Guyanas to England, so changing arrangements at the drop of a hat was impossible. They did play in the end, but because Hull City play quite roughly compared to people in this part of the world they got a lot of booing; they won one match and drew the other.

All in all I was away four days. And I am very glad I went as it was interesting to see the other two Guyanas and I certainly learnt a lot about the lives of professional footballers of the third division.

22 June 1973
My darling Timothy,

It was lovely to hear you on the phone this morning and you sounded very clear and close. We were going to send you a cable but decided we would rather speak to you. Well done again. [He had done very well in his common entrance exams.] You seemed to do particularly well in maths. We are very pleased and proud of you. You asked me to tell you how to spell the house at Harrow you are going to. It is The Knoll, and the housemaster is Raymond Venables.

23 June 1973
In spite of what you say about our plans for Lucy we are still convinced it is best for her to come back to England. The business with the Indian family, whom no one else will speak to now, and to whom she is completely loyal, means that when she walks up the road with them the other kids jeer and whistle, which is most unpleasant. They are sweet kids, the father no doubt making a lot of money from his typical Indian sell everything store, but the social and racial tensions in the area and in Guyana as a whole are very strong. It is just not good for Lucy not to be able to play with anyone else, which is what it is now boiling down to. The plans are still in the melting pot as far as Michael's next posting goes — and we are determined to get Lucy organized.

Thank God this is our last year here. I really couldn't take any more. It does get you down after a time. The rains have started. I am drenched in sweat writing this. It is very enervating at the moment. [At this time I began to feel very ill with severe headaches. The medical situation in Guyana was not good; there was no neurologist in the country, so my medical advice was basically across the Atlantic from my father, a consultant physician in Guildford. But, as usual, communications were not easy.]

5 July 1973
You will have had my letter with more details of my illness. I am feeling slightly better now; I certainly could not have typed yesterday. My doctor has been very sweet, though obviously does not know quite what to do with me. He is not actually practising at the moment as he is so busy with the forthcoming election on 14 July. But he has dropped in and been on the phone to me and prescribed various pills, some of which needless to say are unobtainable.

There has already been one violent pre-election incident with four people killed. Forbes Burnham has since spoken on the radio and things have quietened. Though my doctor says that at his meeting last night stones were being thrown and the mounted police did nothing about it, his is an Indian party, and one of his colleagues ended up in hospital. So we shall be glad when it is all over.

I look forward very much to hearing what Desmond Carroll [a neurologist in Guildford] advises.

[Two weeks later, and feeling very unwell, we decided to take matters into our own hands and that I should fly home. There was little or no advice from the FCO in London, and colleagues from other missions were amazed I had not been flown out much earlier. My father met me at Heathrow and took me straight to Guildford Hospital. Following tests I was transferred to the National Hospital, Queen's Square in London and operated on by Dr Laurence Walsh, who removed a benign tumour, or meningioma, 'the size of an egg' from my head. I was very lucky to be alive. Michael flew out of Guyana for two weeks on 'compassionate leave', Lucy stayed with her Indian friends and Tim and Andrew, who were in Guyana for the summer holidays, were parked on kind colleagues. We were due to leave Guyana at the end of November, and we had a battle with the Foreign Office to pay my return fare to Guyana after the operation as it would be for less than three months. Despite letters from doctors that for my health and recovery I should be with my husband, and backup support from the DSWA — our wives union — we lost the battle. Nevertheless I returned at my own expense, basically to say goodbye and to pack up.]

18 October 1973

Can't say I am feeling all that great; I was tired in England but am far tireder here, which I suppose is not surprising as everyone is always tired here. I went to one cocktail at the US ambassador's which I enjoyed, but felt ghastly the next day. So I shall not go to any more standing up dos and really go very slowly. It is hard work making conversation with the new security guard and his wife, for example, when out of duty we have them in for lunch.

And next stop Turkey. The job sounds interesting and from all we hear, apart from problems like smog and no water, Ankara is a good posting, with opera, concerts, theatre and cinemas which will be paradise. Luckily there is a British primary school in Ankara so Lucy will be able to come with us before going to Downe House. [Lucy, aged ten, had now left Guyana to spend a term to re-anglicize herself at a primary school in Guildford.]

Nothing more from the FCO about paying my fare. Wives certainly get very little appreciation or recognition for all the unpaid work they do overseas. I think this used to be accepted without question but times are changing and some wives are beginning to complain that they are unable to have careers of their own, contribute tremendously to the work of their husband and the Embassy or High Commission, and at the end of his career, after 30 years or so, receive nothing in the way of thanks, or more important, some form of pension.

See you soon!

4
Turkey

After a fairly quick turnaround in England we flew to Athens — Lucy was with us — and went by boat from there to Istanbul, where we stayed for two nights in the Pera Palas Oteli. We arrived in Ankara in February 1974. Michael, in his posting as first secretary (Economic and Aid), had little to do with Turkish politics and was loosely attached to the Commercial Department with responsibility for reporting on economic developments and a separate role supervising the UK's aid programme.

9 February 1974
After a super trip have come down to earth with a bang. Ankara is a hard place to settle into, and I think the best way to describe what I've found so far is to list the goods and the bads.
Goods:
- People in Embassy are helpful and friendly.
- Lucy is very happily settled in the British Embassy School.
- A maid, Efina, who cannot come till next week, but it will be good when she does as she speaks a little bit of English.
- Shops are reasonably full of food — there is good local lamb and beef, but peculiar things (like tin foil, tin opener and oven cloth) are unobtainable.
Bads:
- No water now for two days. Can buy drinking water from a van which comes up our street periodically. Water situation varies over the city but there are perpetual troubles everywhere; our flat is worse off than most in the Embassy. We now fill our one bath when

the water is on and two large containers, which we bought today.

- Everything gets filthy due to the smog over the city caused from burning wet cheap coal. Ankara is 3000 feet high in a basin of hills. When there is no wind the smog cannot escape and settles for days.
- Turkish is an impossible language to learn; like Finnish, it has no common roots with English. But we must try as most people speak nothing else. So getting anything done is very difficult, and getting organized generally very hard.
- The flat is too small, is hopeless for entertaining and has pretty ghastly furniture.
- It looks as though our luggage will take weeks and weeks. There are hold-ups everywhere, always. We could do with at least a gramophone or radio for cheering-up music, not to mention some more clothes.

We thought of moving, but larger flats are difficult to find and furnishing would take months. So we think we will stay and put up with the inconvenience of no water and no space.

The weather was very cold when we arrived but is now warmer. Flats are very heated from October to May and get hot and dry but if we open the windows the filthy, smoggy, greasy dust pours in. It still gets in even if we don't open the windows, and things get covered in dust and have to be cleaned twice a day. Michael needs to change his shirt when he gets back at lunch time, which is difficult as we have no water to wash it in.

Michael's immediate boss, Alan Elgar, who is head of the commercial section, is a very charming ex-naval officer with a lovely French wife, Maryse, and they are being extremely helpful and friendly. They took us out to a super restaurant last week (Lucy came too) and Turkish food is interesting. Tonight they are giving us a smart dinner for 12 to meet some high-up Turks. I only wish we could wash first.

19 February 1974
The chap in the Embassy who looks after these things came to look around our flat and was shocked at the state of furniture and carpets. So we did have something to be fed up about. We have the OK to order nearly all new stuff from the UK. I do not know how long it will take. They may tell us to get some things done locally, I hope so, as otherwise it could all take a year.

The water situation is really ghastly. We never know when it is coming on. Yesterday we had four minutes in the morning and five minutes in the evening, while we were out. But we have to try to keep the bath permanently filled, taking out water in a saucepan for cooking and washing and severely limit the flushing of the loo.

After the First World War Mustafa Kemal, or Ataturk, the founder of modern Turkey, decided to make Ankara the capital instead of Istanbul as he wanted to get away from European influence, and also be right in the middle of the country.

Apart from the ancient city of Ancyra, built around the old citadel, Ankara is all new and surrounded by barren, waterless areas similar to Russian and Siberian steppes. Ataturk thought it would never be too large a city, and water would be OK. There are now around a million inhabitants, the population is growing and Ataturk got it quite wrong. [The population in 1995 is over three million.]

Smog also seems an insoluble problem. The temperature can drop to minus 30 degrees in the winter. Everyone has to keep warm somehow, so they burn cheap fuel. They cannot burn smokeless fuel as first there is none available and second, if there were, they could not afford it. So the smog hangs heavily over the city. On some days it is so dense you really cannot see out of the windows until there is a wind to blow it away. And then we start again.

[The smog problem has now been solved. For the past few years piped gas has been used for fuel instead of coal; it is piped to Ankara from Russia. Also the water situation is now much improved since the building of a very large dam.]

The American Embassy does not allow any families with children in the post. Apparently living here is equivalent to smoking 40 packets of cigarettes a day.

But Lucy is surviving so far. There is a complete mixture of nationalities at the British Embassy School, which she enjoys, but she has huge gaps in her overall knowledge because of all the changes in her education.

The Turks we have met are certainly very pleasant. But apart from the well-educated ones who will speak French or English, the language problem is bad. We will *have* to learn quite a lot. Heaven knows how, for at the moment it is like learning gibberish. *Bir, iki, uc, dirt, bes, alti, yedi, sekiz, dokuz, on* is their way of counting from one to ten!

We have now completely lost track of our luggage and have no idea when, or if, we shall see it again.

Efina, the maid, is very sweet and works very hard. Also I have a lovely old man called Mehmet Yuksel coming in once a week to cook; soon he will come twice. Some friends, Jeremy and Wendy Varcoe, who are colleagues in the Embassy, employ him but apparently not many want to because he smokes very strong Turkish cigarettes, continually, like most Turkish men, and there is always ash in the food. But Wendy and I are far too sensible to worry about things like that. The ash is not going to hurt us and the food is very tasty! [Turkish cigarettes were banned from Britain in 1992 — much to the dismay of the playwright, John Osborne, among others.]

But entertaining will be easy — I hope. Mehmet will cook, and bring a helper if necessary for cocktail parties and we shall have to start soon. Though it will be difficult without our glasses, plates or cutlery, and with only the meagre office float of four plates, four knives, four forks, four spoons, two saucepans and a frying pan to keep us going. The Turks are very proud of their cuisine, which they regard as second only to French, and we are beginning really to enjoy Turkish food and eat out quite a lot, for anything is preferable to cooking in a kitchen with no water.

19 February 1974
Cento, which is the Central Treaty Organization, rather like a south-east European NATO, has its headquarters in Ankara and celebrates its nineteenth anniversary this week. It consists of Turks, Iranians, Pakistanis, Americans and us and exists to KEEP RUSSIA OUT.

We went to a ball to celebrate, which was full of generals, medals, smart uniforms and was all very military. Michael is chairman of the Economic Committee this year. Apparently he chaired his first meeting admirably with the old schoolmaster coming out in him and keeping all the soldiers in order and making the meeting go the way we, the British, wanted.

The Hittite Museum, which is the archaeological museum in the old part of Ankara, is fascinating. The history of the citadel probably goes back to AD 640 and the museum is housed in a covered bazaar which was built in the second part of the fifteenth century. It is really beautifully laid out and covers the history of the civilizations of Anatolia dating from the Palaeolithic period right through to the really modern Urartian times which were during the first quarter of the first millennium BC! The Hittites themselves were around during the twelfth century BC.

Turkish lessons start tomorrow. We are having two a week to start with as we *must* learn some or living here is impossible. If only it was not so difficult. I am still struggling with *bir* to *on*.

Our luggage from Guyana is in Istanbul. And we should have it in two weeks or so, but the customs are awful here and everything takes ages. Our luggage from England has not even left yet, and the packers took it from Warwicks Mount [our house in Guildford] in early January. It is maddening as so many things we need are with that lot, including warm clothes, and now we shall not see it until the end of May or so.

And our entertaining will have to start soon. We cannot possibly wait for all our luggage, and people sitting on battered dining room chairs with ripped and torn covers will get a more accurate impression of poor old England in the 1970s than if it were all spick and span and new and good.

26 February 1974

Had a nice weekend with Robin and Teri Seeley, a fellow first secretary from our office. He's an excellent linguist and speaks several European languages; his father had also served in the Foreign Office in Turkey and is still remembered here. Teri is Japanese and we eat lovely seaweed with them, which she has sent to her from home. We visited a mountain lake, Abant Golu, 4750 feet above sea level, three hours' drive away. It was frozen over and surrounded by pine trees and snow capped hills. There was brilliant sun all the time, really lovely. The motel was extremely basic but had individual verandas overlooking the lake and running water.

As Ankara is 3000 feet up and surrounded by the Anatolian plateau, which is really miles and miles of nothing until you reach the coastal areas, we were very pleased to find the lake — even though it was not exactly close.

8 March 1974

You will be glad to hear things are looking up here, mainly because we have decided to move flats. The smallness of this one and the lack of water were driving me around the bend. I don't think I am as resilient as I should be following my operation. The office gave us no help or encouragement and just said if we wanted to move we would have to find something ourselves, and we have.

It is an enormous flat, four minutes from the Embassy near the top of a hill overlooking the town, which has constant cold water. It never has hot water, but that is a minor problem. It is in the same block as Mr Cagyliangl — the Foreign Minister — which explains the water luxury. He is an elderly statesman-like figure, very impressive, and he smiles at me when we pass on the stairs.

I feel immensely relieved, and much better already.

Turkish Airlines sadly has the worst record in the world for air accidents. You will have read about the ghastly Turkish plane crash. We have problems getting from Ankara to Istanbul and vice versa. The road between the two is extremely dangerous — with the bad Turkish driving and far too many accidents, Embassy staff are not allowed to drive that way — and the Turkish Airlines' internal flights are also terrible. That leaves the train, which apparently is very slow, goes overnight, but is quite comfortable except for the rats.

13 March 1974

Our new flat is now being painted and we hope to move in next week and to get our lift vans from Guyana in and unpacked before the boys arrive. But there is no furniture so we still do not know what we shall sleep on.

Lucy has had a cough for days — probably a result of the smog.

Yesterday we had lunch with the ambassador, Sir Horace Philips, in his very grand Embassy. He is small, bright, twinkling and amusing; he speaks 11 languages well and left school at 16 when he joined the board of the Inland Revenue. He is unusual for an ambassador as he can do his own typing, decode his own messages and operate radio transmitters. He spends a lot of his time touring the outposts of Turkey in his Rolls-Royce. We had good food and we met some more nice Turks. They are difficult to get to know very well; everyone says it takes years for that, but they are very pleasant, though formal.

We went to Goreme in Cappadocia with the Goatlys, our British Council friends whom we met on the boat coming to Istanbul. They have a Range-Rover which makes travelling in the winter months on the terrible roads around here possible and we love being with them. John is a bearded, larger-than-life figure who survived a terrible period as a Japanese prisoner of war. Frixie is a Freya Stark-type lady and they are both getting very involved in Turkish life and Turkish history.

Goreme is about 190 miles from Ankara and the landscape is spectacular. A wide valley of red and yellow earth has been moulded by the weather over the ages into hard pointed cones and pyramids and strange shaped formations, which all started in prehistoric times with ashes from a nearby volcano. And dotted all over the valley there are vineyards and poplar groves. Strangely this area produces the best wine in Turkey.

Monks being persecuted in the seventh century went into hiding in chapels and churches created from the underground rock caves and, because of the darkness, the paintings in the chapels are still full of colour.

We went down a very narrow shaft to visit the *Elmah Kilise* (Church of the Apple), which has domes, apses and religious paintings. The guide then took us to the *Yilanli Kilise* (Serpent Church) and the *Karanlik Kilise* (Dark Church), where there were some lovely frescoes. There is so much to see in the area we shall certainly be going back.

9 April 1974

The boys arrived in excellent form and we are now moved. Having spent hours estimating the local cost of furniture here, and with a visit from London from a Department of the Environment man, the decision was finally made to get us furniture from London. They swear it will be driven across in a container lorry from London to Ankara and arrive here by mid-June, and meanwhile we are using a motley collection, mostly pretty unsuitable and pretty uncomfortable.

So all is going fine. We now have lots of cold water and space. Thank God we moved; I am feeling miles better. If we want a bath we heat water up in saucepans in the kitchen and bring it to the bathroom.

We have finally unpacked the last packing case from Guyana. It was a horrible business as a lot of damp had got in. It had all been very badly done in Georgetown, with soggy newspapers as the main packing material, for nothing else was available. Our books and pictures are all mouldy and there are damp patches all over the linen. But in spite of the problems it is marvellous to have our belongings again, at least some of them.

Now I am being a lot more venturesome about driving around Ankara, although the drivers are appalling. They become doubly bad when they see a woman behind the wheel as the men do not think women should drive. They do their best to frighten you and you just have to keep a cool head. But I think using public transport, what there is of it, would be a far worse alternative.

There are some very impressive women in Ankara. Although not encouraged to drive and left at home by their husbands when the men go out in the evenings, they are encouraged to work and have achieved very high positions in several fields. Nearly every Turkish woman I meet here has a career and they are still in the happy situation that their mothers think it their duty to look after the grandchildren, which of course helps tremendously.

Social life has not been too hectic and I have missed several cocktails. Wives do here, luckily, because of the Muslim influence. Ataturk, whose photograph you still see in every shop or restaurant you enter, decreed that Turkey should be a secular state, and the more sophisticated Turks are very happy about this. But driving in the countryside around Ankara we see the smallest, poorest villages in the process of building large new mosques they can ill afford.

19 April 1974

The Mediterranean coast here is beautiful and nearly unspoilt, with few hotels and few visitors [it is now very developed]. We stayed in simple guesthouse accommodation, which was unbelievably cheap and very clean. It reminded me of our first visits to the Costa Brava in the 1950s before the tourists arrived.

We saw Perge and Side, which are beautiful Greek and Roman ruined cities with theatres, baths, temples and acropolises, some in surprisingly good condition. One can walk over the mosaic floors and climb anywhere, for there are no barriers or guards.

There is so much to see, and ruins, when you have them nearly to yourselves with no other tourists, are so evocative.

We also visited Alanya and Antalya, the first a sweet little fishing village, the second a larger town, but attractive against the blue sea with snow-capped mountains behind it. Sadly it takes eight or nine hours hard driving from here, but Turkey is a very large country, over 300,000 square miles.

3 May 1974

At last they have changed the tour arrangements here. FO doctors now realize that smog is unhealthy. So we will do two tours of 18 months instead of two of two years. It will all work out very well and we shall be home for the next summer holidays and be able to get Andrew to Harrow that September. I badly want to come back and see him starring in *Androcles and the Lion* next term at Edgeborough, but unless something cheap comes up, perhaps someone driving with a spare seat, I shall not be able to manage it.

13 May 1974

First dinner party for 14 was a great success. I made vichyssoise soup, apricot mousse, remembered all the guests' names and Mehmet did the rest.

21 May 1974

Luggage from Guildford, which was sent in January, has at last arrived having been lost in Istanbul for seven weeks. It is such a relief.

We drove with the Varcoes and Goatlys down to Silifke for a weekend, which was quite a long way, five hours or so, but worth it. The sea was fabulous and the weather gorgeous. We stayed at the BP Mo camp. Lunches and breakfasts we cooked in the communal kitchen, all clean and nice, and we had supper in the attached restaurant. But as a result of our suppers, or the water, one or other of our group had the trots or sickness every day from Friday to Sunday inclusive — when we drove back.

It was a really lovely spot, but far too crowded with masses of Germans and Americans from the military camps nearby, who park their cars and put their tents right close to the sea, play their transistors and make a hell of a row.

30 May 1974

Bags are as hopeless as ever; today's has not arrived at all. I see I last wrote on the 21st. Since then I have been suffering from the food poisoning I picked up at Silifke. I was not too bad there, but as soon as we got back I began to feel sick. This got worse and worse and I felt like death. Two doctors were called, in case it was hepatitis, but I am beginning to feel better, though I have lost pounds and am very, very thin. Apparently we had all eaten bad goat meat, which was being passed off as shish kebab, and the effects can last for ages.

The weather is now fabulous — sunny, hot and gorgeous. The Embassy has a lovely little pool, set in beautiful gardens, where Lucy has great fun with her friends. Having had a lot of rain, Ankara is looking green and pleasant and the trees are covered with blossom.

Fruit and vegetables here are lovely now. The strawberries are really delicious, but their season will be short. All fruit and vegetables are seasonal — frozen food has not been invented here and tinned food is virtually unobtainable — so sometimes there is lots around and sometimes very little.

6 June 1974

You will be glad to hear I am feeling completely better now from my (?) hepatitis. In fact I am beginning to feel really healthy again for the first time since before my operation, which is a great relief.

However, running battles with the Embassy continue about our flat; it has been a nightmare getting it organized. Next week a lorry from London arrives with furniture, though we heard today that several items have not made the van.

Turkey is incredibly inefficient too. All the phones are liable to be out of order at any time. For the last few days no one in this area has had a working phone as they are changing the numbers — but of course have not managed to tell anyone what they are changing the numbers to. But our cold water is lovely.

And it is a beautiful country. We had a wonderful drive down to Kusadasi on the Aegean coast and had a lovely four days there with Liz and Jerome O'Hea, our friends from Chichester; he works with the family firm of Colt International. They are great travellers and love to see everything there is to see, and there is a great deal. The ruins are a joy — Ephesus, Didyma, Miletus. If I had my life again I think I should become an archaeologist. That part of the coast is gorgeous, but sadly there are signs of it being spoilt — I give it ten years. Ephesus already gets rather crowded with parties in coaches, but lots of the places are still empty and idyllic.

On the way down we were planning a picnic lunch and we took a little unmarked turning off the main road to find a suitable spot. And just up the lane, with no signposts in sight, we came upon a little old Roman theatre at a place called Nysa. Apparently a few years ago it had been cleared of the earth that had covered it and it is in very good condition. There was an old temple as well, olive trees and views of the sea with complete tranquillity and no signs of twentieth century life. So we sat in the theatre and ate our picnic of Turkish bread and wine and goat cheese and the only human in sight was a goatherd and the only sound was his flute. A very special place indeed, and very difficult to leave.

18 June 1974

Last night we had a cocktail party here, it went fine, but I am completely flaked today. We went out each night last week and have to go out each night the next week. All very exhausting indeed. Events have included the annual Queen's Birthday Party for hundreds of people and a military attachés' and their ladies' reception!

27 June 1974

All our new furniture has arrived and it meant virtually moving once again. Everything had to be taken out, carpets laid, all drawers and cupboards emptied, complete confusion for days. This on top of endless nights out and the prospect of cocktails and dinners to be given here today, tomorrow and on Monday — it is what is known as really overdoing it.

But before the chaos we had a good exploratory weekend with the Varcoes and Goatlys at the Black Sea. It is a six- or seven-hour drive, but worth it for a weekend, and we have decided to go for ten days in August with the Goatlys and the children.

The hotel is very simple, about £2 a day all in, and it is right on the beach in a completely unspoilt area of Turkey as far as tourists are concerned. The loos are the basic squatting-on-the-ground type and not too clean, but we shall set forth armed with masses of disinfectant. There will be so many of us we shall virtually take over the whole hotel. The place, named Cakras, is not on the map at all, but it is near Amasra, which has a lovely harbour and a beautiful ruined castle. The scenery is green, lush and gorgeous. There are a few jellyfish, but not the stinging type, and it rains a bit, but never for very long. So we look forward to August.

Jeremy and Wendy Varcoe and their daughters Chesca and Lucy, who are Lucy's great friends, are very sadly off to Zambia next month. We shall miss them a lot. Wendy has been an understanding friend and help to me. Jeremy is an ex-university law lecturer and is small and dynamic, and they both managed to learn Turkish well.

24 July 1974
[At this time the invasion of Cyprus by the Turkish army took place after years of resentment by the Turks of their treatment there by the Greeks.]

We have been really cut off — no post, planes, telegraphs, phones, nothing! I do not know if the airport is open today or not, or when this letter will get out. You will have been hearing all about the goings on here. Thank heavens, with today's news of the change of government in Greece, it really looks as if things may now stay calm. It has been tense here, but except for a blackout each night there has been no difference to our normal lives. And, as Michael is not in the political section, he has escaped staying up at nights, with four-hour shifts, as the political lot have been doing.

Thank heavens Andrew left school early — if the boys had tried to fly here two days later there would have been no plane and they would both be still with you for the holidays. They arrived in great form.

Sorry for this rather dull letter. I should have told you more about the war. But I am sure you know just as much as I do, more probably, from the telly and newspapers.

PS. Have just heard airport is working today, so all should be OK for Rozy and kids' expected visit [my sister and her two children].

16 August 1974
Well, here we go again, trouble all around. The airport was closed again yesterday just after Rozy and the children left and we thought she was lucky to get away, but it has apparently opened again today, so I'm writing this in haste to get to you in case it closes again. The Turks are being quite impossible as you will have gathered and no one knows what the outcome will be now.

We have been advised to keep a low profile as after Jim Callaghan's

Left: Michael and Sally James with Andrew and Lucy at a beach near Wellington in 1964

Below: Michael with Tim and Andrew at a paddy planting ceremony in 1967

Above: Masanam outside the James's house in Colombo (now the Iraqi Embassy. *Below:* Sally James with children and friends on a beach outside Colombo

Above: Sally James on a trip up the Demerara River
Below: Tim and Andrew in Ankara in 1974

Above: The countryside around Ankara
Below: At home in Guildford before leaving for Ghana in 1980

Above: Lucy buying vegetables in Accra
Below: Sally James shopping at the local greengrocer in Accra

Sally James's mother, Helen Bell, in Singapore in 1919

Above: Michael meeting Lee Kuan Yew. *Below:* Andrew, Lucy, Tim and Sally James at a cricket match in Bridgetown

Above: Michael and Sally James at a historical site in Barbados
Below: Heward and Helen Bell, Sally James's parents, with Michael
and Tim at a formal occasion in Barbados

statements which, at least in the Turkish view, were very much in fa-vour of the Greeks, and other British activities, we are not very popular [Callaghan was Secretary of State for Foreign and Commonwealth Affairs]. I was called *chok fena*, very bad, in the butcher's yesterday, but apart from that have not personally noticed anything.

Colin and Angela Stansfield-Smith [he played cricket with Michael at Cambridge and was the RIBA gold medal winner in 1991] were due to arrive here on holiday today and just did not know what to do. I managed finally to get through to them on the phone and, since we had heard that the talks had broken down and the second war was in progress, we advised them not to come. So we will keep fingers crossed that all will be quiet in a month's time for your arrival. So far no more blackouts, but I have stocked up with a fair amount of groceries in case of shortages.

The Black Sea with Rozy plus children and the Goatlys was a great success.

We ate lovely meals outside by the beach and drank lots of very good and cheap Turkish wine. Each morning the proprietor asked us what we would like for dinner and each morning we asked him what there was. He always said fish, a delicious whitebait type, so each night we had fish! We had one or two tummy upsets, but not bad. There was nothing to do in the evenings, but we had brought several plays with us from the British Council library and all enjoyed reading them under the stars. It must have been the cheapest holiday ever.

There was one worrying incident when the girls were wandering along the beach in bathing costumes and they were physically accosted by some local village boys who of course were not used to girls dressed in this way. It was our fault, we should never have allowed them to roam around in such a provocative fashion.

We had met the local schoolmaster and he had spent one or two evenings with us, practising his English. When he heard that the boys had behaved like this he was extremely upset and said they had brought shame on his village. He told us that they would be punished in the traditional way, but when we discovered that this would mean breaking their legs, we managed to persuade him that a verbal apology would be enough.

There was an appalling crash, which we witnessed on our drive back and also heard about on the World Service. Two buses collided head on and 47 corpses covered by sheets were laid out in rows on the sides of the road. We were just about to stop for lunch when we passed them, but changed our minds and drove on as we had lost our appetites. If only driving here were better.

Thursday 22 August 1974

It was good to hear you just now on the phone and as I had only just put the call through, very quick indeed. I repeat what I said, we think it is quite all right for you to come in October. If anything does flare up again you can come up to Ankara and we will work from there. At the moment the only fighting that may break out would be retaliatory attacks by the Turks on the Greeks for their supposed atrocities in Cyprus. As the Turks have got more land than they really want in Cyprus they are even prepared to give some of their gains back to Greece.

4 September 1974, Bodrum

Bodrum is the best place I have seen so far in Turkey and we are having a really fabulous time. The town is divided with a line, not visible, running up from the castle in the harbour to the hills with the Turkish inhabitants on one side and the Greeks on the other. The Greek side on the right is bright and clean with sparkling white paint and cleanly swept streets, whereas the Turkish side on the left is not quite so impressive.

But we are lucky and staying in a private Turkish house, which is very well looked after, spotlessly clean, really pleasant, about 15/– a day each B & B and run by a very charming ex-naval officer. The loo is of the squatting type in the garden, and the shower is also outside with not much privacy. Our Turkish friends who have organized our accommodation are staying next door with a strange American who teaches English literature and is crazy about Virginia Woolf and the Bloomsbury Group — he cannot believe he has actually met a relation of Clive Bell's [my father, Dr Heward Bell, and he were cousins].

9 September 1974

Yes, stay in Pera Palas Oteli in Istanbul. Ataturk always lived there and the whole place is full of grandeur. It is where we stayed when we first arrived. The rooms are vast, the bathrooms are enormous with hand basins the size of baths, enormous old creaking lifts and very heavy shining brass fittings everywhere. I am going to join you there, so see you soon.

23 October 1974
BBC news at 8.00 a.m. this morning of a bomb at Harrow was ghastly, but at 9.00 a.m. we were extremely relieved to hear there had been no casualties. Guildford, Harrow, where next? [These were both IRA bomb attacks.]

4 November 1974
Turkish medicine is basic. I am suffering from shoulder calcification, which has been very uncomfortable and driving is almost impossible. So I went to the bone man and he arranged for me to have injections of cortisone and it was agony. He plunged the needle in for about ten minutes and turned it round and round. It was extremely painful, then I thought it must be over — but *no* — that was supposed to be the pain-killing one. The real one followed and the needle was gouged in again and turned around for what seemed like forever.

When the agony was over I got up, went out and with great difficulty found a *dolmus* (taxi) and when I got home an hour later I was shivering from shock. When I told the doctor what agony it had been, he said that if he had known I was in pain he would have given me a local anaesthetic. Apparently he normally does. So much for the stiff upper lip.

Thanks to Claudia, Maryse and Alan Elgar's daughter, I have got a teaching job at the Lider School, which basically caters for adults. I teach English two evenings a week to groups of senior soldiers. The lessons require lots of preparation and I did find Turkish generals a bit intimidating at first — the Turkish army is the fourth biggest in the world — but military discipline amongst the pupils is very helpful for a teacher.

Social life is busy including a farewell dinner at the ambassador's for our counsellor and his German wife, Dick and Gaby Fyjis-Walker, who are leaving — he is to be the press counsellor in Washington. Dick and Gaby have an excellent rapport with Turks. He is a very good Turkish dancer and, with his large black luxuriant moustache, looks very much at home here. It was a bit chaotic because three ambassadors there, including ours, were suddenly and unexpectedly summoned to go to another presidential dinner in honour of the visiting president of the European Parliament. It was very grand and they all turned up later for coffee. I made a big hit with the Dutch president of the European Parliament, but it was rather hard work as he was a bit pompous.

13 November 1974

Lucy is taking her common entrance today. She did maths and English this morning and both went well. I shall be glad when we hear she is in. Now she cannot wait to go to England. Though we have been having all her age group for lunches, teas, nights, and she has been to jolly parties and is extremely cheerful at the moment, she now says she hates Turkey — perhaps they all say it. But she is now much the oldest at the school.

15 November 1974

We went to the French ambassador's for a cocktail party and it was terrible. It is an extremely grand residence, like a palace, but there were no waiters anywhere; the only ones in sight had empty glasses and tomato juice on their trays. Everyone stood around looking lost. Eventually word passed around that one could grab a drink of champagne from a table at the end of the fourth salon and everyone made a mad rush for it. Also, though the electricity was off when we arrived, they had lit only one or two little candles in each of the enormous rooms in which candelabra, with candles, were left unlit. Then the lights came on, then off, and this went on for three quarters of an hour. It was supposed to be a Common Market party — not very encouraging with the French being difficult again.

28 November 1974

Lucy has passed her CE, so that's a relief. We knew she had done the papers well, but it's jolly nice to know definitely.

Now I have a private pupil who comes approximately four times a week for two hours at a go and it is quite lucrative. He is rich. His father, whom I met at a party, is the most famous lawyer in Turkey, but I don't think he has got his brains. But the lessons are quite fun. He's coming to me instead of the Davis School at Cambridge, for the time being anyway. Also the Lider School, where I teach, will have another midweek class for me soon — so my time will be taken up profitably.

New carpets have arrived and a new stove and men are coming and going trying to lay them and fix it and are all incompetent.

The local dentists seem a bit wild. Suffering from toothache I went to have a filling and, on inspection of my teeth, was told that I needed eight more fillings. This I cannot believe, so please would you fix dentist appointments for us all when we are home? [The dentist in England said no fillings were required.]

6 December 1974

My shoulder is much better. I saw Dr Bayinder again and we are going to leave it now and hope it will all completely clear up in time. He had heard I teach English and wants his son, Yusuf, to have private lessons with me. So that's one good result of having a calcified shoulder.

There has been terrible trouble with our *kapici* — you remember the caretaker who lives downstairs and generally looks after the block, and goes shopping for us each morning? He says we have never paid him, which we have every month. Sadly though I have not kept all the receipts. He went up to the Embassy and made a dreadful scene, then came back here and physically attacked me and I had to fight him off. The police had to be called to speak to him and calm him down. All very unpleasant, and he doesn't shop for me any more.

20 December 1974

Many thanks for sending the boys, who arrived in excellent form. Thank you too for all the shopping, presents and so forth. A cheque is enclosed.

It is now snowing hard again and we are gradually getting skiing equipment together as we are supposed to be going in a large group to Uludag, near Bursa, on the 28th for five days. But the hotel is being difficult so it is all slightly in the air. We booked months ago and sent vast deposits, but it seems that rich Istanbul Turks have offered more for our rooms and the hotel wants us out. But we hope to make it.

And on 8 January we shall arrive on flight BE 487 at 16.00 — so see you next year. Lucy is looking forward to starting school at Downe House, near Newbury, Berkshire in January! Happy Christmas!

7 February 1975

No letters from the kids. The bags have gone astray as usual and it is

Timmy's fifteenth birthday today. It is so sad not to see him or speak to him. It has been a mad rush ever since I got back. Alan and Maryse Elgar are very sadly leaving and their replacements have arrived. In ten minutes we are giving them lunch and next week we, in conjunction with Arthur and Beryl Amy, he is the first secretary (Commercial), are giving them a vast reception (250 guests) at the ambassador's house. Oh dear!

13 February 1975
It is frequently 15 degrees below freezing at night — so cold and so smoggy, and altogether horrible. Last Saturday we were going out, there had been snow, so we skidded everywhere and finally left the car and took a taxi. Everywhere we passed cars that had crashed into each other, or into lampposts, and been just abandoned. Four lots of Embassy people had prangs that night. In this backward city it is too much to expect that they could put salt or sand onto the roads.

Our water is OK, touch wood, but Ankara electricity is having trouble. We have cuts each day at specified times and they also just cut it each evening for an hour or two in a completely *ad hoc* manner, so candles are always at the ready.

American aid is being cut and no one knows what is going to happen now. The Americans are irritated with the Turks, who will take no positive steps to negotiate with the Greeks over Cyprus and will make no concessions. This does not worry the Turks, who seem completely indifferent to public relations. They think they are in the right and that this should be obvious to everyone. The Greeks behave very differently, and in the Turkish view have no pride at all and are prepared to wheedle, lie and ingratiate themselves with whoever is necessary in order to achieve what they want.

20 February 1975
Parties and dinners galore, mainly because Michael has been chairman of a Cento economic committee meeting with delegates from the five countries. It has all been very difficult as the Pakistanis have been impossible and the Turks and Iranians fairly impossible. Thank God for the sensible British and the USA!

Yesterday I had 20 wives from our wives association [DSWA] in for tea and demonstrations of batik in the kitchen. They came in two shifts and they now all want me to give lessons, but I have said no firmly to that idea. Last Saturday I taught my usual three hours in the morning, then two more in the afternoon to a class of doctors. They were very pleasant, but five hours a day is a bit much.

25 February 1975
The mail via the bag has been utterly hopeless this term and letters are taking forever to reach us, if they reach us at all. Lucy had had no letter from me for ages and we have been writing religiously regularly. This week we have had cocktails every night, including a 2000 people 'do' at the historic Ankara Palas Oteli on Monday to celebrate the twentieth year of Cento, which was so noisy and crowded we left after one hour.

12 March 1975
Last week I went to a funny Turkish ladies' tea party. The American ambassador's wife, Mrs Macomber, was there and other smart social Ankara Turkish ladies all hatted, gloved and overdressed. What a waste of time and effort, and how fattening, but the cakes were delicious. And this afternoon I have to go to another tea with Mrs Macomber and we are going to hear a talk about indoor gardening, which I suppose as we live in a flat could be quite useful. Americans are very unpopular here now as they have stopped their aid over Cyprus and, I suppose, think it is their duty and mission to do their utmost to be seen to be friendly and loving. Kissinger has just been over and the US ambassador spends lots of time flying back and forth to Washington for consultations.

There are lots of problems here over drugs. The Turks are very sensitive about accusations that they are conniving in the opium trade. Farmers here grow poppies, for vegetable oil so they say, but some cannot resist the lure of huge profits from allowing their lovely white poppies to be harvested for opium. Surprisingly the Turks themselves do not have a bad 'drug habit', perhaps because there are horrendous punishments in Turkey for anyone found to be pushing drugs or taking drugs or involved in the drug trade in any way.

A letter from Lucy who is down in the dumps; her French teacher says she has to have extra lessons in the holidays as she is so far behind. And she is worried she'll never get any O or A levels as she is so unclever. Pathetic and a bad advertisement for frequent school and country changes. If only I could see her.

117

17 March 1975

Have just had two very large dinners, which went fine and Mehmet cooked extremely well, although his smoking seems to be getting worse all the time. But I have managed to persuade him that when he comes into the dining room to clear plates away it would be better if he did not have a cigarette in his mouth with ash falling everywhere.

20 April 1975

Lovely holiday with all the children at Side on the Mediterranean coast where we stayed in a pension on the top floor of a simple house with a flat roof. It was all fairly basic and Heath Robinsonish but just about worked and had a proper loo and cost £1 a day! There were views of the sea 25 yards away and was right in the middle of Side which is a mass of gorgeous old ruins including the remains of a Roman amphitheatre with pillars in the harbour. What a shame all these places are so far from Ankara. Back here it is awful, smoggy, cold, rainy and grim; we seem to have had months and months of gloom.

8 May 1975

We were giving cocktails for 100 in connection with a Cento seminar on fertilizers, but at the last minute had to cancel all arrangements as the wretched Iranians have said it is inconvenient for them to attend and want to postpone the seminar. What a nerve after masses of preparations! It just shows what you can do with oil behind you.

20 May 1975

The weather has been absolutely ghastly — rain, rain, more rain and cold, almighty thunder storms, hail storms — and the road outside has flowed like a raving torrent down to Kizilay. Off to Beirut soon — so let's hope it all calms down there — to stay with Neil and Cynthia Bratton; he was at school with Michael and is now teaching at the university there.

4 June 1975

Thank God the fighting in Beirut broke out the day we were due to leave. We were having breakfast when we heard on the World Service of the trouble. This was three hours before our flight and we did not know if we could, or should, get there or not. We could not get through to the Brattons on the phone and we eventually cabled our Embassy there, and they said don't come — thankfully, as it certainly all got a lot worse after that.

Did I tell you that I met Henry Kissinger at a Cento reception? Another British Embassy wife, Arlene Fullerton, and I rather determinedly stood in his path, and when the American ambassador said 'Hi,' Kissinger saw us and came over and talked for quite a while.

It was a big thrill and he is very charming, with a lovely smile, but his wife, who is inches taller than him, was obviously tired and looked very bored with the whole proceedings. He is surrounded by bodyguards (royal progress is not in it), there are machine guns on all the surrounding roofs, roads around are closed to the public, and a special bulletproof car flies with him in his special bulletproof plane for use wherever he goes. This security is all a real twentieth century phenomenon and I am delighted that we were able to see it so closely in action.

Bill and Arlene Fullerton go off on long adventurous expeditions in their Range-Rover to remote areas of Turkey; Bill loves the remoteness and by contrast Arlene, who is American, is extremely sociable. [Bill Fullerton would enjoy the emptiness of a later posting as Governor of the Falklands.]

No one was in the least interested in the other Cento foreign secretaries. Michael was landed with our Roy Hattersley, who is Minister of State at the FCO, for ages and could not pass him on to anyone else. The Turkish papers described him as 'fat and fidgety' but Michael quite liked him as they talked cricket together.

I shall be home in two weeks. I am really looking forward to a long stretch in England and shall spend lots of time in front of the telly, and watch Wimbledon nonstop.

29 September 1975

The flat was fine, we have seen friends and caught up with news, but still feel disorientated.

Mehmet is very well and thrilled with his tie. He is determined that when you come to Turkey we shall all go and stay with him in his house in his country village where Lucy once visited with Wendy, Chesca and Lucy Varcoe.

Efina has not been at all well and may be hospitalized soon, at our expense. And knowing Turkish hospitals that could be for a long time.

10 October 1975

Last night Angela [Michael's English secretary] and her husband Haki Aydinoglu [governor of the Central Bank] had us to a pleasant dinner party. They are a very happy couple whose company we enjoy very much; Haki gives Michael lots of interesting information and Angela gives me a lot of local advice. It is not easy for foreign girls to marry into Turkish families and spend their lives here — the fall out rate is very high — it requires a strong character to survive and Angela has adapted brilliantly.

Turkish men go overseas to study, frequently to America, fall in love, marry and bring their foreign wives home. These girls have no idea of Turkish society and of how their husbands are likely to be dominated by the powerful family system when they return home again. Also when an English girl married to a Turk lives in Turkey she is regarded as subject to Turkish law and the British Embassy cannot help her to leave against her husband's will, even though she still has a UK passport.

Am now teaching French four mornings a week at the British Embassy School to all sorts of nationalities, and four evenings a week teaching English to Turks; it all keeps me pleasantly busy and I have a bona fide excuse to miss lots of cocktail parties.

Electricity problems now: our electricity should be connected to the mains, but our landlord should pay 3000 Turkish lire and cannot be found. Though the Embassy has said it will pay, the electricity corporation has to see the landlord. Three times men have been around to cut the electricity off and each time we have hedged them off.

But finally it was all cut off. The Embassy sent its electrician who managed, illegally, to connect us up, then next day it went off again. We are now running off our neighbour's meter and have no idea how we shall sort the bills out. Meanwhile the Embassy's admin section has done its best, spending hours with the electricity authorities arguing and achieving nothing. Today the matter has been reported to the Turkish head of protocol at the Ministry of Foreign Affairs and we now have a lawyer acting for us. It is all incredibly chaotic.

Our Danish neighbours, the Steenstrups, have been kicked out of Turkey at two days' notice. They have been here for five years, having built up a business from scratch and done masses for the country. They say no foreigners can stay for more than five years. The Turks are more and more impossible, and getting into a dreadful economic position. The inflation is ghastly.

10 November 1975

I have had a very busy nine days with Haydon and Caroline Warren-Gash and their newborn baby; Haydon is second secretary at the Embassy. Officially the Foreign Office likes wives to go back to England from Turkey to have their babies, but as all seemed to be going fine Caroline had decided she would rather stay here and I had offered to have them to stay when she came out of the nursing home.

But the nursing was nil in the home and Caroline came out four days after a Caesarean in a very weak state — apparently Caesareans are normal practice here — and of course could hardly even walk. We discovered that the baby, Alexander, had not been changed once in his short life and had the most appalling nappy rash. Caroline also had no clue about feeding him as she had not been shown how, but I was able to help her as the memories came back and the baby was very good. He also had a bad tummy and we had to get the doctor in to deal with that.

The other problem was that her luggage had not arrived from London and we were very short of nappies and clothes, so it was nonstop washing — in cold water. I had to make out to be very competent and efficient with newborn babies, but it is amazing how much one has forgotten after all these years and I was absolutely flaked for a few days after they left.

And now Efina has gone into hospital for her gallstones. We have paid for masses of X-rays, and the last one they did showed her gallstones, but they had already told her back in September that that was what was wrong with her. There are a lot of crooks, and inefficient crooks, in the medical profession here and I think we were rather rash to say we would pay for her treatment. I can see why we are sent home for hospitalization. The hospitals here are so backward, and so dirty.

21 November 1975

Have had very cheerful letters from all the children who seem to be enjoying school, which is comforting.

Here there is general bad health in the Embassy, though as the smog is already bad and the weather freezing it is not unexpected.

Our electricity has been cut off twice more. It seems our landlord is bankrupt. We have now paid money to the electricity corporation, having been told numerous times by the crooked landlord that he was doing so. Do hope we don't have to move in view of all this. The saga has gone on for too long and been taxing on the nerves.

Last Tuesday we were woken by a loud bang at 1.00 a.m. We looked out of the window to find a large crowd and police gathered. A petrol lorry, which was full, had careered down the road out of control, the driver was drunk, and had hit a taxi coming the other way. The lorry then swerved into two parked cars — completely destroying one. The taxi hit two cars, including ours, and did quite a lot of general damage, and completely stove in one back door. The drunk driver and his three drunk comrades tried to run for it, but luckily police, who guard our flats because the Foreign Minister lives here, chased him and caught him.

All the car owners went to the magistrates' court the next day. The driver had spent the night in the cells — 100 per cent of the blame was put on him — and he will be sentenced in two weeks. Poor chap, Turkish gaols are not the most comfortable places, as witnessed in the film *Midnight Express*.

1 December 1975

The weather here is terrible, smog everywhere, but our electricity has at last been sorted out and a meter installed.

Yesterday we went with friends in two Land-Rovers up to Baynam Woods, lovely snow covered pine forests where the sun was gorgeous. Looking down on Ankara was quite a sight. A gigantic black cloud covered the city spreading over a vast area. It is such a relief and so vital to get out at weekends to be able to breathe properly.

Had a lovely time in Istanbul. We travelled by train, which was quite comfortable except for the ominous rat-like sounds in the sleeping cabin, as the train chugged slowly along and it was a lot safer than driving on the horrific Ankara–Istanbul road, or flying courtesy of Turkish Airlines, the world's most dangerous airline. We arrived at the Consul General's for breakfast. It is the most beautiful old historic house, with marvellous views over the city, and was a real joy. Our hosts, John and Jasmine Blakeway, were super and we all got on very well. John's great hobby is restoring old Meissen china. He spends hours pouring over Sotheby and Christie catalogues, so is delighted to have Topkapi Museum nearby. Jasmine is great fun, very energetic and puts on plays with the office staff and friends. They have spent most of their time in European countries. It rained nearly all weekend but it was such lovely fresh air I did not mind. We saw wonderful sights, met all sorts of people, had delicious meals, and I had a really good haircut for a change.

9 December 1975

There has been fog and smog and snow and sleet for days on end. The airport was closed for almost the whole of last week. This afternoon, for the first time in days, I was able to see out of the window beyond the neighbouring tin roof to the snow capped mountains beyond; a change of wind direction has brought about the smog's temporary departure.

We went with the Goatlys to Konya, where the whirling dervishes have their base. These form part of an unusual ancient Muslim order, but are only allowed to perform in December because Ataturk banned them from whirling all other months of the year. We left a cold, smoggy, foggy Ankara to arrive, three hours later, in a cold, smoggy, foggy Konya. Still it was a change. The hotel was pretty awful and primitive. We had a double bed with dirty sheets and one single blanket, and we both froze all night long.

We duly arrived at the dervish place of action, a basketball stadium with a few bits of crepe paper decked around, where we sat on very hard benches. For one hour we froze and slept intermittently through long and dreary semi-religious speeches in Turkish. Then we were subjected to Turkish music on Turkish instruments for 45 minutes. Then followed a ten minute interval and we were thankful we had brought with us suitable alcoholic refreshment to warm and keep us going.

Finally, at 10.45 p.m., they started to whirl! — 20 men in long white dresses with tall green hats turning nonstop anti-clockwise with one hand facing heaven and the other facing earth. This continued for 45 minutes, their endurance was impressive, and they moved very gracefully. Since Ataturk officially abolished their religious order in 1924, it is not really religious any more, and they did not seem to go into real religious raptures. On the other hand, neither was it a very successfully stage-managed performance, so the whole thing rather fell between two stools. But it was an experience, and we were glad we saw it.

The next day we visited the dervishes' Mevhlana Centre, which was very impressive with lovely gardens, fountains playing, minarets and old buildings. We also spent a lot of time with a carpet seller who showed us bazaars and spice shops and other places off the beaten tourist track and finally in return for all his help we bought a lovely Yuruk carpet.

The restaurants had very little food, due to the influx of visitors, and the Konyans on the whole treated us with suspicion. They stared at us wherever we went and were far less friendly than the Turks in other areas we know.

There seem to be three types of Turk. The sunny Mediterranean types, the hard-working dour hill types and the suspicious Anatolian plateau Turks.

But the Anatolian plateau is so vast it seems to stretch barren forever. Turkey is so large it seems like a continent itself and the last hour of our drive home was quite alarming — thank heavens we were in the Range-Rover. Even so we were nearly in the ditch once. Snow, ice and darkness were causing innumerable accidents all over the place. We took an hour to do about ten miles.

After this experience we have decided not to go away by car for a few weeks.

11 December 1975

There are great problems in getting the kids routed on from Istanbul on their arrival, but we have finally managed to get them on a supposedly connecting flight. Other colleagues have not been so lucky and as all the trains are booked and roads liable to be impassable, it is not funny.

But we are still having terrible trouble trying to get flights back in January. Lucy may have to arrive late for school as we do not want her to have to change flights in Istanbul on her own and would rather she was with the boys.

I apologize in advance for any inconvenience all this may cause you, but we are really stuck and frantically doing the best we can.

Lots of love, and if I don't write again before Xmas have a lovely time and we will think of you and drink to your health.

21 January 1976

The weather here is utterly terrible. It is 25 degrees below zero, there is very thick snow, it is the worst weather they have had for 15 years, and most roads are impassable and have been for well over a week. Our car is sitting outside unable to move as we cannot get the chains on it. Ankara municipality is doing nothing to clear the roads and the whole place is really seizing up. Poor Mehmet takes two and a half hours to come to work, walking most of the way — no buses, *dolmus*es, taxis or anything. Added to that the smog and fog are awful and the airport is closed more often than open.

The *eskijee*, the rag-and-bone man, has just been up the road. He goes around the streets in Ankara with a barrow, ringing a bell, and buying anything on offer. Nothing gets wasted here.

31 January 1976

Bags have been really up the creek recently. One has been lost in Beirut and one in Nairobi. All sorts of people are waiting for vital communications of one sort or another and have no idea when they will receive them.

Full of anticipation we went to the cinema, a rare event, to see a film advertised in the *Daily News* as Charlton Heston and Ava Gardner in *Earthquake*. Not until we were inside the cinema did we realize that it was an entirely different *Earthquake*. This one, which was made in Japan, had no Heston or Gardner, was incredibly badly dubbed from Japanese into English with Turkish subtitles and was, I think, the worst film I have ever seen.

Timothy's sixteenth birthday is on 7 February. I see he has an exeat on the 8th which is super for him. I just wish I could be there. We have had cheerful letters from both the boys, and a marvellous letter from Lucy — 14 sides.

4 February 1976

There was an exhausting, hard working official dinner at the commercial counsellor's and, as we had to help out, we could not leave till the end at 1.00 a.m. — last night cocktails, tonight the opera and tomorrow a barbecue in the snow followed by a Japanese puppet show in the evening.

I have been feeling very flaked and headachy and am now trying to take it easy. I cannot wait to do nothing but sit in a stupor in front of the telly night after night.

The weather continues foul with snow and smog, and now the Embassy School has had to close because the Turkish Oil Company has not delivered the fuel oil, despite countless reminders. The only good thing is that I can rest.

Leap Year Day 1976

Had a lovely week in Izmir, or Smyrna, which is on the Aegean and is a thriving commercial centre and, after Istanbul, the most important Turkish port. The history of Izmir dates back to the third millennium BC, with a long, long story of battles, earthquakes and fires. After the First World War it was occupied by the Greeks who in 1920 were granted the right to the territory, but two years later Kemal Ataturk managed to restore Turkish rule in the course of which a lot of the city was destroyed by fire and it is now very twentieth century in appearance, but sadly has lost its original character.

We stayed in the Aydinoglus' flat, which is a penthouse on the seventh floor overlooking the harbour. Michael spent two days at the university, the rest of the time we visited sites, had barbecues and lazed. Though cold for Izmir (it even snowed one day) and windy, we had the chance to sit out on the balcony with coats on, and it was a gorgeous break and treat to breathe fresh air.

Izmir is a lovely area, lush and fertile, with orange groves and olive trees and cotton. It is all very beautiful. The people are more relaxed and happier than the dour dark Ankarites. There are also a lot more fairer people because of the big Greek community that was there at one time.

We visited Mereyamana, near Ephesus, where according to some the Virgin Mary lived after Jesus died. It is now a place of pilgrimage tended in loneliness by a French priest and two nuns. It is high in the hills, on a very spectacular site overlooking the sea, and they hold services in the open air for the thousand or so pilgrims who visit in the summer. At the time we were the only visitors and we met the priest who has lived there for over 20 years and the whole situation seemed unreal and timeless.

We also visited Pergamon on a windy, snowy and freezing day as the site is on a hill top. But it is impressive, with a restored theatre which used to seat about 4000 people and the ruins of a massive amphitheatre, which would have held 50,000. The whole region is littered with historical sites, mostly uncommercialized. It is so evocative to walk around these sites with no one else around, no barriers, and no signs of modern life.

8 March 1976

Spring is hopefully on the verge of being around the corner, but sadly I have been under the weather. It started with an upset stomach and the typical Turkish symptoms before our holiday, and while there it continued in spite of all the usual drugs. Then I started feeling very sick and was summoning up courage to go to the Turkish doctor when, luckily, I saw what looked like a worm. So I wormed myself, contacting an Australian doctor friend of mine for advice on the subject, and feel better.

Thank heavens I did not go to a Turkish doctor with my complaints as I would have been admitted to hospital, had barium enemas and anything else they could think of. My doctor friend has a Turkish friend who had been suffering for weeks in hospital here. She had tests galore and they were all set for an 'exploratory' operation when she decided to come to London. She went as an outpatient to the Middlesex Hospital, roundworm was diagnosed, and she was home, cured, a week later.

Letters for the last few months of the Turkish tour have been mislaid, but there were complications over departure dates. We finally left in July in time for the school holidays, but sadly missing our long-planned trip to Lake Van in the far east of Turkey, which can only be reached in the summer months.

Hence followed a home posting for four years with Tim and Andrew at Harrow and Lucy at Downe House and at Charterhouse for the sixth form.

Michael worked first as desk officer for Iran and Iraq in the Middle East Department then as assistant head of the Information Policy Department. In the Middle East Department he was on record as recommending against encouraging the shah to liberalize too quickly — not many years later the shah was swept away by Khomeini. In the Information Policy Department he had the uncomfortable role of trying to negotiate cuts in the budgets for the BBC External Services and the British Council.

I did several jobs, for example I taught batik and worked as fund raiser for a local school, but found it difficult to settle to anything very satisfactory as the first question I was always asked when applying for a serious job was — 'When will you be going away again?' And unfortunately I could never give a definite answer.

By 1980 we were looking forward very much to another posting, preferably close by in Europe, as Tim had started at Reading University, Andrew was due to start at Exeter University in September and they would only get one fare a year paid to come out and see us.

5

Ghana

Michael telephoned one afternoon and told me to sit down as he had news for me. We were to be posted to Ghana for three years. West Africa had always been somewhere we were not particularly keen to go to, as there are so many problems there and the climate, with the terrible humidity, is difficult to cope with.

But Michael, by now a counsellor, was to be Deputy High Commissioner. This was a good job considering it is a large post, and we would get our fares paid back to England every 12 months, so I began to think perhaps it would not be so bad after all.

A few days later he telephoned again. He had just heard from the travel department that it was necessary to take everything we would need for a year in the way of food, household goods and clothing, as there was nothing available in Accra. Thence followed several weeks of frantic shopping, including hiring a lorry and going to a wholesale grocer to buy as much as we could possibly afford for shipping out with us.

In 1957 the Gold Coast, as it was then known, received independence from the British and was renamed Ghana. Nkrumah was the Prime Minister and when Ghana became a republic in 1960 he became the first president. There followed years of turbulence and several dramatic changes of governments by force.

Nkrumah was known as the Emperor of Africa, but he reduced the previously rich country to hopeless penury very fast. In 1966 he was overthrown by the army and the National Liberation Council, a military government, ran the country. In the elections of 1969 a civil administration with Dr Busia as Prime Minister was elected but in 1972 there was another military coup led by Colonel I. Acheampong who was subsequently overthrown in another coup led by Flight Lieutenant Rawlings. He voluntarily withdrew after less than a year to be replaced uneasily by a civilian government under the nominal leadership of President Limann who was there when we arrived in June 1980.

24 June 1980

Having just come in from the garden after giving the daily banana to our fairly tame wild monkey, a rare animal in Accra as they have mostly been killed and eaten, I then walked upstairs and saw the most attractive bright emerald green snake about four foot long moving towards our bedroom from the veranda. I screamed and the whole house came to life with people running from all directions and the snake was killed with a broom. I am told it was a green mamba, and they are hardly ever seen inside houses.

In our garden there is an enormous nest of vultures, and the mangy dog we have inherited from our predecessors keeps trying to bite us and looks rather rabid. Doves and pigeons have taken over our veranda, which is rather unpleasant. We are trying to move them and have built them a cage in the garden, but they are staying firmly put. Oh, yes, in the kitchen there are rodent-type animals, not quite rats or mice, but near enough if you walk in at night, put the light on and see them scurrying across the floor. They say there are no lions or elephants.

Apart from the wild animals and anti-burglar barricades and mosquito nets at every window our house is airy and spacious, surrounded by a large garden in a pleasant residential area. Nasa, our head servant, or boy as they are still called here, is from a northern tribe near Upper Volta [now Burkina Faso], is very efficient and has worked for Deputy High Commissioners for 16 years. Sam, the cook, is old — how old he does not know — comes from Liberia, is Muslim and has lots of wives and children in both countries, and is very sweet.

At the back of the house are the servants' quarters, which are a complex of outhouses large enough to house a small village. There always seem to be lots of people around and we never know who they all are. In Africa the extended family system is very much in evidence; if a third cousin four times removed arrives on the doorstep he is automatically given board and lodging for as long as he wants. Africans would never dream of asking visitors how long they intended to stay.

30 June 1980

Accra is really very pleasant, though in the most terrible economic doldrums. There is really nothing to buy, but the people are marvellous and smile, laugh and are very friendly and cheerful — they must be fantastic when things are going well. They say you go to East Africa for the animals and West Africa for the people. Lots of people have told us that you immediately feel at home here, and it is certainly true.

We had a three-day trip upcountry on an official visit to Kumasi, which is the second largest town in Ghana, and a nonstop programme was organized for us, including a fascinating audience with Asantahene Otumfo Opoku Ware II at Manhya Palace.

The *asantahene* is chief of the Ashanti tribe, or the supreme Ashanti king, and is the most important chief in Ghana where chiefs' moral and social authority is recognized by the government and their influence in the community is encouraged.

They really have a lot of power, from forming the link between the government and the population to organizing the important traditional festivals in the region. In fact they are really responsible for local government.

Historically the Ashantis were also of great political importance. In the 1870s they tried to extend their power to the coast of Ghana, but this led to the British sending in an expeditionary force against Kumasi and to a war which lasted for two years.

After this the British officially founded the Gold Coast colony. But troubles continued. At one stage the *asantahene* was exiled to the Seychelles and the British refused to recognize the Ashanti throne, or golden stool, but this merely caused more war and devastation in Kumasi.

We were ushered into his presence at his palace (signed photographs of famous people were prominently displayed) where he was seated in full tribal regalia, with very large gold rings and bracelets, surrounded by his courtiers, who were traditionally clad in colourful Kente cloth.

He spoke to us through an interpreter in Twi-Fante, which is the Ashanti language, though, having graduated from the Inner Temple, he does speak perfect English himself.

English is the official language in Ghana, but the tribal languages, Twi, Ga, Ewe and others are the Ghanaians' main languages.

We were offered local drinks and were not sure whether they were

131

alcoholic or not — our audience was at 10.00 a.m. — but the after-effects assured us they were. He was charming and courteous, but I did find it a bit frustrating not talking directly to him in English.

The roads are quite appalling and my neck [injured by a whiplash while in England] suffers a lot. We had a five-hour drive, a lot of it extremely potholed and very bumpy, through tropical rainforests, passing little villages of wooden shacks with tin roofs and, on each side of the road, abandoned broken-down vehicles of all descriptions. We stayed in a guesthouse belonging to the Kumasi Brewery, which is run by a larger than life Englishman, Denis Beasley, and took all our food and drink, apart from beer, with us. We took an office car and a driver, and only had one breakdown, which was very lucky on those roads.

26 June 1980

No luggage has arrived yet. It is on a boat down the coast at Takoradi and sadly the crews of the Ghana shipping line, Black Star, are on strike and the captains have just been arrested — so we have no idea when, or if, we will see our possessions and food.

Meanwhile we have just six suitcases of air freight to live on, plus some frozen meat we have got hold of and for which we have had to borrow a freezer. It is all very difficult as there is virtually nothing to buy locally. I have just hopefully planted lots of vegetables in our enormous garden.

Yesterday Chief of Staff Sir Patrick Howard Dobson, who is here for four days, took us up with him in an eight-seater plane on a two-and-a-half-hour flight around the country arranged by the Ghanaian army. We saw a lot — the lovely coast here, old forts and gorgeous beaches.

30 June 1980

After lunch we are going to Togo, which we cover diplomatically from Accra and which is a three-hour drive, but apparently the roads are not too bad in a Range-Rover. Michael will pay official calls and I shall frantically shop for food and, hopefully, parts for my little Renault, which has at last arrived, albeit slightly bashed and vandalized, i.e. with no radiator or headlights. We have no idea when the Peugeot will arrive.

Lomé, the capital of Togo, the neighbouring country down the coast from Ghana, is a strange little bit of France in the middle of Africa

132

where there is an abundance of everything; so we all go there as often as we can and bring back food and vital everyday necessities.

A lot of French have stayed on since independence in 1960, and every day a plane flies in from France bringing the required fresh food and drink.

The French still do everything from advising the military government, led by President Eyadema, to running shops, cutting hair and driving taxis. Eyadema is known as the 'saviour of the nation' and he took over the presidency after a coup in 1967 when he was alleged to have personally shot his predecessor, President Olympio.

There is such a difference between ex-British colonies and ex-French colonies, basically because the French came in at all levels of society, whereas the British came in only at the administrative and supervisory levels and left at independence. Because there are so many permanent French settlers there are arrangements whereby the Togo currency, CFA, is tied to the French franc and the French government can prevent the worst mistakes and also pump money into the country when needed.

Today the High Commissioner, Jimmy Mellon, goes on three weeks' leave, so Michael will be acting High Commissioner and social life too busy. It will be pleasant being driven around in the flag-flying Daimler, but it does break down rather too often, as does everything here, and it is really too heavy for the potholed roads — a Range-Rover would be a lot more practical. Telephones more often do not work than do work, so a car is vital for communication as there is not much public transport in working order either.

The High Commissioner is taking this letter to post in London as the bag only goes once a week, and you must never write using ordinary post as it will never arrive. Please could you contact Lucy and try to organize her ticket and passport? The international phones hardly ever work from here, and I think there are muddles over her holiday flight arrangements. She should be coming in two weeks or so, but I have as yet no ideas of the date. And remind her to start taking her malaria tablets before she leaves.

9 July 1980
Letters via the bag can take an incredibly long time. I do hope Lucy's passport situation is now OK but we have not heard yet. Please will you tell her we are longing to see her next week and, as our luggage is still

133

at the strike-ridden docks, perhaps she could bring her small cassette player with her — or she will have no music in the house.

With the help of Mark Pepera, a charming Ghanaian who was at Harrow with Tim and Andrew, we are organizing a seventeenth birthday party for her. His father is the head of British Leyland here, but also owns a gold mine and an electrical business and has fingers in very many pies. Mark has very kindly postponed a visit to the UK for six days so that he can show Lucy around. He has also organized a reception for her at his house — so she will be bursting onto the Accra social scene on her arrival — and has offered her a car and chauffeur for as long as she would like.

Time goes by incredibly fast here and life is very busy. Last night we had ten people for dinner and today we have 12 for lunch. It is rather difficult as we have nothing (apart from the office float of a few basics) in the house and I spend a lot of time driving all around Accra borrowing everything — food, drink, knives, forks, plates, glasses, saucepans and washing up liquid.

12 July 1980

The Ghanaians are really great fun, so friendly, cheerful and easy. The country is in the most ghastly mess and there is no sign of it getting better. There is, however, no need for the chaos, for they have lots going for them in every way. They are better educated and have a higher literacy rate than any other African country. The schools were formerly very good, but are now of course suffering from problems like no books. There is also a shortage of teachers, for if possible they are leaving the country to teach elsewhere.

And the corruption is appalling; nothing gets done without a bribe or 'dash'. Tribal jealousies are also very fierce. The Europeans drew lines down the west coast of Africa demarcating countries' boundaries, but these frontiers really mean very little to the Africans, who regard the tribe they belong to as far more important than patriotism.

Daniel and Seidu, our two gardeners, are very sweet, but it is difficult to find them when you need them; they spend a lot of time asleep as they are obviously undernourished. We try to get hold of rice for them, and for Nasa and Sam and for the two security guards who come on duty each evening armed with cutlasses, bows and arrows and catapults and sleep all night long.

134

It is incredible how fast things grow. We are planting lettuces, tomatoes, peppers, aubergines, cucumbers, parsley, thyme, sage and courgettes and we pick soursop, papaws, pineapples and corn from the garden. If you take a cutting and stick it in the ground, it will be sprouting two days later. As any vegetables you can buy are exorbitant, say £1 for four tomatoes, £1 for five potatoes, 75p for one mouldy lettuce, self-help is the only answer here. Eggs are £1 for six.

Most foreigners working here, and a lot of diplomats, too, change their money on the black market and they get approximately 31 cedis to the pound, but we are sadly not allowed to do that and only get seven cedis.

PS. Please could you ask Lucy to bring lots of cigarettes with her. They are needed to 'dash', tip or bribe policemen and others.

24 July 1980

There were torrential rains last night and sadly some of my seedlings were flooded. Golf is going well and my neck survives, just, with protest — sadly I cannot get proper treatment for it out here, physiotherapists do not seem to exist, but life would be ghastly without exercise, so it will have to cope.

Food here is really a problem. Rice is like gold to find.

PS. Please could you send me dried onions, instant mashed potatoes and soap.

15 August 1980

Lucy's postcard was from Togo, where we went for three days for Michael to work and me to shop. This takes a great deal of time, as although you can get lots of things it is not an efficient system and it is very tiring going from market stall to market stall, negotiating, haggling and wilting in the heat with perspiration pouring down. We went in the office Range-Rover, and once we had got the roof rack piled high with crates of beer, sacks of rice, tins of fish, boxes of tinned milk — most of my shopping was for our brigade of servants and their very extended families — we were so heavily loaded we broke a shock absorber, and the journey back was so bumpy on the terrible roads that it really flared my neck up. In future on trips out of Accra I shall wear my collar.

But Lomé is a life saver, especially as our luggage is still sitting unloaded at the docks with great pilfering going on apparently. The whole situation is very depressing as the only thing to do is to borrow or do without. But we have to eat something.

Had a nice colonel to stay last week — all official visitors have to stay with High Commission staff as all the hotels are impossible. He was so moved by our plight that he arranged for an RAF plane, which was coming, to bring me in some basic supplies — or emergency rations. His official brief here was to try to persuade the president, the vice president and the chief of defence to cut down on the armed forces and to advise them on efficiency — but he doesn't think they will pay much attention.

Must stop, and go to airport to give this to a departing businessman to post in London.

5 September 1980

Our luggage has finally arrived. We were lucky to get it at all as it came in at the wrong dock and, as there was no chance of it ever getting to the correct dock, people from the office had to go on the boat themselves and virtually bodily remove all three tons of packing cases and hire a lorry to drive it the three hours back to Accra. Luckily it is in good order with very little missing or broken — a great relief all round. Now comes the problem of returning all we have been borrowing to live on for the past three months. The lists are endless.

We had a good trip away for six days visiting British people and British interests, including Obuasi, the massive Ashanti gold mine, for two nights. This is owned by Tiny Rowland, or Lonrho. There are a lot of English people working at the site, which is an enclosed camp about 45 minutes from Kumasi, and there they lead an unreal existence completely shielded from the outside world; they are provided with food, drink, tennis, swimming and film shows — they could be anywhere. They have no desire to leave the camp or explore and know very little of what goes on in Ghana.

There is masses of gold in Ghana, or the Gold Coast, but this mine, 48 per cent of which is owned by Lonrho and the rest by the Ghana government, is the only efficient one in the country. The others, which are wholly Ghanaian run, do not succeed in extracting the gold very successfully and what they do extract is mostly smuggled out over the borders for foreign currency. We went down a shaft in a lift a mile underground and saw a gold bar worth £250,000 being smelted.

The vegetables are doing very well. We are nearly self-sufficient. I am, however, worried about our very large grapefruit tree and our four lemon and lime trees, as they all have an ominous black mould on them. We have been spraying like mad, but sadly have now run out of Melathion which is necessary but unobtainable here.

16 September 1980
Last week we went to Togo to give a medical aid parcel to a remote little village in the country where there was no sign of French influence. Eight mothers and babies and a dozen or so other patients were lying on rather dilapidated mattresses (beds do not exist) in two bare rooms with virtually no equipment. They were thrilled to bits with the £300 worth of selected equipment from London, but I was only sorry I had not brought Dettol, which I have at home, as they had no disinfectant and no access to any. They are dependent for water from a well, which completely dries up in January and February. But there was no hospital at all ten years ago, so it is all an improvement. The women average seven babies each and there is a 7 per cent infant mortality rate.

Most of the rest of the trip was spent buying sacks of rice, cans of fish, milk — and cans of infant milk for a sick baby belonging to a member of our extended family in the garden, who when I got back had sadly died — and I spent a lot of time haggling over cloth for the servants in the market. But we had a very good French meal one night and a marvellous help yourself buffet at the hotel the other night, which was a real treat — you really forget the sophistication of European life when in Accra.

24 September 1980
I am busy trying to arrange a reception for 200 people on 30 September and am hoping only half turn up and I remember some of their names. It is quite a business trying to make food for that number, we are busily filling freezers now, and I am trying to borrow glasses, soda water, gin and all other cocktail party necessities.

3 October 1980
The reception was a huge success and it is a great relief that it is over. About 160 came. It was all very cheerful and jolly and thankfully the weather was good. I have now learnt to provide twice as much food as

you think necessary as guests like to smuggle food home in their pockets for their families, and in the kitchen waiters and drivers all have a very good party too. But now my freezer is almost empty and there is an overdue order from Kenya of frozen food, which apparently is now not going to arrive for some time.

The Belgian ambassador gave a farewell party this week as he is off to Strasbourg. His wife never lived here; she couldn't stand it. Last night we went to the Guinea national day celebrations, which were a complete shambles. There was nothing to eat or drink and chaos all around. No wonder their country is in trouble when they cannot even organize their national day — and there were fewer people than at our party.

They are installing an extra water tank in the attic of our house because of all the cuts and shortages. There has been tremendous banging and crashing in the roof for two days now. I was sitting on the loo this morning and there was an almighty crash and a face appeared above me. They had made a hole a few yards from where it should have been. Ghanaians are incredibly inefficient, but terribly nice!

30 October 1980

Went to a lovely *durbar* at a village in the middle of the country. These are ceremonial occasions when chiefs receive homage from all their subjects. The chiefs are borne on palanquins made of carved wood surrounded by henchmen carrying large coloured umbrellas and there is colour, dancing, drumming — the lot, really exciting. I am now inspired to do a batik of it.

Must go to attend a British Wives' Association meeting; this is basically a morale boosting organization for ex-pat wives.

PS. Please could you send me Bradosol for sore throats, dried onions, soap.

24 November 1980

Apart from the strain and aggro of trying to make all the children's travel plans for the Christmas holidays, which seem to be totally confused with all the delays in communication, life is fine.

The weather is just perfect and we have now got a lovely plot on a beach for Sundays. The nearby beach five minutes away is also not to be sneered at and, although it has a bad undertow, there is a fat, very jolly Ghanaian beach guard in attendance, so we all feel relatively safe.

Must fly as I have to get this to the KLM chap for posting. I shall be glad when the children are here safe and sound — oh, for a phone.

PS. Please could you send out with the children a large Xmas cake, crackers, a Xmas pudding, cauliflower, aubergine and pepper seeds.

2 December 1980

It was lovely to talk you to on the phone in Togo [we were there on a business trip] and hope all is finally in order with the kids' tickets — it had taken two and a half hours waiting to get through. The president of Chad and other presidents were in town (supposedly signing the Lomé Peace Treaty but only half the signatories turned up) and I imagine they must have been using all the lines.

When we came back from Lomé we found two of our gorgeous lemon trees had burnt down. Seidu, the gardener, had lit a fire just underneath! Is wood ash any good for the garden?

Crisis — crisis — our frozen food arrived from Denmark and, as there was far too much to fit into my freezers because I had just received my long overdue delivery from Kenya, and as our phone had been out of order again for the past three weeks, I drove around to friends trying to beg for some freezer space, but to no avail. Meanwhile hundreds of pounds worth of food was rapidly defrosting in the back seat of the car in the African afternoon heat.

Finally I ended up at the High Commissioner's where they had no room, but luckily did have a working phone. I rang around from there and finally, at 7.00 p.m., delivered 12 boxes of food to three different houses where they could just squeeze it in. By then the food had been defrosting fast for five hours. But I hope for the best.

Today has been a typical day in Ghana. No phone, no electricity for six hours, therefore no cooking, no food. There is a gas cooker for us, which should have been installed ages ago, but a vital piece that attaches the gas cylinder is missing; of course we cannot get it here and the office does not seem able to order us another from London. So the gas cooker waits unused in the shed.

6 December 1980

Many thanks for your letters and presents, which arrived with Tim and all the shopping. Everything was fine except for the Xmas pudding, which seemed to have vanished. Sorry you have been having a panic about the tickets. It has all been such a muddle, but we did get them very cheaply — thanks to our friendly KLM man this end who, incidentally, has just ordered a large batik from me.

Tim had not begun to take his anti-malaria pills before he left and you should start several days before. It is too late to tell Andrew and I bet he has not either. Please could you remind Lucy.

18 December 1980

Lucy finally arrived after a terrible journey. There has been a bad harmattan here — this is a wind that blows sand down from the Sahara, which covers everything, obscures visibility and makes everyone cough and splutter — and the airport has been closed on and off for several days.

Her plane was diverted to Lomé where they landed at 4.00 a.m. Of course with no communication between Lomé and Accra no one here had any idea what had happened to the plane. And a lot of parents who had very young children travelling on their own were extremely concerned. Apparently the passengers, who were mostly children, were left hanging around at Lomé airport, which is a hut and not much more, and the air crew vanished to their luxury hotel and deserted them. Finally they were all put on buses and arrived here at 8.00 p.m. — 16 hours late. They were given precisely one coke to drink and nothing to eat in all that time.

The harmattan this year is the worst since 1973, so I suppose it may go on for weeks yet. Here's hoping it does not as the de Baritaults [sister and brother-in-law and children from France] are all arriving soon and all on different flights.

Last night we had a dinner here for 24, four days ago a dinner here for 28, and tonight a commercial section drinks party for 30 with a few extras. There are parties all over Xmas and they start with a vengeance next week; we shall be out, all of us, nonstop. I am organizing a dancing party for the younger generation on 29 December, a disco and supper hopefully, a sort of five week early 21st for Tim. He and Andrew are both on excellent form, playing lots of squash and tennis, socializing and doing hardly any work, though both have exams at the beginning of next term.

Lucy wants to stay here next term [she had left Downe House] and teach at the International School, which seems an excellent idea and we hope we can arrange something.

I have had to put the servants' wages up by nearly 100 per cent and prices of eggs are now nearly 50p each and fruit and vegetables exorbitant. So we wish we could join with the vast majority of the ex-pat community here and live off the black market, but, along with the respectful US Embassy and the Canadian and Australian High Commissions, we don't. Most others do!

Have a very happy Xmas!

4 January 1981

Last week, at 12 hours' notice, we were invited to say Happy New Year to President Eyadema in Togo at a diplomatic reception. We left home at 4.00 a.m. and at 8.00 a.m. we were ushered into his palace, lined up and the 'saviour of the nation' walked along shaking hands with us all. We noticed he had a lot of armed guards surrounding him and did not look too relaxed. Then followed a diplomatic cocktail party. By this time it was 8.30 a.m., with a band playing, lots of very good French champagne and cocktail eats. It was all very peculiar.

We had to return the same day to Ghana to say Happy New Year to the president at Christianborg Castle. President Hilla Limann is a gentle, respectable man, apparently regarded by the government as a safe choice and rather a front man — though perhaps not as pliable as some would like.

The castle, which is dramatically sited on cliffs on the outskirts of Accra, was originally built in 1657 by trading Swedes. It was also owned by the Danes, the Portuguese and, in 1693, by the dangerous Akwamu tribe. It eventually ended up as the British Governor's and then the head of independent Ghana's headquarters. It was a splendid occasion with the Africans in their flamboyant robes making our men look very dull in their suits. There was drumming and dancing, but only beer to drink and inedible eats, which reflects the Ghanaian economy. They say devaluation is on its way.

8 January 1981

I wanted to tell you the good news. Lucy has been accepted by York University. The letter was posted on 23 December and has only just reached us.

11 January 1981

We seem to be very busy with dead bodies and wakes, including the funeral yesterday, which lasted for three hours, of Dr Benjamin Obeng. He was a Ghanaian gynaecologist working in England who had come back to Ghana just before Xmas for the first time in 13 years. He was a charming man who had dinner with us and tragically died of a heart attack two days later.

Lucy came with us and had rather a shock when we were greeted by the body lying in the open coffin in the aisle. It was shut before the service which was full of eulogy and praise: a simple family produced this boy who did so well; he had a Harley Street practice and worked at hospitals in Essex and elsewhere.

Then, just when three hours was nearly up, there was a great palaver of chiefs, drums, robes, umbrellas and a delegation from the *asantahene* strode up the aisle with a message and gifts of two gold rings to be put on the deceased's fingers in view of his great services to the region, as he was Ashanti. There followed dramatic proclamations from the pulpit, and the coffin was opened again, the chiefs and henchmen encircled it and put the rings on the dead man's fingers, one from the *asantahene* and one from the Queen Mother. Probably because the corpse was already becoming stiff it was very difficult to get it back into the coffin; I am not sure if it was imagination but I thought I heard bones crack as the lid was sealed down.

The whole occasion was a mixture of Christian religion and tribalism, which exists in Ghana at all levels of society. It was all rather strange and macabre, but fascinating.

Last night was the Italian ambassador's fiftieth birthday party. There were 200 guests in a beautiful setting in the garden, with tables decorated lavishly, lovely food, wine especially flown in, an orchestra and dancing. It was a really luxurious occasion.

The newly arrived German ambassador was rather drunk and upset, so we gave him a lift home. We went in with him and heard all his problems. He is a bachelor and, because of all the difficulties here — no food, no drink, no honesty — he cannot organize his life or do his job. Poor, lonely chap, it is very sad for him.

16 January 1981

Lucy came to Togo with us for General Eyadema's fourteenth takeover parade plus banquet and ball. The parade lasted for five hours and was very impressive. I only fell asleep once. Everything and everyone was praising the 'great man and saviour of the nation'. There were jets flying overhead, tanks, soldiers, trade unions, boy scouts, lovely dancing — the lot. If only the wooden seats in the stands had been a bit more comfortable; we could hardly walk after five hours.

PS. Please send some soap, toothpaste and Smash potato.

22 January 1981

In two hours' time 60 people are coming here for cocktails for the Leicester Chamber of Commerce, who are on a trade visit. It is good that they are coming and showing interest in poor Ghana but, alas, we are not optimistic that they will find much business now and foreign exchange is in short supply. One can only hope that Ghana will reap benefits when times improve, but memories here can be short.

Ghanaian ladies used to walk around the streets selling lots of useful items from trays on their heads, but sadly we do not see these around any more; their wares now consist of rather tired, wizened fruit and mouldy vegetables.

2 February 1981

We made a trip down the coast last week where we had to present a gift of medical equipment to a village. We drove through remote countryside, which all looks very barren now with the drought, with the flag flying and for once the Daimler did not break down over all the bumps.

They had laid on a *durbar* (celebration) in our honour and after a slight hitch — consisting of sitting around for one and a half hours making conversation and getting hotter and hotter as the sun rose higher and higher — the Regional Minister arrived.

The whole village had turned out for the occasion. We all sat on specially erected stands on the flag-decorated square. There were bands playing and we heard masses of speeches, including one by Michael, first in English then translated into Twi. The chiefs all decked out in robes and crowns with the most incredibly elaborate gold sandals looked quite magnificent. Then followed dancing, ceremonies and the pouring of libation. The whole occasion lasted for three hours.

We then drove on to Takoradi, which is a very pleasant place by the sea and the original port for Ghana, where we had two days in a firm's guesthouse. This gave us some time to rest and to see the lovely castles built by the Europeans from the fourteenth to nineteenth centuries on our journey back up the coast.

Some of these have terrifying dungeons where Africans were held in chains before being shipped out to the West Indies and other regions as slaves in years gone by. The one at Cape Coast is still used as a prison.

This morning I spent two hours driving around trying to get soda, tonic and beer for the three parties we have to give this week and next. If the office lorry goes to Lomé it can bring stuff back for us, but if it is not we have to try and find it here and this is virtually impossible.

A very large gold conference has just been convened and everyone is generally more optimistic about the economy than they were when we first arrived.

We just pray that President Limann's civilian government, which is supported by the West, can survive after several years of military rule, for then foreign investment in all fields will gain confidence.

But the president is such a civilized and gentle man and is not really tough enough to cope with a country on the verge of bankruptcy or with his own self-seeking senior ministers and advisers. And they will probably have to devalue later this year, which is liable to cause further trouble.

12 February 1981

Many thanks for your letter of 29 January which has only just arrived as it overflew into Lagos or something. Our letters seem to cross non-stop at the moment. This is being sent out with a friend, so hopefully will reach you soon. Oh, for a telephone.

Life has been completely and utterly chaotic here, far too busy, out nonstop and we are badly in need of a break. It is also terribly hot, 101 degrees at midday, very overcast and oppressive.

Everything is dry, there are terrible water problems and everything in the garden is dying.

There is a flour shortage and, if it can be found, they are now charging over £1 for a tiny loaf.

Lucy is teaching English privately and French at the International School, playing squash and going out a lot. We have now converted a bedroom into a studio, as she is painting and drawing while I do my batik. I am working out what to say next week when I have to talk at

the university to a group of French-speaking Africans for 20 minutes. I
am already nervous.

18 February 1981
I was greatly honoured to be asked to give a tea party for the *asan-
tahene* with one of his wives and his entourage as he is *en route* to
London to open an exhibition of Ashanti treasures at the Museum of
Mankind. It was like receiving royalty. In fact he is royalty.

He arrived with his drummers and when he alighted from his large
black car the guards held large coloured umbrellas over his head as he
walked to the front door, purely for effect, it was not raining. This time
he was far more relaxed with us, and spoke in perfect English without
using his interpreter.

I don't think Lucy quite realized his importance as she marched over
to him, sat next to him on the sofa, and chatted animatedly to him
throughout tea. He told her in lots of detail and with great enjoyment
about all his wives and his very many children. A lot of his treasures
will be on display at the exhibition and he is obviously delighted with
the idea.

I am still too busy. A lunch party we had to give for 14 was chaotic.
At 10.30 a.m. there was an electricity cut, so at 11.30 a.m., in desperation, with raw meat and potatoes to cope with, we transported the cook,
plus all the food, down to the salt and pepper, to the High
Commissioner's Residence to be cooked there. He is away so
everything in the kitchen was locked up. Then we brought it all back
and tried to serve it before it got cold. Luckily in this heat things stay
hot for a long time. Our gas stove has still not been fixed. And in any
case it is impossible to find gas cylinders.

28 February 1981
The electricity has been terrible recently. We had none upstairs for four
days last week, so we all ended up sleeping downstairs on sofas or on
the floor as, with no fan or air conditioning, the heat is rather too much,
especially since this relatively modern house is not designed for natural
living. There are constant water cuts; luckily we had the very large
extra tank installed last year as without this we would be without water
frequently.

See you soon for the Easter holidays.

28 April 1981

Ghana is the same as ever, but we seem to have avoided the threatened general strike and the 72-hour water cut only lasted for 12 hours.

The garden is like a wilderness. Seidu and Daniel have done virtually nothing for the last six weeks. The grass is far too long, but the mower is broken as the gardeners are not too good at avoiding stones when mowing and, as usual, it cannot be fixed without getting hold of some elusive vital part.

The Islam influence is getting stronger and stronger in this part of Africa. Nasa has now converted to Islam, for which he received a radio. He also has to change his name, though he does not seem to take much notice of that.

Sadly, when I tried to play my piano it sounded most peculiar, so I opened it up and found that a family of mice had used most of the felts to make a nest. I contacted the dear old piano tuner I know, but he is very gloomy about fixing it. Even if I get some felt from England he very much doubts whether it will ever sound quite right again. But I shall certainly try. At times here the piano is vital therapy.

But Accra is looking fantastic. It is a mass of blossom with scarlet flame trees everywhere, as well as large yellow laburnum-type trees and flowery mauve jacarandas — the whole place is a mass of vivid colour and a pleasure to drive around. Not much rain yet, but things are much greener than when I left. There was a massive storm on Easter Day, which sadly demolished three of our banana trees with young bananas on them.

Today we have eight for lunch. Tomorrow there is a meeting of 20 here in the morning, so biscuits, cake and coffee. Tomorrow night is the Queen's Birthday party, 600 invited, but luckily that is not our responsibility. On Saturday we are going to the races where Michael has to present the Queen Elizabeth Trophy, and on Sunday it is the beach. So life is back to normal.

PS. Please send old plastic bags from Sainsburys, or wherever, for use for storing. They are unobtainable here and are used and used. Nothing gets wasted in Ghana. Dustbin men do not exist, bottles and newspapers are recycled. In fact if you have no empty bottles you can get no drink which makes things very difficult for newcomers. We dig pits in the garden for rubbish, have a large compost heap and very occasionally have a bonfire.

146

6 May 1981

There are slight problems at the beach. Friends with a beach hut near ours found it being used as a public wash house and loo, not very pleasant. They took sanctuary with us and the local chief came around to organize things and promises it will not happen again. But we wonder. Also, crowds of villagers came and sat around staring at us all until the chief got them to move. There has been a lot of pilfering and we have to be very careful, but it will be sad if they drive us away as they will lose the income they get from their plots.

The economic situation is as dire as ever. I have not bought anything since we came back — except eggs. Now a loaf of bread is £2.50. Vegetables and fruit are exorbitant. Thank heavens for our garden, or we should live on tins.

19 May 1981

Life has been interesting here with frequent electricity cuts of up to ten hours when one gets worried about all one's worldly food supplies going off in the freezers and only two portable generators to service the whole office staff. And we have just finished four days without water. Today it is real luxury as we have water and electricity, but of course no phone.

Last week we went to Togo for four days as the Minister of Overseas Development, Neil Marten, who was in Accra last year, was in Lomé for a large international conference. He retires soon and is clearly going on as many trips as he can and doing as little work as possible. He drove us mad when he was here last time as he was so idle and would not do half the things we had planned, or see the people we wanted him to see.

Well, he was just the same in Togo. It was all very funny as his permanent secretary was there trying to organize him. Everyone calls him minister — so it's 'Yes Minister', African style, a lot of the time. Anyway, we were landed with him to get him out of his permanent secretary's hair, but as the weather was lovely and there is a pool at the hotel the minister was very happy, so that was no problem. Michael went to conferences in the day time and there were vast receptions in the evenings. It was all quite jolly, but I got a bad tummy — which always happens in Togo however careful I am — and there were flies everywhere.

147

I have done some good batiks since I got back, but with no water or electricity and an African tummy output has slowed down recently. I am in the middle of two large, brilliantly coloured ones, which have been commissioned and are on the theme of the *asantahene durbar*.

15 October 1981
It's good to be back [from a trip to England] although one of our freezers broke down in our absence and we have lost an awful lot of food. We've already given two lunches and a dinner, had most evenings out, played golf and been to the races. There are several demands for my batiks and the country, as usual, is in complete chaos.

And a week ago I was in Guildford!

PS. Please could you send dried onions and Smash potatoes.

9 November 1981
Our trip to Bolgatanga, northern Ghana, via Togo and Ouagadougou, Upper Volta [now Burkina Faso] was an unforgettable experience. Upper Volta is the third poorest country in the world and you get a real insight into African life and realize what a very backward and very vast continent it is. We drove for hundreds of miles through parched, desolate countryside, passing simple villages with no signs of twentieth-century living and were invariably greeted by villagers and their children running alongside our Land-Rovers; fortunately we were well supplied with sweets, pencils, cigarettes and cans of food. The drought is making life very difficult indeed for the Upper Voltans.

Ouagadougou, the capital, is an oasis that caters for the French people still living and working in the area. The electricity and water both work and fresh food and wine are flown in regularly. We stayed in a simple but comfortable hotel, which even had a little, and clean, swimming pool.

The highlight of the trip was having dinner at an open air restaurant in the centre of Ouagadougou. This restaurant is run by nuns and the local girls they have 'saved' from trouble. At 10.30 p.m. the nuns and ex-fallen women stood in a group and, with one of them playing the piano, we all sang hymns from a song sheet on our tables, with Ave Maria as the finale. It was all very bizarre and somewhat unreal under the starlit African sky.

Northern Ghana feels remote and unspoilt and very different from the coastal regions. Bolgatanga was certainly worth visiting. But there are quite a lot of British interests in the area; the chief one being a massive irrigation scheme by Taylor Woodrow.

16 November 1981

I am having great garden problems. The main one is a blight called mealy bug, which is now all over this part of Accra. Though we have managed to get the garden sprayed several times, it keeps coming back; we are now out of spray and it is unobtainable here. It is a little white bug, which leaves a black film all over the trees and finally kills them. Our mango trees are terrible, but we are hoping they will survive. Our three frangipani trees, beautiful old trees usually covered in blossom, have been killed and have to be taken down, and our citrus fruit trees are in a terrible state. The mealy bug even affects the vegetables, so efforts at living off the land are not so successful this year.

The other problem is that one of the gardeners, Daniel, has vanished and we are left with only one, Sedu. This may not sound a problem to you but with the amounts of watering required, all from taps which usually have a thin trickle of water at most, and cutting all the lawns by hand as not one mower in the whole office is working, I am almost beginning to regret our very large garden. But as one mouldy lettuce at the official rate of exchange is £1 we have to persevere!

27 November 1981

We have just sent an order off to England for vegetables, meat and groceries, which are being flown in every six weeks or so by an enterprising firm in Worthing; our food situation has consequently vastly improved. We even have the eggs flown in and I have ten dozen locked in the storeroom at the moment. How long do fresh eggs last before going bad? Or should I store them in water glass as we did in the war?

At the weekend we visited Akwatia, the diamond mines. The drive through the wet zone was lovely, really tropical with lush vegetation, and reminded us of Ceylon. They are doing very badly up there because of the financial situation, which is diabolical. Ghana is expecting 200 per cent inflation next year.

The IMF, International Monetary Fund, is here under conditions of great secrecy to consult the office (Michael) about the possibility of getting the English banks to provide standby credit. The loan is on the verge of materializing, but with accompanying devaluation and much against a lot of people's wishes, there is much nervousness on the part of the government — the last two governments to devalue fell.

16 December 1981

We had no idea what had happened to Tim and Jon Williams [a friend coming out for the holidays], what plane, if any, they were on and had received no communication from the FCO at all regarding their flights. We had been hopefully meeting every plane from London for three days and were getting rather desperate about the whole situation and wondering if they had vanished for ever when we were woken at 6.00 a.m. by ringing on the door bell and there they were on the doorstep. They had spent two days at Heathrow trying to get seats on a flight.

It was a great relief all around, but I am sure the taxi driver who brought them from the airport, whom they had paid in pounds sterling because they had no cedis, was the happiest of all. They had paid him £30 for the two-mile trip, which was an absolute rip-off, but at that un-earthly hour they had no choice and there was no phone to contact us. The taxi driver can now change that on the black market and live in great comfort for some time.

There have been endless problems with air traffic over the last few days and a lot of violence and trouble at the airport, which has not helped the situation, but it all seems calmer now.

Sadly Tim developed malaria very soon after his arrival. Apparently he must have contacted it on his last trip and as soon as he got back to the tropics it emerged. He felt pretty ill, but thankfully it was not cere-bral malaria and he responded quickly to treatment. We have to take two lots of tablets now, one lot daily and one lot weekly, as there is drug resistance in the malarial parasite and no drugs are 100 per cent effective. Lots of people find they have side effects ranging from mouth ulcers to dizziness and blurred vision; I need glasses now for reading, but whether that is due to drugs or age I am not sure.

There have been nonstop official visitors and entertaining to do and I never have time to do my batiks, for which I have several commissions. The biggest and most difficult event, thankfully over, was the party we gave for 90 last Friday for all the office, plus the British Council, and the few British Army personnel we have here. We started with carol singing around the Xmas tree, to try to get a Xmas feel on a very hot and humid evening, and the tables were laid out in the garden. There was a panic when black clouds loomed and there were drops of rain, but luckily this passed over. After the dinner we had a disco fixed up in the study and dancing. It all went well, but was quite a feat of organization and, as usual, I had to beg and borrow food, drink and equipment from all over.

I am writing this while waiting for another plane to arrive, this one containing food parcels from Worthing. It should have arrived at 6.00 a.m., now it is supposed to arrive at 11.00 a.m., but one never knows anything in this place. There was a very large shipment of food and drink last week from the UK, but it had been vandalized *en route* (in Sierra Leone) and lots of people got nothing.

There was a drama when a lot of people had no electricity for five days due to a power cable breaking and the office generators not working properly. As we do not have our own generators, boosting people's freezers with only one mobile generator was a 24-hour job for the office. If we were Americans we would have completely self-sufficient generating systems in our houses, but we cannot get London to recognize all our problems.

The situation is deteriorating all around. The IMF loan, which could be coming through, is being mucked around by the government, which is too apprehensive about being seen to kowtow to the IMF. It does not dare announce the conditions just before Christmas and in March it is the silver jubilee. But if it does not do something soon civil unrest is not far away. There has been trouble at the docks, now supposedly controlled by the navy, and the airport. The universities are now on strike in Kumasi, and so it goes on.

A Happy Christmas!

[At 3.00 a.m. on New Year's Day we were awoken by sounds of shooting from the direction of the Burma Army Camp, just down the road from our house. As communication is so difficult it took some time to piece together what was happening in the country. Nine hours after the shooting started Flight Lieutenant Jerry Rawlings, the son of a Scottish father and Ghanaian mother, delivered a speech on the radio telling us that he had taken over the country and demanding 'proper democracy' in Ghana. For two days after that nothing was heard of Rawlings, but random announcements were made over the radio breaking up the broadcasting of nonstop music. We were told of a dawn to dusk curfew. This was the 'second coming', as Rawlings had led a successful revolution of junior officers on 4 June 1979, but after three months had handed over the reins of power to a civilian government.]

6 January 1982
We are all fine, but what is happening to Ghana is not so fine.

I expect you have been hearing about the goings on here and the kids will fill you in when they return. At the moment the airport is still closed and we are not quite sure when it will be opened, but I am just dashing this off as there is a chance it will be opened tomorrow.

For the first two days we were very close to the action with lots of shooting nearby at the Burma Army Camp, from where the new regime is ruling. I only stayed on in the house as I had four strong men to guard me with golf clubs. I found sitting at the sewing machine sewing lots of old sheets sides to middle in the good old-fashioned way fairly soothing, as it was impossible to concentrate on very much else.

On the first day of the revolution the boys went out onto the balcony to sunbathe in their usual fashion, but came in quickly when a shot was fired very close by indeed. And Lucy, who had somehow slept right through all the shooting, emerged mid-morning in her tennis clothes asking for a lift to Burma Army Camp where she had arranged a game of tennis. She could not believe that there was a revolution happening and thought we were teasing her — until she heard some very loud gunshot.

7 January 1982
Tomorrow has come and the airport is still firmly closed. We are now trying to make evacuation arrangements for the kids, perhaps a special British Caledonian flight or a flight from Lomé, Togo, if we can cross the border, which is doubtful.

It is all very dodgy and difficult, and there are about 80 kids to get out. I sincerely hope we get them off in the next few days as people are rather pessimistic and think that this is the lull before more trouble.

Life here is very restrictive at the moment as the kids are not allowed to leave the house, but I have been out a few times with Michael in the official car flying the Union Jack bravely and we have been able to visit people and tell them what is going on. There is some joyfulness amongst working-class Ghanaians, but it is not in the least overwhelming. The regime is organizing rent-a-mob lorries to go around town shouting revolutionary slogans.

It has all been incredibly busy and the day never ends. The High Commissioner is on leave — he was on leave during the last coup too! — but is trying to get back via Nigeria, Benin and Togo.

The Libyans are involved in this coup — Rawlings spent a month in Libya last year — and guns are coming from other unfriendly sources as well. So far the electricity and water are both working and the phone has never worked so well in all the time we have been here.

Fortunately the shooting has calmed down now (only odd shots can be heard) but the future is dicey. Apparently the coup two years ago got far more out of control and there was a lot more violence — this time they reckon on about 60 military dead. Rawlings has announced on the radio that the constitution has been suspended, Parliament has been dismissed and all political parties have been banned. There is now a massive round-up of old government supporters who are to be tried before people's courts. They have arrested President Limann and the vice-president and quite a lot of ministers — there are around 90 political prisoners in all — but many are still in hiding. According to Rawlings, it is this group, with its greed, corruption and negligence, that is responsible for the bankruptcy and ruin of the country.

Nasa came in to talk to us in a very surreptitious manner and said he had someone in the kitchen who would like to see us. It was the Ghanaian High Commissioner in London, Francis Badzie, who had come home to Ghana for Christmas, had not managed to get out in time and was on the wanted list. He was asking us to give him sanctuary. So we all sat down to discuss the situation over a glass of whisky.

Francis was extremely concerned about being unable to get out of the country. He had left his whole family in London, there was no way he could catch a plane (even if there had been any flights) and driving out would be impossible because of the many road checks. We managed to contact London by radio to confirm that we could offer asylum and were told that we must as he had shaken hands with the Queen and was a friend of Britain.

So we told him that he could stay with us secretly. Although we were apprehensive about the situation he was after all an accredited diplomat in London for the Limann regime and the new regime had not as yet been recognized by anyone. Nasa we knew would keep quiet as he is of the same tribe as the High Commissioner.

He was very relieved but said he must go out for a while and talk to his brother. Later we heard that during the night he had, by various means, managed to cross the country through the bush and get over the border into Togo, from where he flew to London. I wonder if he will ever return to Ghana?

10 January 1982

Still no one is certain what will happen now Rawlings is back. What, for instance, will be his attitude towards the Westerners, including nearly 1000 British, in Ghana? Luckily Michael is one of the few diplomats who was in touch with Jerry Rawlings during his time in the wilderness. In theory, under President Limann, Rawlings was free to come and go as he pleased after the 1979 revolution, though his movements were regularly monitored by Ghanaian security forces and from time to time he was harassed.

The other day the High Commission got word from Brigadier Nunoo Mensah, head of the Defence Force, whose English wife runs a flower shop in Accra, that Rawlings would like to contact the 'West'.

The problem is that if any head of mission sees him formally this will constitute recognition of his government. However, our government has not yet decided whether to like him and is not in a hurry to give him its blessing. On the other hand, as he and his slightly uncontrolled and wild supporters are now undoubtedly in charge, we need reassurance that Rawlings is not ill-disposed towards Western foreigners in Ghana and is not, for example, going to chuck any into gaol, close their businesses or throw them out of the country.

To cut a long story short, Colonel David Jones, head of the army team at the Burma Camp Staff College, who with his wife has involved himself intensely in Ghanaian life during his posting here, unusually so for a British soldier, was contacted by Brigadier Mensah and elaborate arrangements were made for Michael, as acting British High Commissioner, and Tom Smith, US ambassador and a good friend who did not want to miss an opportunity to make informal contact, to meet President Flight Lieutenant Rawlings in Burma Camp. [David Jones was later deputy director of Oxfam and his wife Nerissa is one of the first ordained women priests in England.]

A military escort of two Land-Rovers and four military policemen on motorbikes, all heavily armed, with sirens blaring, called at our house and Tom Smith and Michael followed them in unmarked cars, no flags flying, through the deserted town, the curfew still in place, and into Burma Camp.

Apparently it was all very eerie and surreal. The entrance to the camp was heavily guarded, with the gates stacked with sandbags, and there were guns everywhere. They drove slowly deeper and deeper into the camp. The soldiers around were all heavily armed, cheerful but slightly manic, partly because they had had days of very little sleep and some were high on Indian hemp or *wee*, as it is known, and were drugged to the eyeballs.

Rawlings received them in a sandbagged bunker in the middle of the camp. He was unshaven and haggard, but neatly dressed in combat uniform.

He was extraordinarily friendly considering he thought that Western countries had let Ghana down by cutting their aid and had been the main supporters of President Limann's regime. Michael and Tom asked him very formally if his government would strictly adhere to all the international rules and would treat foreigners with courtesy and guarantee their protection. He seemed only too happy to give these assurances and said he intended no harm to any genuine 'friends of the people'. His revolution was on behalf of the people, to protect them against corruption and exploitation by self-seeking adventurers, i.e. capitalists, and the feeble and disloyal middle-class Ghanaians who thought only of themselves.

Michael and Tom welcomed the assurances, said they would put in a good word with their respective governments and left quietly and in a dignified manner, which was apparently not easy with so many nervous and obviously aggressive and hypersensitive armed soldiers everywhere.

But this meeting, which was his first contact with the West after the coup, was apparently regarded by Rawlings and his regime as a crucial breakthrough in diplomatic relations. [In the following months Rawlings is known to have maintained contact with his allies, the Russians, Libyans and Cubans. But the communist bloc countries were all rather embarrassed by Ghana and were not ready to pour in massive aid, nor would Rawlings allow a heightened military presence from the East.]

13 January 1982
Many thanks for your letter of 28 December, which arrived yesterday when they finally managed to get a bag through. It was certainly nice to get some mail and newspapers.

Rawlings has now appointed a council. Apart from the one decent and sensible Brigadier Mensah, who is trying to keep things under control, he has a priest who is about to be defrocked, a Marxist student, a corporal, a militant sergeant, and a head of security, Kojo Tsikata, who won the silver stick at Sandhurst and gives people the heebie-jeebies. So there is not much hope. Though Nigeria delivered oil last week, it is unlikely to do so again — we [Ghana] now have a five to six week supply. There are Libyan 'advisers' here now. There is certainly a great deal of unrest and anything could happen at any time. And so the holy war, as it is called, continues.

People are worried about food supplies drying up completely. Prices came down for about two days but are now sky high again. Either that or the goods are not on sale any more and being hoarded away. The police vanished completely for three days during the coup, there was not one around, and are now only back to half-strength. So much for security.

Sadly the beach we like to visit nearby has been closed by the army. It is apparently now used for shootings. We have a curfew from 8.00 p.m. till 6.00 a.m. so social life is restricted.

25 January 1982
Hope the kids got back safely. It was quite a hassle to get them on the first flight out.

The situation here is one of uneasy calm. The curfew has now been extended to 10.00 p.m., but no one likes being out that late and, apart from a few working lunches, we have virtually no social life. Our video is helping to keep us sane. The army is rather out of control. We still hear shooting, sometimes just down the road from Burma Camp, which can only be executions. And, in spite of the curfew, burglary is rampant, so the atmosphere is not pleasant.

It is getting more worrying as all the market 'mammies' have had their stalls burnt down. These are the women who make vast profits from black marketeering and Rawlings did the same thing to them during his previous coup two years ago. As a consequence there is no food around and people are getting restless and hungry.

Togo opened its border for about three days, but after a shooting incident last week, it is now closed again, so we do not even have that safety valve.

Sadly, the service which last year started bringing us food by plane every two months or so does not dare risk flying in at the moment as the airport is extremely unpleasant and the harbour services are now slower and more unreliable than ever. So there is very little to eat save the fast-dwindling supplies we still have in our freezers and our storeroom.

We are desperately trying to get sacks of rice for our vast household of servants and their very extended families, but until we can get over the Togo border this is impossible.

There are a few things I would be grateful if you would send me via the bag. There is no bread at all, but I still have flour, so please send two tins of yeast, six tins of Nescafé, two large tubes of toothpaste and six tablets of soap.

29 January 1982

The headlines in this week's Ghanaian newspapers are unbelievable. They are all about a plot by the USA, Britain and Nigeria to get rid of Rawlings and his men and to get Limann back — apparently 1000 SAS troops are already waiting in Lagos to fly in! As the press is now controlled by this lot it is all rather unpleasant and we are hoping that it was just some madman who released the story. Needless to say the accusations are completely false. Britain and the USA are making strong protests to the 'government' and have formally denied any involvement in any such plans, describing them as 'totally irresponsible and without foundation'.

There is a leading article in the *Ghanaian Times* of 26 January headed 'We Won't Die Twice'. It talks of the aims of the revolution and how the British and Americans should be playing a useful role in ensuring its success.

Whoever is tempted to take action to reverse the revolution or sabotage it in any way must be prepared to contend with several realities: The progressive Ghana People's Armed Forces are ready to defend the revolution to prove that they are the true salvation of the oppressed masses of the people. Every Ghanaian soldier will fight any invader to the finish because soldiers have suffered deprivation and insult from the greedy and wicked Limann regime.

All workers will fight fiercely to defend the revolution because it is the only hope they have to control the nation's economy and make sure that the fruits of their toil benefit they themselves and not those who exploit their valour to live in luxury.

30 January 1982

Things here go from bad to worse. There was an announcement on the news today that all 50 cedi notes must be handed in to banks by the end of next week in exchange for a receipt. No inkling is given of when money will be given in exchange, or what money. This is very hard for people like our servants who in this way will lose all their savings, which are usually kept in 50 cedi notes under the mattress.

They are trying to catch hoarders and there have been some nasty incidents of houses being raided and the inhabitants badly treated. The French are preparing to evacuate their citizens next week. This is because of rumours of massive military house-to-house searches on 11 February which, given that the army is rather uncontrolled, could be dangerous. We are not advising evacuation for the time being, but there are very few British wives still around. Of those that are, some are very nervous and dare not go out on their own.

Very sadly it seems that Rawlings's few moderate and sensible advisers are being overtaken by his radical and ignorant revolutionary ones. It is getting more and more depressing and we're becoming increasingly pessimistic about the future of the country.

Stories abound every day. Gunshot is heard quite frequently — probably misbehaving soldiers being killed. Bodies are seen by the side of the road. But apart from the terrible nonsense being written in the papers we have not experienced any anti-European sentiment.

The fate of President Limann is still unsure, though Rawlings did say in a BBC interview the other day that he did not think he would be shot. He also said that he had reluctantly taken power again because he believed Dr Limann's administration was returning Ghana to corruption, denial of human rights, victimization, prison without trial, economic crimes and constitutional abuses. [Limann did survive under house arrest.]

Meanwhile my keep-fit and keep-sane golf campaign continues. It is a lovely course, though one never knows whether it will have been mown or not and there are children and animals all over it, but the Ghanaians, being such marvellously cheerful people in spite of everything, lift one's spirits.

In fact golf, played mostly by Ghanaians, has never before been so popular and busy. But whether the course will be closed, like the one in Ankara, and made into a people's park, we have yet to see.

Driving home from golf the other day some very shabbily dressed and unshaven soldiers stopped my car and pointed a gun through the window at me. They seemed high on drugs, or alcohol, their English was very limited and communication between us was difficult. But they did not seem too aggressive and I tried to explain about our CD plates, but that did not get me very far.

I then realized that what they really wanted was cigarettes and sadly I had none to hand. So I showed them my empty bag and they grudgingly let me through. It was a bit frightening, and now I never go out without cigarettes.

22 February 1982

Things are deteriorating at an alarming rate. Violence and revolutionary fervour are on the increase, food is on the decrease, and the army is getting more out of control every day. We frequently hear guns in Burma Camp, and people we know of are beaten up badly and have their heads shaven.

Up to now the European community has not been too badly treated, but the English manager of the Unilever factory here, Harry Pease, dares not go to his factory today. This is because his managers were beaten up and illiterate armed soldiers and members of the Workers' Defence Force spent a whole day moving in and out of his office pointing guns at him.

The curfew is at 10.00 p.m., but if you do go out and drive home any

159

time after 9.00 p.m. the roads are eerily deserted, so our social life is now confined to lunch time.

Two trips around the country, which we made to see how the British were getting on, went fine. There are road blocks all over the place but only one aggressive soldier, high on *wee*, insisted on looking in my bag, the others let us through with a smile because of our CD plates and cigarettes.

Kumasi, where there has been a lot of violence, now has an uneasy peace. By contrast, the majority of the 50 or 60 European families working at Obuasi, Lonrho's gold mine, are so curtained in their apartheid surroundings that they have no idea at all what is happening in the rest of the country. I suppose that is one advantage of isolation behind fences.

Anyway, we saw as many Brits in the region as possible and gave them news of the situation. With phones not working, the roads ghastly, and newspapers and radios just spouting revolutionary nonsense, it is very difficult for people outside Accra to keep in touch with events.

After two nights at home we set off down the coast, thankfully on a far better road, to visit Takoradi and various factories and plantations in the countryside where British people are in control. They were all very happy to see us and get information at first hand, but I find it exhausting going from one place to the other seeing people, advising, consoling and generally morale boosting.

Back here tension is high. Several Europeans, particularly French, have left, though only a few British in very small concerns have got out so far. But business is completely seizing up and the future utterly depressing. We really live from day to day, wondering what ghastly news we shall hear.

Now I must go to the duty-free shop. I hear they have some Farex there, which I want for the babies I have got involved with at the Osu Children's Home. We manage to get dried milk to them sometimes via the erratic supply at the duty-free shop and from some tins I brought up from Togo. The babies really are starving, but we have discovered that unless we stay and feed them ourselves the staff at the home will take the milk for their own families — who no doubt are also desperately in need.

I have at present in my storeroom two sacks of rice for our servants and their apparently ever-extending families. If members of the

People's Revolutionary Party come to the house searching for hoarders, which they are doing a lot now, we will be in deep trouble.

And we now also have three crates of very good champagne, found on our doorstep with a note from a German friend of ours, Jörgen Heinel, who was worried about his future in Ghana. We heard the following day that his house had been ransacked and that he had fled the country. We have big signs on our gates saying we are diplomats, so hopefully they will not worry us, that is as long as they are not illiterate.

I try to console myself with the thought that it is a fascinating experience to live through a revolution that has completely changed the character of a country in seven weeks. It is so tragic that their attempts to achieve their stated aims — no more corruption, people working honestly and hard for others, the country before everything — are having such unpleasant side effects and completely disastrous economic results.

28 February 1982

Things continue in a very uncertain fashion. Stories of the army getting out of hand abound and rumours are rife. The economic situation gets worse by the minute. I am really looking forward to a break.

This week there has been an ultimatum that public servants who cannot cope with the present revolution must retire within 48 hours and that no public servant should be seen wearing a suit to the office. Public servants are also to be deployed to undertake a moral crusade to improve the living conditions of the rural people and help stem the perennial food shortage problem; presumably that means they are to become farmers.

The country has been desperately low on oil, but we have just been informed that Libya is now going to supply Ghana with a large quantity free of charge as a demonstration of the Arab *jamahiriya*'s solidarity and goodwill towards the people of Ghana.

Since November we have not been down to Togo, though it is supposed to be part of our job. But the frontier has been closed either on the Ghanaian side or the Togo side, or both sides, for months. Rawlings accuses President Eyadema of being hostile to his 'revolutionary' cause and the feelings of distaste are mutual.

Oh, yes, our car has been stolen. The Peugeot 504 was parked outside the High Commission office in the morning in the main street in Accra

— Michael had both sets of keys. He reported to protocol who alerted border posts, or so they said, but the fact is that Peugeots are the car used by the army here and it is likely to have been commandeered by them.

Must stop now and write to the kids as I have a friend flying out tonight who will be able to take the letters with him.

PS. I was not able to give this to my friends as everyone is being searched, having bags opened and letters read at the airport. So it will have to go in the bag and will no doubt arrive after I get home.

See you soon!

2 May 1982

Everything was in good order when we got back. Nasa and all the families were very pleased to see us and the various things they had requested — from watches to cigarettes to lengths of cloth. Social life is picking up despite the 10.00 p.m. curfew.

Ghana is in the same chaotic and economically disastrous situation, but we have noticed a considerable change in the atmosphere, which is far less tense, thank God. There are not nearly so many soldiers around, though we were greeted by tanks pointing our way when we landed at the airport, I have not heard any shooting yet and there are not the hair-raising horror stories that abounded when we left. Food is still in desperately short supply, but luckily the office lorry got into Togo and has brought us back a sack of rice for the servants.

Our phone, which is dead, apparently cannot be fixed until they lay new underground cables. These are at present stuck in a boat at Takoradi and will have to be brought up the coast in another boat, so it is highly likely that we shall be phoneless for the rest of our time here, which is a great nuisance, though thankfully we are all supplied with radio telephones for emergencies.

The World Service is giving us the Falklands news, though I cannot get a clear reception even with our very special radio. It is certainly not the same as hearing it morning, noon and night and on telly and in the papers, but all extremely worrying. One does feel very out of touch.

Now for the monthly golf medal. I am rather nervous, but the ladies are all jolly and friendly in true Ghanaian fashion, and a particularly helpful lady is going to fix the draw so that I shall play with her — she will probably fix my card as well!

14 May 1982

Life is very busy with official visitors to stay. If only there were hotels in Ghana! Dinners, lunches, and not a free day for the next two weeks — thank God for the curfew, it does make a difference.

The country is collapsing around us. They have at last appointed a finance secretary, Kwesi Botchwey, a former university lecturer in geography, but he seems quite sensible, so perhaps something will be achieved — [he was still Finance Minister in 1995] — but the outlook is not good. A lot of people are leaving or are about to leave; the next 18 months will be filled with endless farewells.

21 June 1982

Yesterday was a typical day in Accra. Although we are already giving two dinners, two lunches and a tea party this week I was informed early in the morning that we had to have eight people unexpectedly for lunch. At short notice these occasions are rather difficult as all our meat is kept in freezers. So I took out two legs of lamb and hoped they would defrost quickly.

Also, we have four house guests from the Ministry of Overseas Development staying in our guest chalet. Apart from the fact that the water never runs in the chalet taps, we have been having very heavy rains and its ceiling is looking ominously close to collapse — materials needed for repair are not available in Accra. Anyway, I sent them off with sandwiches so that I wouldn't have them returning for lunch too.

All had been going quite well, though there was drama in the garden when our new second gardener, who had only been with us for three weeks and did not seem to work very much, came and asked for an advance on his wages. The chief gardener then appeared on the scene to tell me that he was a very bad gardener and ought to leave. I then got Nasa to help me with negotiations and, after half an hour, the situation was resolved and the second gardener was dismissed with his month's wages.

Then, at half past ten, the electricity went off. Our alternative gas stove is at present unusable because we cannot get any gas locally to fill the cylinders, which are now both empty. We had two uncooked legs of lamb, not to mention raw vegetables, and guests due in two hours. And, of course, there was no phone and no car, as Michael is now using mine. Luckily Nasa, who is very good on the African bush telegraph, set off on a trot to neighbours to borrow a cylinder. He proudly returned with a cylinder, but it had a different fitting and was of no use to us.

Meanwhile we lit a wood fire and valiantly tried to cook the lamb and veg. Everything looked rather raw and unappetizing, but I was very hot and sticky and the guests were on their way, so I laid the table and tried to shower and look presentable, which was difficult with only a trickle of water in the taps.

The guests, none of whom I had met before, arrived, plus Michael, and we poured them very strong drinks. They were extremely pleasant and, when faced with a rather odd-looking lunch and a mild explanation of the problems, seemed rather to enjoy the scene — 'how typically African' — and conversation and laughter flowed. Finally, when the lunch guests had gone, the house guests returned and the ceiling of the guest chalet collapsed! And the electricity did not come on again for 30 hours!

3 July 1982
A letter from Tim telling us of his degree, about which we are delighted. He sounds on very good form, and the Surrey 2nd XI cricket is going well too. If only we could watch him.

The British and Americans have only now had their first official contact with this regime. The High Commissioner, Jimmy Mellon, and Michael went into Burma Camp the week before last and spent an hour with Rawlings and his henchmen. He did not talk much, kept completely out of financial affairs and really does not know very much. But he is more relaxed than he was.

A massive hydroelectric power project has recently been completed and the dam was opened by Rawlings. I met and talked to him for the first time at a social gathering afterwards and quite understood why the masses loved him. He is very handsome, charming and charismatic and I would certainly vote for him if he had sensible people around him.

A Foreign Office chap was over from London, via Lagos. He could not get a flight up from Lagos to Accra so eventually hired a plane, but by the time he arrived the office cocktail party I was giving for him to meet the staff was almost over and he could only stay ten minutes before his next engagement. So that was rather a waste of time and effort.

The frontiers with Togo are open again, for the moment, and we went with him down to Lomé for two days, which was pretty chaotic. As Togo will be on the UN Security Council for the next two years and is consequently rather important, we may have to visit it more often and perhaps even open a permanent office there. Michael rushed around seeing people, including their Foreign Affairs Minister, to explain our point of view on the Falklands, for their votes are vital to us.

On my first day in Togo I took a few supplies to a clinic only ten miles from Lomé where they had no disinfectant, no piped water, no electricity and very little medicine.

On the next day, by contrast, we went to a fantastic and very lavish government banquet for about 18 people. There were nine courses, all provided by French chefs, with food especially flown in from France, and it was very difficult to remember that we were in the same country. The Foreign Office chap, Michael and I were the only visitors; all the rest were high-powered African Togolese. The whole evening was quite an experience, marred only by the fact that it was rather lengthy, I had to speak French all evening to the Togolese sitting around me (Togolese French is rather different from Parisian French) and I was not very hungry, for we had had an enormous lunch that day at the German ambassador's house.

12 July 1982

I shall now be coming back one week earlier — Friday 23 July. Things have been extremely difficult recently and tension is high. No doubt you will have read about the kidnapping and murder of the three judges in Accra; we knew two of them personally. A lot of people think Kojo Tsikata was responsible. The High Commissioner of course went away the week before it all happened. He always goes away just before any crisis and it has all been very hectic and worrying.

This week we had 45 medical people in for drinks to meet six visiting English doctors who have been examining at the medical school here. They were most impressed with their standard in spite of the lack of facilities available.

The trouble is that when they have qualified the doctors usually leave the country because conditions of employment here are so bad; many go to Nigeria. The fact that I have promised a doctor friend to bring X-ray film back with me from England, as apparently at the moment there is none in the country, gives one some idea of the problems they face.

Must dash and get this letter to the airport. I still have to find some kind person going on today's plane who will post it for me in the UK. Will you be able to meet me at Gatwick?

Please let Tim and Andrew and Lucy know what is happening.

6 November 1982

Everyone greeted us rapturously when we arrived home in Accra just before the 10.00 p.m. curfew, which is not surprising considering we were bringing badly needed food.

The house was fine — no freezers defrosted, cars stolen, or any other horrors — and the garden is looking lovely with lots of vegetables planted. As the border with Togo is shut again this is vital. Thank heavens supplies are now quite regularly being flown in to us again from the firm in Sussex. But it is too expensive to bring in the servants' rice, or potatoes and onions and other heavy luxuries of this life.

The atmosphere in Ghana is much more relaxed now. There were no machine guns pointing at us when we got off the plane this time, the soldiers are keeping a much lower profile and there are not nearly as many tanks around. Economically the situation is as hopeless as ever.

Last weekend there was panic for two days with rumours flying around of violent fighting amongst those at the top. There are great rivalries and the situation is volatile, so something is bound to happen. But let's hope it stays within the army camp headquarters and does not turn into tribal fighting, which is always possible.

On the negative side of our return we have already had two power cuts, though they only lasted about two hours, and there is no trace of the four suitcases we sent air freight over a week ago. And they were all full of commodities we badly need, such as food and soap.

PS. Please could you send with Andrew or Lucy some light bulbs as we have none and cannot get them.

11 November 1982

Our lives have been dominated since Sunday by the death of Lieutenant Colonel Tony Whittall, our fairly newly arrived defence attaché, at Mile 7 Beach. Michael and I had gone with a picnic, but having felt a very strong current and undertow when swimming had decided to leave early. We were just getting into the car when we saw three people about 50 yards out obviously in difficulties and shouting for help.

Tony Whittall was one of the first to react and ran into the water and started swimming towards those in trouble, followed by a further 12 to 15 people. They all, in turn, found themselves swept out of their depths. There was no panic, but several were quickly becoming exhausted trying to fight the current and were in need of assistance.

We all felt very helpless on the shore standing watching everyone being swept out to sea. There were no boats of any description, or life belts, but a very efficient Ghanaian, aided by the Canadian first secretary, who is himself a former lifeguard and a very strong swimmer, organized everyone to find ropes from wherever possible. These were then tied together and a human chain was formed into the water; the people most in distress, including the three who had originally called for assistance, were helped or managed on their own to reach the rope and were then hauled in.

But Tony Whittall in his efforts unfortunately overtaxed his energies and collapsed about 60 yards out. He was got back to the shore but efforts at resuscitation were unavailing.

It was quite horrific standing on the beach helplessly watching so many people in such danger, including Michael, and trying to find rope, which took a long time to organize. Michael came out OK and went on helping, but it was awful to see so many people looking so ghastly laid out all along the beach.

And to make the nightmare even worse the Range-Rover running Tony to the hospital ran over and killed a little girl who stepped in front of it in a village, and they had to drive straight on because of the possible crowd reaction.

At the hospital conditions were hopeless. We took along two very badly shaken men but there were no doctors and the people who had been dragged in and needed attention were laid out on the floor with no one around to help them. And this at the best hospital in Accra!

Everyone who was there has been extremely shaken. The poor widow, Pat, flew home today. Yesterday they had a book of condolence to sign at the Residence and she was marvellous and sat and received people as they filed through. It was a real nightmare.

15 November 1982
Our four large suitcases of food-filled air freight have still not arrived. I am just praying they are not lost forever. We need them.

17 November 1982

The black market is now offering 120 cedis to the pound — we change at under 5 cedis. Also, as the borders now seem permanently closed, we have not been able to get to Lomé for food. Luckily my pineapple bed is producing rampantly at the moment — hope it will still be OK at Xmas time — and we are working very hard on the vegetables. It is hot now, getting hotter, and it will rain less and less. But the tomatoes, lettuce, beans, corn and spinach (African variety) are coming on. And we are living on vegetables I froze earlier in the year, corn and beans mostly. Thank God for the garden. Sadly we have this ghastly mealy bug disease, which in spite of all our efforts has now killed all our citrus trees, so no more grapefruit, which we used to live on, lemons, limes or oranges. Also the mango trees are badly affected. I would not like to be a farmer here, particularly as you cannot buy the necessary sprays.

19 November 1982

Thank heavens our air freight has now turned up. All is OK except that lots of chocolate (After Eights and Mars Bars intended for Xmas presents, as well as for us) had melted all over everything in one of the cases. But it was rather stupid to send chocolate anyway.

As all our frontiers are now closed we are incredibly isolated. Oh for an international telephone service that worked! Rumours abound, but so far nothing seems to be happening.

PS. Please could you send me black and brown shoe polish, Coffeemate and four jars of mincemeat for our office Xmas party mince pies.

27 November 1982

I expect you have heard that we have been having a little trouble here in Accra. All seems to have quietened down now, though we have a curfew from 6.00 p.m. till 6.00 a.m., which is a nuisance.

It all started on Tuesday evening when I was driving home at about 5.00 p.m. and noticed people running in all directions, as I have said, we live near the military camp, and a general atmosphere of panic. When I got home Nasa said that a Ghanaian lady, who had two children with her, had driven in and asked for sanctuary in our house. But he did not know her and as I was out he sent her away. Also he said there were soldiers with guns on the other side of the road.

Then I started to hear shooting; it was now about 5.15 p.m. I tried reaching people on our radio telephone to tell them what was going on, but no one in the office was aware at that stage of anything untoward. Michael is away in Dacca. Soon the shooting spread all around and obviously something serious was happening. It lasted for about three hours; then road blocks were put up on all the streets. This worried the people in the office because they could not get me out and I was in a very vulnerable position.

In fact I was getting rather nervous and had told Nasa, who was nervous too, that he and his family could stay in the house for the night. I did try to appear calm and in control of the situation though, and told him what I would like for supper. And luckily we have plenty of whisky. Suddenly the two Pepera boys, the Ghanaians who had been to Harrow with Tim and Andrew, appeared on the doorstep. They were stranded and could not get home because of the road blocks. Fortunately for me they were able to stay the night. I was much happier with two strong men in the house and we had a very jolly evening. We listened to the radio to try to find out what was happening (nothing but military music), watched *High Society* on the video (amazingly there was no power cut) and listened to sporadic gunfire.

Next morning I went around to the High Commissioner's house and spent the day there. It all quietened down very quickly. This time it had been an unsuccessful coup, with odd isolated shooting. There were announcements over the radio that the soldiers and civilians who were involved were being hunted down. Like last time there was a lot of revolutionary nonsense being spouted over the air nonstop. The airport has opened again, but not many planes are coming in. I have no idea when Michael will get back. The 6.00 p.m. curfew makes air schedules very difficult to manage.

So I am spending the days at home and nights at the Residence. No one yet knows the exact details of the coup, but it seems that very few people were involved and the army stayed firm. The day before the chief of defence staff, a good friend of the West, had announced his resignation from the PNDC, or People's National Defence Council. We think he is safe; there is a possibility that the lady and the children seeking sanctuary were his, but no one really knows where he is. Rawlings has had a mass meeting and has made his usual hysterical rabid anti-imperialist speeches.

I do not know when the next bag will go or the next one arrive. All very irritating. Sincerely hope they lift the curfew soon. Luckily there is no more news for the moment.

3 December 1982
At last some mail has arrived, Michael has got back and the curfew has been lifted, at least until 10.00 p.m. This is a particular relief as Andrew and Lucy's plane would not be able to get in as long as the curfew continued. So we just hope nothing else happens to close the airport or produce a curfew before Monday 13th when they should arrive.

If I can find someone travelling I am hoping to get this letter off this weekend, otherwise we have a queen's messenger to stay next week and he will bring it, plus Xmas cards, for which I have no stamps. So please would you very kindly post them for me?

PS. Please could you send with the children one large tin of Mansion floor polish, ten packets of dried onions and four packets of Flash. And a Christmas pudding and perhaps a Christmas cake. And I enclose Nasa's watch, which needs a new battery.

But, most important, please could you send me some Batik Procion Dyes. The demand is very good at this time of the year.

5 December 1982
Here is the best card we have received so far:

> *To Brothers of the British High Commission Accra*
> *The People's Bureau of the Socialist People's Libyan*
> *Arab Jamahiriya presents its compliments to you and*
> *on the occasion of the Birth of Jesus Christ, has the*
> *honour to extend best wishes to you.*
> *Glory be to Him and peace to mankind*
> *and to you my brothers.*
> *From the secretary of the Libyan People's Bureau.*

Our friend Kwame Pianin, former head of Ghana's Cocoa Marketing Board and now a businessman involved in many projects, has been imprisoned with 16 others for being behind the recent coup attempt. Apparently he had sent Cornelia, his Dutch wife, out of the country, so she was safely out of the way.

He is now in prison with the 16 others awaiting trial; heaven knows when that will be, and the conditions in prison are dire. Approximately 23 political prisoners have been executed since the coup. Poor Cornelia is now back and spends most of her time trying to get food to him.

14 December 1982
Many thanks for all the parcels and shopping you sent with Andrew and Lucy. They arrived in very good form after an easy flight. Today we have a lunch party for them to meet all the young people we can rake up who are out for Xmas, as they know very few here and most of the friends they made on previous holidays have left.

Some firms are not allowing families out for Xmas, and some are sending wives and families home, as they think the situation is so unstable. But these are mostly American and they are rather hysterical.

This is probably the last letter before Christmas. We shall certainly miss you all — and Tim — and hope you have a lovely time. We will be thinking of you. Happy Christmas!

4 January 1983
Our imprisoned friend, Kwame Pianin, is going to be charged with complicity in the November abortive coup. His wife, Cornelia, is not allowed to visit him any more and is finding it difficult now to get food in to him. This is extremely worrying as the conditions in the prisons are, needless to say, pretty appalling. Sadly there is very little we can do to help.

Andrew and Lucy gave a party which started at 6.00 p.m. and the dancing had just got started when all the guests had to leave because of the curfew at 10.00 p.m. Two days later they extended the curfew till midnight and the fashion for the young now is 'curfew parties' from midnight till 5.00 a.m.

On behalf of Her Majesty the Queen we had a trip to Togo in an official convoy to say Happy New Year to President Eyadema again. The border has now been closed since August and this was the first time it has been opened to let accredited heads of mission through for this special occasion. But more important, it was an extremely useful shopping expedition as we were able to get rice, fish, milk and other necessities for the servants and their families and our supplies were all running very low.

We did the shopping, the border was opened again for us, we drove through, and the border was closed behind us and we do not know when it will open again.

On our return we had a message from London that mercenaries from the UK were *en route* to Lomé to assassinate President Eyadema, so we had to get a warning through to him. Due to lack of communication between Ghana and Togo we had to send someone by plane via Abidjan and, with West African airline connections, it took him two days to get there. But he did manage to deliver the message and the president has not been shot, so far.

[President Gnassingbe Eyadema survived attempted coups and unpopularity until 1991 when, at the country's national conference, he was forced to agree to elections, for which he would not be eligible, and to allow a transitional government to rule in the meantime. Thence followed a year-long terror campaign on his behalf by the army, including a near assassination of one opposition leader, a successful murder of another, and the deaths of hundreds of people in political violence. Mr Eyadema is, in 1995, allowed to stand again for president, to chair cabinet meetings and to represent Togo abroad. France has now withdrawn its friendship.]

10 January 1983
There has now been a New Year speech saying that they are going to nationalize the foreign banks by the end of the month. There have also been many threats of takeovers of international companies, so the business community here is in a state of severe panic.

We are really watching at first hand the collapse of a Western orientated society. The exodus of Ghanaians is faster than ever and Accra is getting emptier by the minute; lots of people are going back to the countryside and their old homes where at least they should be able to grow something to eat.

Sam, our cook, Lucy and I went to the market today to buy local ingredients for groundnut stew, not exactly an elaborate dish, and the total spent was 180 cedis (divide that by 4.7 to convert to sterling). And that did not include onions, which I had at home dried in a packet, they would have been about 15 cedis each, if obtainable, and tomatoes, which sell at 25 cedis a pound. And the minimum daily wage is 15 cedis, which is equivalent to one loaf of bread.

There are far fewer cars on the roads now, which means that we lucky ones all get about faster and the ordinary Ghanaian stands in never-ending queues for non-existent taxis and buses.

21 January 1983
A very busy week. We had to give two large lunch parties and have been out to dinner eight nights running.

31 January 1983
Life is pretty frightful here now. A million Ghanaian refugees, and that is not an exaggeration, are pouring into Accra after having been kicked out of Nigeria. Ghanaians have always worked in Nigeria, but with the collapse of oil prices Nigeria has had enough and, at a seeming whim, has declared that all Ghanaians must be out of the country within two weeks or they will be arrested and beaten up.

They pass by at the end of our road in a seemingly endless stream. We have seen some incredible sights — enormous, overladen lorries with loads of people, exhausted and hungry after a long journey through Dahomey and Togo, clinging to all sides and fighting to stay on. They are pathetically clutching their few possessions (packets of Omo, boxes of matches and torch batteries), which will be traded here on the black market in exchange for yams, or dried fish, or sometimes, their pride and joy, a transistor.

On arrival they are taken to the trade fair site, which is just up the road from us, to have medical checks. The authorities are trying to get them out of Accra as quickly as possible for reasons of security; there is so little food here that there are fears they may ransack the area in desperation and there is a risk of disease as there is virtually no sanitation available and an absence of toilet facilities. All available lorries in Accra are being commandeered to take them back to their home towns or villages.

The only good thing that may come of all this is that we may get skilled men like teachers and engineers back here to work again, which we so badly need. At present it is all just a rather terrifying chaotic scene.

We were pleased to escape for a three-night break. One night was in Obuasi at the Lonrho gold mine. Their main problem now is security. They reckon that, however stringent their checking system, half the gold is smuggled out over the border to the Ivory Coast and, with the prices it fetches in hard currency, the miners reckon it is worth all the risks. Also they do not work very hard because, like all Ghanaians, in order to survive on their meagre wages they have to do more than one job, for example growing things to sell on the side. And they have endless worry about how to feed themselves and their families. So their hearts are not exactly in their work.

Kumasi, which used to be known as the Garden City, is now known as the Garbage City and it is certainly looking very collapsed. The main reason for the visit was the graduation of doctors from the university there. The British government has given generous aid, along with the Dutch and Germans, so we were all there in an official capacity.

At dinner in the evening Michael was put in the place of honour next to the *asantahene* in the middle of the top table. In front of His Majesty was a bottle of whisky, to which he and Michael helped themselves liberally throughout the long and drawn-out dinner, whilst the rest of us had water if we were lucky, though at the very end we did get a glass of wine.

Back here the seemingly endless stream of thousands of refugees is continuing and seems utterly hopeless and depressing.

PS. Please send dried onions, dried potatoes, soap and toothpaste. And please ring Tim on 7 February to say happy 23rd birthday for me.

19 February 1983

We now have more water problems as they have cut off the entire supply for Accra for three or four days and, knowing them, it may be longer. The other day I came home unexpectedly to find a queue of market mammies in the garden with buckets helping themselves to water from our newly installed storage tank, which as yet has no lid. I had to ask them to leave and locked the gate behind them. I felt terrible, but as we seem to have about 15 people living in the servants' quarters at the moment, our reserves are dwindling far too fast. I am pretty sure that Nasa was behind the whole exercise and was selling the water; it has probably happened frequently, but up to now been undiscovered.

Our cook, Sam, is very sweet, but he must be at least 73, so gets confused sometimes and his standards of hygiene are rather questionable; when there is so little water it all gets too difficult. But don't worry, we have all had cholera jabs recently.

When we leave he will retire to Liberia, his home country, and I am not quite sure how he will manage with all his wives. He married his fifth a year ago. She is 20 and now having a baby and he is terribly proud of that. But he does not keep her with him in Accra; she is deposited out of harm's way in the countryside, with three of the other wives, all in different areas of Ghana, so he does not see them very often. But he seems most concerned about his first wife who is in Liberia and is very happy when a letter comes, rarely sadly, which will have been written by a letter writer and which I help him read.

Here is a letter he wrote to Lucy the other day:

Dear Lucy,

I have received your letter with the gift and I thank you very much for your kindness towards me, Lucy. God will Bless you in all your Life. I will never forgot you in my life and I hope you will continue copy your parent in good doing and I know you will Be Good even than your parent. I now in your Father and Your Mama hand.

After they go I will not stay here any more longer and I will ask there adress so when I reach home I will write you all. I wish you Good Luck that anything that you Touch may be Bless by God and God may give you Long Life.

I end here with Best Greeting to your Brothers and Friends, I
Remain Your Faithfull Old Man Samuel S. Jacob.

[Just before we finally left Ghana we arranged for Sam to get a plane to Liberia. We have heard nothing since waving goodbye at the airport and worry about what may have happened to him in the violent troubles in that country.]

The finance secretary, Kwesi Botchwey, has been having talks in Washington for two weeks and we are all hoping there may be a big IMF loan and devaluation, though last time this happened there was a revolution.

27 February 1983
It is hot and oppressive now with everyone saying the rains will come soon, but although there are black thunderous clouds around nothing ever actually happens.

Sadly poor Sam has had to go away as his eldest son has died. We have been terribly busy and given two dinners for 26 and a lunch for 14, all in nine days.

On top of all this I have had a bad tummy, so I had some tests, which showed an infection from bad water or dirty food. The office then did some research and found our water supply highly unsatisfactory, even though it is always boiled and filtered. There are various reasons for this, but the chief ones are not enough pressure and very old split pipes.

Hopefully we are getting our supply improved, but the overall water situation is getting extremely bad. Sadly it will not be cured by this year's rains as over the last few years the level of the Akosombo Dam has been gradually dropping to a dangerous low. When the Volta River was dammed and a huge valley flooded, this was supposed to end the water problems here once and for all, Ghana even exports electricity, but sadly the rainfall estimates did not allow for so many years of drought.

Our other main problem is electricity, which is also supposed to come from the Akosombo Dam. There are many more cuts nowadays. London has at last recognized our problems and is sending us small generators, by air thankfully; they will only cope with our freezers but will at least make the food situation less acute. We have been asking for generators for the whole time we have been here. [In 1995 the low level of the Akosombo Dam is causing severe problems. The growth in the economy has led to a greatly increased demand for electricity. There is rationing, no more exporting and talk of another dam.]

A lot of food aid arrived for the refugee camps, but sadly many of these supplies have found their way onto the black market. Also a lot of the refugees who were sent back to their villages found their situation so bad that they are now back in Accra with nothing to do and very little to eat. Everyone thinks, hopes, that after the forthcoming elections in Nigeria they will be able to return. Sadly we have not got the doctors, teachers and other professional people we need so badly back here as they were for the most part legally able to stay on in Nigeria.

4 March 1983
Enclosed is some mail for other people, which I would please like you to post, including letters written by an English lady whose Ghanaian husband, who was a minister in the last government, is sadly still in

prison, untried. She has great problems with communication as she cannot use the ordinary mail.

The High Commissioner and his wife, Jimmy and Philippa Mellon, had their farewell cocktail party. There were over 400 guests and it was complete chaos as there were not enough servants, not enough glasses and people were fighting for drinks. At one stage Philippa and I were in the kitchen madly washing up glasses as people were having to drink out of cans.

The following day we had drinks here for 70, electricity problems all day and of course the endless lack of water. But we survived somehow. When Ghanaians get invited for drinks from 6.30 to 8.00 p.m. nowadays they arrive at 6.15 and stay until 9.00 p.m. to eat and drink everything in sight and take anything they can find away with them in their pockets.

Oh, yes, that was yesterday. This morning Michael had 12 people for a working breakfast for our house guests and they all arrived at 7.00 a.m.

Our cook, Sam, has thankfully now returned from burying his son. The train in which he was travelling broke loose from the engine and careered uncontrollably down a hill, so lots of people jumped from the train in terror and there were many injuries. Luckily Sam stayed in his seat and was all right.

Another attempted coup at the weekend. This time we heard nothing at all and did not know it had happened until Tuesday. They are connecting it with the November plot.

We had a visit from Sir William Ofori Atta, known as Paa Willie. He was a founding members of Independent Ghana and was imprisoned by the British for freedom fighting. He is an incredibly old man who has really lived the history of this country and knows more about it than anyone else; his contemporaries are all dead. I love talking to him. To make ends meet, his wife does dressmaking and, at the party at the Residence, he told me she could not get any material. I mentioned I had some I was not using and, lo and behold, the next day they called and were so happy I could help. It is tragic that the most distinguished old Ghanaian should have so many problems.

Nasa came screaming into the house carrying his two-year-old baby, who looked terrible, and said please could we go to the doctor fast. Luckily our doctor and very good friend who lives nearby, Harold

Philips, was having a surgery and was able to see her immediately. She was having convulsions caused by malaria. He injected her, and treated her, and she is much better. I suppose if they had been living in the bush she would have been one of the million Africans who die of malaria each year.

Harold Philips was dean of the medical school here, but had to resign and go into private practice because he was not paid a living wage by the government. Even so, he has had such difficulty feeding his own family that once or twice we have left some rice on his doorstep — anonymously to save embarrassment.

Thank heavens I am at last feeling better. The infection caused by dirty food or water lasted four weeks and, after a succession of medicines, hopefully I am cured.

And so we go on with life in Africa. But at least we have an endless variety of activities and happenings. You will remember that I did find life in New Zealand rather dull.

10 May 1983
Here the situation is deteriorating very fast. We were supposed to be visiting Kumasi, Mim and Obuasi this week, but have had to postpone the visit. There are calls for a general strike and there have been a lot of rather violent incidents over the last few days between 'revolutionary workers' and students, which have now resulted in the University of Lagon, Accra, being officially closed. In fact the students had nearly all left anyway as it was getting too dangerous. It was announced today that the university will stay closed for three years and that its accommodation will be used by the workers.

There is no food in this part of the country and the rains are failing. This, together with the bush fires, which have been appalling and have destroyed two thirds of the crops, leave a crisis situation. We may be getting a massive UN food donation, but nothing definite yet.

Four babies at the children's home to which I take milk (when I can get it) are in a state of real starvation and I reckon they will be dead very soon.

Nan Burns, the wife of the newly arrived High Commissioner, Kevin Burns, comes with me to the home, which helps a lot. Kevin and Nan are a great asset to life in Accra and we get on very well with them. Nan, who is sweet and artistic, comes from Ceylon. Kevin met her

178

when he was on a posting there and we have lots of mutual friends. Kevin has a very relaxed manner, which Ghanaians enjoy. He is extremely laid back about Ghanaian life and problems; nothing seems to upset him or get him down. He is Irish and completely without pomposity, and is a very good story teller.

But for the time being Rawlings and his men are managing to keep the army reasonably content foodwise, and this is the only way they will hang on. The nasty thing about the situation in Ghana now is that the normal, cheerful, friendly people here are getting out of hand and the violence is increasing with lots of punch-ups and injuries and a general loss of control. Apart from the food troubles, the situation has been made worse by a strict devaluation budget, complying with IMF instructions even though the IMF loan has still not come through. Also, the findings of the tribunal on the judges' murders last year have still not been published, but everyone thinks that Kojo Tsikata, the power behind Rawlings, was responsible for organizing them.

We went to the teaching hospital last week to present £80,000 worth of equipment, which we had managed to get into the country under the Nigerian refugee aid programme, to the children's wards.

Life is as busy as usual — people to stay, drinks, dinners, lunches. There are a lot of farewell parties, some for diplomats who arrived with or after us, as well as for various British people who have been here for years. The UK population here has halved in the last three years.

And of course the Ghanaian exodus is continuing fast. The latest friend of ours to leave is Francis Nkrumah, son of the first president of independent Ghana and self-styled Star of Africa, Kwame Nkrumah. He is going to Zimbabwe, which is a popular country for emigration. He is a paediatrician and his wife is a headmistress — both professions desperately needed here right now. When we arrived three years ago he used to say it was terrible the way people were deserting their country.

I shall be coming home in July on leave, ahead of Michael, to try to find somewhere to live. And we hope very much we shall know the definite date of our final departure soon.

[In August, whilst we were away, Kwame Pianin was gaoled for 18 years for his part in the plot to topple the government of Flight Lieutenant Rawlings on 23 November 1982. He was one of two civilians involved in an otherwise military attempt. This was one of four coup attempts since the revolution. Three months previously, in June 1983, about 52 detainees from three prisons, some of whom were involved in the 23 November plot, had escaped in a mass prison breakout. This had been organized by other former servicemen who had escaped arrest in the wake of the coup attempt and had been sentenced to various prison terms *in absentia*. They had gone into exile in Togo and had infiltrated the country with heavy arms and ammunition.

After releasing prisoners and holding the Ghana Broadcasting Corporation for a few hours, they were routed by loyal troops. They then scattered into small bands, where they remained on the run or in hiding. Those who were captured were shot.

Kwame Pianin did not take advantage of this breakout. He was finally released from prison in 1992 and is now secretary of one of the new political parties. His two sons had been sent to America for their education after his imprisonment and one of them married the daughter of the newspaper tycoon, Rupert Murdoch.]

22 October 1983
Well, here I am, back in Ghana for a very short final tour. Thankfully the atmosphere has considerably eased since I left. We even have a picture in the paper this week of Rawlings talking and smiling with the new US ambassador.

The Libyan/Russian bloc is now no longer in full control of the government. Having received cool responses to his appeals for support to the Soviets, Cubans and Libyans, Rawlings has apparently now swallowed his pride and turned to the West again. This pragmatic streak, his genuine patriotism and extraordinarily popular appeal to the poor of Ghana, are enabling him to survive far longer than any of us thought possible in January last year.

[Not all went smoothly. The Rawlings government remained eccentric and dictatorial, though not too murderous, and we felt deep disquiet over many of the things it did. Nevertheless, our relations with Ghana steadily improved. In 1983 the World Bank and IMF agreed to give Ghana $400 million per annum in exchange for accepting a rigorous and austere programme of development.]

There is more food around now and the small harvest has helped, though sadly there has not been enough to store and it is all being eaten rather too quickly.

But I am jolly glad we are leaving soon as the rainfall is way below what it should be. Everything should be green and lush at this time of year, but our garden is dry and brown with lots of things dying. The Akosombo Dam is getting lower all the time and water and electricity cuts are increasing.

Just for the moment things are generally more relaxed and there are fewer soldiers, tanks and road blocks around. But the universities are still closed and the hospitals have no drugs. The hospital was thrilled with the X-ray film I brought back as apparently there is still little or no film obtainable in the country. The brain drain is continuing, and there is a severe shortage of petrol.

So the end is really in sight now and I am enjoying myself very much because of it. I would not be as happy if we had another year to do, but I would love to know where we are going next.

[Since the World Bank and IMF agreement of 1983 came into operation, Ghana has received $2.5 billion and, unlike other African countries, has fulfilled the terms of the agreement. In the words of a World Bank official, 'The Ghanaians have kept their word and done it.' The economy has grown by one-third since 1982 and the country's infrastructure has improved considerably, but the austere and rigorous programme laid down by the agreement has led to great dissatisfaction.

In 1995, following elections in 1992, President Rawlings is still in power, now at the head of a civilian government. Kojo Tsikata also is still very much alive — and in office.]

6
Singapore

During our time in Accra we had sold the house in Guildford and I had flown home and bought a flat in Highgate, north London. We spent three months in the UK, after which Michael was appointed Deputy High Commissioner and commercial counsellor in Singapore, one of the busiest posts in the world for commerce. He was pleased.

I was very keen to work in Singapore and heard that there was a big demand for English teachers. Although I had taught English before, I had no formal qualifications and, hearing that Singapore is a very organized country where it would be impossible to get work without paper documents, I did a TEFL (Teaching English as a Foreign Language) course at International House in London.

This meant arriving in Singapore in May 1984, a month after Michael had taken up his appointment.

Since independence Singapore had been under the control of Lee Kuan Yew, an Oxford starred first, barrister and former freedom fighter, whom the British had once imprisoned. His autocratic government had transformed Singapore into one of the best-organized and most modern hi-tech city states in the world.

5 May 1984
My flight was awful. I was stuck at Muscat airport for eight hours and then, when I finally arrived at 4.00 a.m., Michael greeted me with the news that we had to give a drinks party that evening for Kenneth Baker, Minister of Trade and Industry, followed by dinner with the High Commissioner, Sir Peter Moon, and his French wife, Lucille, who live

next door to us. Surprisingly I enjoyed it all, though I had very little idea of where I was or to whom I was talking. Perhaps entertaining is easier if one is suffering from lack of sleep and jet lag, and Kenneth Baker, though a bit smooth, was very friendly, articulate and easy company. He was over here dealing with information technology; apparently Singapore is mad about computers.

I had only been in our house for 48 hours when we had to move out again into the house of a colleague who is away on leave. This was to allow our house to be reroofed, painted and refurbished, which it badly needs since water pours through whenever it rains, which is rather often.

On May Day Bank Holiday we played 18 holes of golf at the Singapore Island and Country Club. Located in the middle of the island, surrounded by jungle and built around a reservoir with hardly a house in sight, this must be one of the most beautiful golf courses in the world.

The next day I went on a shopping expedition: the shops here are quite fantastic and the country is a food paradise. You can buy anything you want at any time, but in case you do not feel like shopping a man from Cuppage Market, a large market nearby, will telephone every morning to ask what you need and deliver it all before lunch.

We had a delicious dinner last night with some old friends from Ceylon, George and Marie Claire Seymour. He is now the Canadian High Commissioner here. Singapore abounds with excellent restaurants of all types — Chinese, Indian, Malay, French, Italian, Greek, anything you like — and if you do not want to go to a restaurant there are hawker stalls.

These are areas with stalls selling all types of food. You go around to different stalls, choose what you want, then sit down and wait for the stall keepers to bring you what you have ordered. It is cheap and tasty. As far as I can ascertain, Singaporeans eat all their meals out and the stalls are open 24 hours a day.

It is incredible to live in such an efficient, attractive place. I spend my whole time comparing it with Ghana. The town is really lovely; there is green everywhere and trees and flowers abound. It is quite safe to walk anywhere at any time of the day or night and there is a feeling of total security. There are very strict punishments for misbehaviour here, including flogging, which is so severe that it often has to be administered in more than one session because the unfortunate victim loses consciousness.

There is always water — you can drink it straight from the taps — and electricity is always available too. The rainy season should be over by now, but we are still getting heavy rains and thunderstorms, usually at night. These are majestic, but it can be quite alarming when they crash overhead.

We eat all our meals outside here. There are hardly any mosquitoes as men come around regularly to spray the gardens.

24 May 1984

The weather is very odd. It is still raining, even though it is supposed to be the dry season. There were torrential rains two days ago, with people wading waist high through floods and cars stranded everywhere. Although the Chinese are incredibly efficient they do not seem to be able to cope with the monsoons.

Sadly the rains are not helping the progress on our house, but we are hoping to be in by early July. Then we will be able to unpack, settle down and really feel at home.

Life in Singapore is hectic. We have been out seven evenings on the trot; and Michael has to go out to one lunch after another as well as to endless business functions. The Commercial Department is very busy here with 3000 UK business visitors a year, 12 or more trade missions and lots of trade fairs.

The foreign community here is extremely large. It includes between 10,000 and 12,000 British, approximately the same number of Americans, 14,000 Japanese and the largest colony of expatriate Swedes outside London.

Some friends from Ghana came through the other day. We all went out to dinner and they were amazed at the endless choice of restaurants. Singaporeans do like their food very much. Making money, eating and shopping seem to be the three main objects of their existence.

Getting teaching work here, even with the TEFL qualification, seems rather difficult, but I think I am onto something quite good. The British Council has won a contract from the Singaporean government to make 60 films to support a programme to teach English in 200 centres around the country. The government, or should I say Lee Kuan Yew, the Prime Minister, is determined to raise the standard of English here. It is now the first language to be taught in all schools and is used by Chinese, Indians and Malays. But overall the standard is very mixed and there are many older people who do not speak English at all.

The British Council has engaged a Singaporean film company, but needs help with the actors' English and with script writing. I have been along twice, enjoyed it and have said that I could work three days a week. If the films are good the British Council hopes to get a further contract for 100 films for television.

Sorry about my scrawl. Oh for my typewriter!

7 June 1984

With this house we are borrowing come two very old and wrinkled Chinese sisters. They are apparently in their early seventies, but look years older. I have found out what they can cook — with difficulty as they speak very little English — and it is not very much, so we have the same very simple menus over and over again. In fact they really run the house for me according to age-old tradition, so I happily go along with all their ways and do what they tell me.

I have spoken to all the children on the phone. What a change from Ghana!

23 July 1984

We have been incredibly busy. We have been moving house and unpacking crates we have not seen since we had left Ghana, which were rather the worse for the journey and storage.

On our removal date, 2 July, we were both stricken at 4.00 a.m. with the most appalling tropical food poisoning/bug. It completely laid us out, made moving very difficult and left us feeling awful for over a week.

But we have now got over that and have moved into our house, Ladyvale. It is lovely and large, has a wing for lots of servants and must be worth millions. There is three-quarters of an acre of garden and it is located just off the fashionable Orchard Road. It is very peaceful, even though it is near the centre of town and the High Commission. There are still lots of jobs unfinished and people keep turning up to do things. The new roof still leaks when it rains and we have come to the conclusion that Chinese workmen are not all that much better than Africans when it comes to repairing houses. Sadly the servants' wing is empty.

185

Ah Foo, our cook whom we inherited from our predecessors and whom I sent for a check-up as he did not seem at all well, has very high blood pressure and, as he is 72, has got to stop work. So his wife, Ah Eng, is retiring too.

Singaporeans do very little domestic work now as factory work is far more lucrative and there is lots of it. We therefore have to employ Filipinos, who are desperate to get out of their country where the economic situation is terrible, but getting them work permits is a hassle and takes an inordinate amount of time and effort. The Singaporean authorities do not really like imported labour and have stringent laws to control it, including medicals every six months, a deposit of £2500 in case they do anything naughty and a return air fare, all paid for by us. As we really need two with a house this size, me working and an awful lot of entertaining, the total bill is very large, but sadly, because we work for the British government, we get no help. Needless to say other diplomats here, bankers and expatriates get these expenses paid by their employers. Still, no doubt we will get it all sorted out soon.

Lucy has arrived, and it is lovely having her here. We are doing super tourist things like visiting the zoo, Chinatown, Sentosa Island, mosques and temples.

24 July 1984

Filming is very busy and yesterday we were out shooting from 10 a.m. to 8 p.m. There is always a lot of hanging around, but often in quite unusual places, and always with all the locals, so I am beginning to feel what Singapore life is really like in factories, hospitals, schools and shops.

We have been shooting family scenes in high-rise flats. The government's policy is to get everyone from shanty-town-type areas rehoused in modern flats, and this policy is moving very fast. Every area being developed is planned with enormous care and all the trees, grass and flowers are planted before the builders start work. Consequently, by the time the people move in there is a feeling of permanence and the soullessness so often associated with new developments is avoided.

Filming means eating! When a scene is finished we all troop off to the nearest hawker-stall centre and have a meal and, in true Chinese fashion, this can mean six or seven meals a day. However, nobody ever seems to get fat from eating local food. The only fat people you see around are kids, who love the American fast foods now appearing on the Singaporean scene. Macdonalds in the fashionable area of Orchard Road is apparently the busiest Macdonalds in the world.

15 August 1984

Andrew has now arrived and he and Lucy are fine and enjoying themselves. We went up to Rawa, an island off the east coast of Malaysia, and had four days away. We drove to Mersin, had a night there in a ramshackle old resthouse, and then had a one-and-a-half-hour ferry ride across to the little island.

It is a coral island with magnificent snorkelling. The weather again was variable, but there was enough sun for us all to get incredibly brown in such a short time. We went with friends from the office, took lots and lots of books and stayed in little wooden huts on the beach. It was basic, but very peaceful.

It was interesting driving through Malaysia. Although rich, it is very much a Third World country and a contrast to sophisticated Singapore. Most of the drive there, three hours or so, was through miles and miles of oil palm and rubber estates. We took quite a lot of food and drink with us because it was expensive on Rawa, despite being so basic. But the east coast is lovely, though inaccessible in the winter months because all the roads get flooded.

Prince Charles was flying back from opening Parliament in Brunei the other day and Michael had to go to the airport when the plane came through in case he wanted to get off. He did and they had a nice discussion about Trinity College, Cambridge and Michael Vyvyan, the tutor they had in common. He seemed interested in everything, ranging from whether the FCO had sabbaticals to the difference between Ghana and Francophone Africa. He thought he would enjoy a sabbatical at Trinity and when Michael asked what subject, he grinned and said he supposed constitutional history. Michael managed to arrange for him to have a look at the new British Aerospace plane, which was on a publicity tour of the Far East. They climbed all over it together to the delight of the crew, who needless to say took thousands of photos. [Prince Charles's memory is impressive. When he met Michael at an environmental conference ten years later (by then Michael was doing a completely different job), he recalled the meeting at Singapore airport.]

We are still slightly in the air about servants. We are taking two

Filipinas on at the beginning of September on temporary permits. They are very good, but have already been here for two and a half years and extension permits are difficult to obtain. But we are hoping for the best. It will certainly help when all this is settled.

We spent three days in Malaysia at Desaru, which is a fairly primitive beach resort about two hours' drive from here on the other side of the bridge connecting Singapore to Johore. We stayed in a do-it-yourself cabin, which had a fridge, a cooker, mice, rats, lizards, mosquitoes, geckos and bats, the last of which had a disturbing habit of swooping down on one at night in bed. It was on a lovely long empty beach, with good swimming and lovely walking, and was a good break from Singapore. But even though we took all our own food and only had one hotel meal, it was expensive.

5 September 1984

Our two new Filipinas have started work but we still have not got their work permits confirmed and just hope they will come through by the end of the month. They are sweet and work very hard and are at the moment cleaning the entire house, which Ah Eng and Ah Foo had not worried about too much as, according to old Chinese custom, an annual turn-out to celebrate Chinese New Year is all that is required.

Today is a national holiday. There are never-ending religious holidays here for Christians, Hindus, Muslims and Buddhists.

10 September 1984

The wife of our last High Commissioner in Accra, Nan Burns, whom I knew so well, has been killed in a car crash on a potholed road outside Accra. A terrible tragedy. The driver was killed too, but the rest of the family are all right, though injured, and they have managed to fly them all out to hospital in London. That makes four members of the High Commission in Accra killed in three years — three on the terrible roads and our defence adviser who had the tragic drowning accident.

1 October 1984

Andrew starts work today at Birkbeck Montagu [a law firm in London]. We had two very smart suits made for him here and he was looking forward to his first day in the City.

Lucy and he have had a few days together in London and he is going to take her up to York to start her teacher training course. I wish I were there with them.

My two Filipinas walked out after two weeks. One decided she must go back and get married, she has to find someone first, and the other decided she must go to university. After two months of hassle getting their papers cleared, I thought it was the last straw, but in fact I think it was a blessing in disguise as another Filipina, Lita Rala, has turned up. She has worked with the Filipino ambassador both here for ten years and in Romania and Czechoslovakia — so she knows what is what, and also she seems to be able to manage on her own, which will save us a lot of money. We are now in the process of getting her papers cleared and I only pray they don't say she has been here too long and must leave. It has taken us seven months to feel settled down here.

My job may well fold up because there are endless problems with the film company, which are now unlikely to be resolved. It is disappointing as I enjoyed it, especially the getting around and finding out about life in Singapore. So it will be back to TEFL teaching.

8 October 1984
The High Commissioner goes off next week for four months leave so Michael will be acting High Commissioner. Since winter is the busy time here when all the visitors come for the sunshine, we are having to arrange a stream of official lunches, dinners and cocktails.

10 November 1984
For some reason we arrived at a reception by the back door and found Lee Kuan Yew standing alone with no one talking to him. He seemed very friendly and talked surprisingly frankly about Singapore's problems with the Islamic revival in Malaysia and about why Singapore needed to be so strict in controlling immigration from less wealthy countries. He spoke entirely without pomposity and as if he were genuinely interested to hear our views.

17 December 1984
Life is very busy indeed. This week we have two or three parties each night culminating in the British Business Association Ball on Saturday, at which we are the guests of honour. And this is in spite of having turned down a lot of invitations.

It is sad we shall not all be together at Christmas, and very sad that none of the children will be with us, but we will be thinking of you all and shall drink to your health.

29 December 1984

It was good to speak to you all on Christmas Day but, though we spent the day with friends, we found it very strange all on our own.

Lovely to think you are arriving on 16 January. I shall meet you at the airport, which is very efficient and impressive and decorated with beautiful orchids.

Happy New Year!

[During her stay my mother, Helen, visited Glencaird, the house in which she had been born in 1913 and in which she had spent the first eight years of her life when her father was working in Singapore. It is now the residence of the Australian High Commissioner and his wife. They told her that the house was haunted by a lady in a long white dress seen often over the years and that the Chinese maid often heard a strange voice calling, 'Helen, Helen'. The maid imitated the voice and my mother said it was exactly like the voice of her mother. No one in the house knew that it had been previously inhabited by anyone of that name. We have many photos of my grandmother wearing long white dresses!]

21 February 1985

Yesterday was Chinese New Year. It is now the year of the ox, which is my year, and particularly important as it is the year of the fire ox, which happens only every 60 years. The elements for this appearance will draw me to power and importance and make me more forceful and prouder than other oxen. But I must beware as I am a fiery ox who can overestimate my abilities. But basically I am honest and fair and can be very protective of my family and friends.

Life in Singapore is dominated by the New Year and it is difficult to live here without a little belief in the Chinese system.

At midday we went to a Chinese multi-multi-millionaire's party, such a spread of food and drink you have never seen, all laid out in great style in his garden. There were some Europeans there, but mostly Chinese.

Ten years ago Europeans would apparently have been in the majority at such occasions, but times are changing very fast. Ten years hence the Europeans will be an even smaller group.

This is not really surprising for although Singapore's growth rate is slowing down, it is still a very expensive place in which to live and it is much cheaper to keep employees in the UK and send them out for four or five visits a year. Also, they are paid in Singapore dollars which, with the exchange rate as it is, makes it expensive for the companies.

The Istana, the president's magnificent house, was open to the public as it was a bank holiday. It is right in the middle of town, with beautiful grounds and a nine-hole golf course.

While we were walking around we noticed a group of people standing by the front entrance. When we got closer we saw that the president, Devan Nair, was standing on the steps and that people were going up to shake his hand and pose with him for their photos to be taken. It was all very informal and sweet. He has mellowed since his early days as the violent communist agitator the British imprisoned for three years.

[Not long after this Devan Nair's time as president came to a sad end. He had taken to drink and on a visit to Brunei had allegedly fondled the breasts of some young dancers, though only the alcoholism was reported in the press. There followed a merciless destruction of the man by the government-controlled media, including his old Unionist friend Lee Kuan Yew, who spoke on television for half an hour about the president's terrible alcoholism and his disgrace to the state. Devan Nair had to leave the country and go into exile.]

27 February 1985
Having made all the preparations and had a drink or two with the guests, I am now in hiding in the study while Michael entertains James Prior, the former Minister for Northern Ireland, and 11 other worthy men to lunch. He is now chairman of the GEC and is here to sign a contract, travelling under a false name so that the IRA do not get him. He is very relaxed and easy company. Apparently, his brother the vicar, who married us all those years ago, is now retired.

And I am about to go off and teach three new pupils — Indonesians. My teaching programme is gradually filling up, as is my knowledge of Eastern life. Conversations with students in English is a great way of finding out about what goes on without appearing nosy.

Life is generally very busy and also far too hot.

27 March 1985

The new High Commissioner, Sir Hamilton Whyte, has at last arrived with his wife Sheila, an artist, so hopefully life will be a bit quieter. He was kicked out of Lagos, where he had been High Commissioner, at very short notice last year as tit for tat following the expulsion of some Nigerian diplomats after a drugged Nigerian wanted on criminal charges had been discovered in a packing case at London airport. With two years to go before he retires, he has arrived here bursting with energy. He is an unusual rather non-conformist diplomat and enjoys wearing way-out clothes to official suit-clad gatherings.

Last week we gave a party to introduce them. There were 180 guests, so thank heavens it did not rain and all went well. The previous week we had a party for 85 for the Manchester Trade Mission. I am now thankfully going to relax and do less official entertaining. Ham Whyte has got a full-time staff of five and they have sensibly taken on an English housekeeper to arrange it all.

16 April 1985

Maggie Thatcher visited Singapore on a long-planned trip to the Far East and our old friend Robin Butler is travelling with her as principal private secretary. [Robin Butler later became head of the Civil Service.] When she arrived at her hotel Michael spent half an hour telling her all about the country as although reams of paperwork had been sent to her in advance, she obviously waits until she actually arrives in a country to sort it out. She started by cross-questioning Michael and luckily he knew the answers. Apparently she always starts by checking people out and if they cannot perform properly she ignores them. After the president's stag state banquet dinner at the Istana she held a postmortem in her room and the day's activities were analysed until 1.00 a.m., with Denis pouring the drinks. Maggie apparently expressed concern about whether she would need a hat for the early morning parade the following day at the Commonwealth war graves. To calm any possible anxiety, Robin quickly left the room to check that she could borrow a hat from one of the staff as, despite all the briefing, this aspect had not been covered.

Michael had spent most of the day with Denis — mainly visiting and having lunch — and they got on like a house on fire. As a successful former industrialist, Denis was on his home ground in Singapore; he was especially knowledgeable about chemicals and was authoritative and friendly.

The only time I saw Maggie was at a reception where we were lined up and she was not in the least bit interested in talking to me. She just gave me a rather unfriendly look and walked on. I don't think she is very interested in women.

Anyway, thank heavens the visit's over. The amount of preparation for it was extraordinary. She works at the most impossible pressure and refuses to take things like jet lag into consideration. By the time she got to Sri Lanka on the next leg of her trip the strain of five countries in as many days was beginning to tell. Her throat was sore and so was her temper and the High Commission and government there apparently got the rough end of her tongue.

14 May 1985

Two weeks ago I met some friendly Chinese, Peggy and Thor Sen Lee, and they very kindly invited us to spend the following day with them at one of their houses on an island called Ubin. From door to door it only takes 40 minutes by car and boat; it is a lovely place, with a comfortable house and nice people. We have an open invitation to go with them any Sunday we want. One feels one is in a different world there, so it is a good way of escaping the claustrophobia of Singapore. One can swim, talk, eat a delicious lunch under the coconut trees, play mah-jong if one wants to, sleep, or look at Singapore's skyscrapers across the waters.

Next weekend we are going with friends to the Malay island of Desaru. This is where we stay in a shack and bring our own food, where it is hot and sticky, there is no air conditioning, and flies and mosquitoes abound. But never mind, it is a break.

It has been far, far too hot — in the nineties with terrible humidity. My energy is waning fast and I long for cold weather.

But we will be home soon now!

4 October 1985

We're gradually settling back into life here, but it takes time after three months away.

Singapore is having problems. Everything is slowing down, there are lots of bankruptcies and a lot of people are becoming unemployed.

Sadly this is having effects on the people who want private English teaching. My clientele has dropped right off and my Indonesians have left the country. I am now advertising in the Japanese newspaper.

16 October 1985

Social life has not been quite so busy. I say that, but looking at my diary I see that we have spent eight evenings out since I last wrote 12 days ago, not to mention lunches. But it just doesn't feel so busy. I suppose feeling resilient after leave helps and several of the evenings have been enjoyable, which makes a difference.

More teaching seems to be looming, for I am breaking into the Japanese market. I am fixing up several groups, including one for Japanese bankers who work six days a week from 8.00 a.m. until 10.00 p.m. and find it difficult to fit in the odd hour for a lesson. I have never taught Japanese men before and am interested to learn more about their lifestyle. I teach a group of well-educated Japanese women, all with university degrees, who seem quite happy once they have married to stay at home and be domestic. When the husband arrives home at 11.00 p.m. there is a piping hot dinner waiting for him and on Sundays he rushes off to the golf course, leaving his wife at home all day to look after the children.

26 October 1985

At present we have a colleague staying with us — Roger Talboys, whom we met on a visit to Houston, where he was Consul General. The poor soul is now 'our man in Hanoi' and needs to escape as often as possible for survival and sanity. The Residence in Hanoi is a former French brothel with a circular balcony and all the bedrooms leading into the centre for ease of access. We had a successful dinner party for him, in fact it was too successful. In Singapore people usually leave by 11.30 p.m. in midweek, but for some reason this time they didn't and by the time we had our nightcap with our guest, it was very, very late.

17 November 1985

Of course our great news is that Andrew passed the ghastly law exams. Tim was with him when the results came through. We had some happy phone conversations and were only sorry we could not be there to celebrate. Andrew is blissfully happy and so are we.

There was a reception at the High Commissioner's Residence for 100 war widows and 200 veterans from the 'forgotten army' in Burma. They are part of a group from England being flown out by the government to Singapore, Malaysia and Thailand to commemorate VJ day in 1945. Here they will be at the fortieth memorial service at Kranji, which will also be attended by the Duke of Kent, lots of old generals, and the Secretary of State for Defence, Michael Heseltine.

When Michael asked the Singapore Foreign Affairs Department some months earlier whether such a visit might cause offence to the 14,000 or so Japanese who live and work in Singapore (and as such be considered unwise by the Singaporean authorities), he was told that all this was history now. The government would allow the visit and, if asked, would also agree to a similar visit from the Japanese. However, Michael was left with the firm impression that our visit would be more welcome as the Chinese still dislike the Japanese and would not mind a bit if they were upset.

The Chinese are very pragmatic. I think Singapore is the only ex-British colony in which we have lived that, on gaining independence, did not immediately change the names of all the British-named streets.

On Saturday morning, after I had got rid of a pupil at 10.30 a.m., Michael and Ann Heseltine arrived to stay, plus entourage of about eight. Fortunately only one of the entourage, the armed detective, stayed with us, very unobtrusively spending most of his time happily talking to Lita in the kitchen.

There were flurries of red boxes and telegrams and then he was whisked off to see Prime Minister Lee Kuan Yew. This is a great honour as the Prime Minister only chooses to see ministers or VIPs who interest him, though a few honoured people he respects, such as Kissinger and the Minister of State of Australia, Malcolm Fraser, visit him two or three times a year for a casual chat. He had apparently refused to meet the previous Secretary of State for Defence — at Singapore airport *en route* to some other destination — despite a request from us to do so. Mrs Heseltine, Sheila Whyte and I went out to lunch at the Cricket Club, which went OK after we discovered we had Harrow in common.

When we arrived back from our respective lunches we all drove up to the Bird Park, which is very impressive and the Heseltines, who both have a passion for birds, loved it. We returned here half an hour late to find TV crews, cameramen and lots of reporters in wait all over the house, including the BBC, *The Times*, French TV, SBC and the *Mirror*. TV interviews were held in our dining room, followed by a press conference on the veranda. Then the press left, Michael went to the airport to meet the Duke of Kent, Ann Heseltine went off to have a rest and I was left in the drawing room with Michael Heseltine.

He began to look at a red box; I offered him a drink. We then started to talk because he caught my eye while he was reading his papers at arm's length. He admitted with a smile that he needed glasses, but was a bit vain and had to think of his public image.

We were still talking one and a half hours later when we realized that we were due to be next door in ten minutes to meet the Duke of Kent for dinner, so we hurried to get ready and to wake up his wife. He was relaxed and charming, far more so than some other official guests we have had to stay over the past 20-odd years.

The next day I managed to produce breakfast at 6.15 a.m. and we went off to Kranji war cemetery for the memorial service. It was a very simple and moving ceremony. The large monument of the war memorial was silhouetted against the sky by the rising sun, and rows and rows of graves, all beautifully kept and all with flowers, stretched far away down the hillside.

It meant a tremendous amount to the widows from home to find their husbands' graves, and to the war veterans, who thought they had belonged to a forgotten army, to take part in such an occasion.

Then we came home, had another breakfast and paid a visit to the botanical gardens, where we were given a good tour by the director. Then Mr Heseltine and Michael went to pay a call on the president. We joined them afterwards at the famous Raffles Hotel where a lunch with lots of speeches was being held for the veterans and war widows. After this we accompanied the Heseltines to the airport and they left on their air-force plane, which was comfortable as they had a bed each and a little sitting room.

They were going on to Burma for another similar ceremony. The Duke of Kent flew in from England for the ceremony and flew back to England the next day.

It is Lita's birthday today. I told her she could have a party here, so she had about 25 Filipino friends for lunch. Thank heavens we have her to work for us, she is so efficient and 100 per cent reliable. I do not know how I would manage without her.

12 December 1985

We are as busy as ever. Apart from parties for three lots of good friends who are sadly leaving, I am giving a cocktail party here for the Deputy Governor of the Bank of England, which will be followed by dinner next door at the High Commissioner's. Earlier in the year we held a dinner party for the Governor, Robin Leigh-Pemberton, who very kindly tried to explain the British economy to me over the soup, though he was much happier talking about cricket. He said he was reluctant to talk to the press, as it made too much of anything he said.

Thank heavens I did the TEFL course before coming out here. I have quite a lot of work at the moment, which is lucky given that the FCO has just cut our allowances by 40 per cent because the pound is strong. The cuts are far too savage and there has been endless complaining, but even now that the pound is dropping, the FCO is sticking to its decision.

The FCO even had the nerve to backdate the cut by several months. Our allowances are based on the cost of living in Bromley and are not supposed to be able to buy us a higher standard of living here than there. However, wives in Bromley can work if they want to, whereas here it is more difficult for them to supplement their husband's income. Though in theory there is no difficulty about getting jobs, in practice it is pretty impossible to obtain a work permit. Singapore strongly believes in job reservation and has its own experts in most fields. There is very little scope unless you have a skill they do not and a qualification to prove it — for example, how to speak English with an English accent and a TEFL certificate.

We are spending this Xmas with friends, very sadly with no children here for the second year running. We shall be thinking of you all and wishing we were there. We shall drink to you on Xmas Day at lunch our time, which is the middle of the night your time. And you can drink to us at your lunch time, when we shall be just about going to bed!

1 January 1986

It was so sad we did not speak to you on Xmas Day; we tried but just could not get through. On Boxing Day life here resumes to normal. The shops are all open and everyone is back at work.

On 3 January, our 27th wedding anniversary, we are off to spend four days in Jakarta, Indonesia, on an official 'acclimatization' visit —

rather late. We then go on to Bali for a five-day holiday. [On our return from Bali we heard that Michael's mother had died and he flew back to England for the funeral.]

While Michael was away for ten days I did very little except teach and I certainly did not feel like going to parties. I spent the two weekends with Peggy and Thor Sen Lee, who were very hospitable and kind. The weather was quite ghastly for ten days, we had nothing but rain, and I really regretted not flying home too.

17 February 1986

If you want to experience bad driving come to Malaysia for Chinese New Year. We drove to Kuala Lumpur *en route* to the Cameron Highlands to stay with Peggy and Thor Sen, who have a house there. We had a terrible seven-hour drive on appalling Malay roads — very crowded, single windy tracks on which lousy drivers, in their impatience, overtake each other all the time on both sides. [These roads have now been dramatically improved.] There was one incredible snarl-up when a solid block of traffic (crammed five abreast and completely blocking the road) met another solid block coming in the opposite direction. The traffic was brought to a complete standstill and we all sat there getting hotter and hotter — it was midday — until finally, after an hour's impasse, the police arrived and somehow managed to get things moving.

We stayed for three days in Kuala Lumpur with David Gillmore, our lively and friendly High Commissioner there, and his wife Lucille, who is French, sweet and very welcoming. [After his posting in Malaysia David Gillmore became head of the Diplomatic Service and his wife president of the DSWA.] The men went off for 36 hours by air-force transport to a conference in Penang and I stayed in Kuala Lumpur with Lucille, which I thoroughly enjoyed; she gave me a lovely time sightseeing and generally getting the feel of the place. They live in the most beautiful house, Carcosa, which was given to the British government by Tunku Abdul Rahman, but which we are now, at their request, giving back to the Malaysian government. One of the reasons for this is that the Union Jack flying on the building both overlooks Parliament and is the highest flag in the city. Carcosa is vast, twice the size of the Residence here, and costs at least £10,000 a month to run, so I think we are really quite pleased to give it back. They have given us money to build a new house, which will be on a small site by the golf course and quite a contrast.

The drive on up to the Cameron Highlands took about four hours and was very windy and sick-making. The weather got cooler and cooler and when we finally arrived the air was fresh and invigorating. We felt marvellous. The Lees have a lovely house up there with a beautiful garden in a wonderful situation overlooking hills all around. There is tea grown up there and it was reminiscent of the planters' houses in Ceylon. There were about 16 of us in their house and a further ten in another family house, so we were a large party.

There was wonderful food, three times a day, and the upcountry air gives you a great appetite. Everyone walked and played golf and tennis. We met quite a few Malaysians, Tunku this and Tunku that. These people are so rich and have an incredible lifestyle. Malaysia is a very fertile country and their aristocratic families who own the rubber, cocoa, tin, tea, timber and everything else do extremely well.

31 March 1986

Please excuse my typing but my eyes have become very bad again. We had to take malaria pills for Indonesia, Bali and Malaysia and, as in Ghana, they have affected my sight.

Lucy arrived in good form, having had a 22-hour journey on Air Romania, the cheapest flight there is, with five stops *en route*. It sounded quite frightful, but they fed them non-stop, though the stewardesses never once smiled.

The day after she arrived we had the Earl and Lady Spencer to lunch. He is much better than he was at the wedding of Prince Charles and Lady Diana when he could hardly walk up the aisle, though his walking is still slightly odd and he wanders a bit sometimes in his speech. But they are having a very exhausting trip to promote his book about the Far East, which is enough to make anyone wander.

Lady Spencer is a formidable lady. Her two-page c.v. covers activities ranging from working for the GLC to being governor of Covent Garden, to organizing wheelchairs for the disabled, to education. And more recently, since her marriage, she has been running their stately home, Althorp (built by Sir John Spencer in 1508 and lived in ever since by the Spencers), and causing a fair amount of controversy by selling off its priceless heirlooms to pay the bills.

During the Spencers' visit a 14-storey hotel in downtown Singapore collapsed in on itself, or imploded, and many people were buried under the huge weight of concrete. Four Welsh miners working on the new Singapore MRT [Mass Rapid Transport] underground system helped with the massive rescue operation. They were used to tunnelling and worked day and night under very dangerous conditions to pull people out. The victims, who were understandably very shattered, were hospitalized and were not fit to see anyone.

The Singaporean authorities were not too happy about publicizing the disaster or allowing VIPs they could not control to find out too much about it, but Lady Spencer wanted to visit some of the victims and as she wanted to she did. She is like that. But he was very sweet indeed; they were relaxed guests and we enjoyed ourselves. He told me he would like to drive with his grandchildren, whom sadly he did not see as often as he would wish, in toy racing cars down the long corridors of the hospital.

21 April 1986
Andrew's 24th Birthday, Queen's 60th Birthday!
The *Britannia* was in town *en route* to China for the Queen's visit and we were invited to a lovely lunch with the captain in his private dining room with a few of the officers and one or two others. The British Navy really know how to do things in style. The only thing I find rather difficult is trying to look elegant while walking up the wobbly gangway onto their ships in high heels being watched by the welcoming committee of officers and men waiting on deck. Sometimes you even get piped aboard and on those occasions you have to try and look even more elegant.

Michael has been involved with the opening of the Singapore Airlines' flight into Manchester and we were invited to the celebratory dinner. It was done in really elaborate Singaporean fashion with a ballroom, containing several hundred guests, all decked up like a football ground and the whole dinner presented like a football match. Lucy came too, but could not sit with us as we were at the 'top' table. However, I think she had a far jollier and more relaxed time with friends than we did making polite conversation to ministers and other high-powered Singaporeans.

Sunday was spent looking after Mr and Mrs Michael Howard, who is the Under-Secretary of State at the Department of Trade and Industry. Lucy very sensibly escaped with the Lees to Ubin for the day. We drove them sightseeing around Singapore and went to a select official dinner with them in the evening.

The next day Lucy and I took Mrs Howard to lunch at the Tanglin Club near our house. It is a very luxurious old club with a lovely pool in which I try to do my daily half-hour keep-fit swim. She is a very charming and attractive lady. In fact, when visiting the washroom at the airport, Mr Howard came out beaming because he had found a photo of his wife on a soap packet — she used to be a model and had been photographed for Lux soap adverts.

In the afternoon the press once again turned up in droves at our house. The dining room was once again transformed into a studio, and Mr Howard gave a press conference and TV interviews. Then the Howards left and we were able to hear the Wells Cathedral Choir sing at St Andrew's Church. [Little did we know that five years later they would be singing at our son Andrew's wedding with Catherine at Wells Cathedral.]

20 May 1986
We spent an evening with the Italian Navy — one of their ships was passing through — and were most struck by the contrast between our two navies' respective entertainment styles. They were really laid back in their organization. People arrived on time, after driving to the north side of the island, to find nothing but a couple of empty tables and a few streamers crumpled in a pile on the deck. Gradually one or two sailors appeared with a few glasses and eventually a few drinks; there was very little choice and ice, which is a necessity here, was hardly seen at all. The streamers were never put up. Obviously knowing the ways of their navy, their ambassador, Alessandro Vattani, and his wife Francesca did not arrive until we were leaving, when the party looked slightly more promising. They are a very sociable, cultured Italian couple who are fascinated by and very involved in the life and culture of Singapore. [We were later to have a marvellous holiday in Venice in Francesca's *palazzo* on the Grand Canal.]

Michael has been playing golf brilliantly recently. He has won a big competition and got lots of prizes including a super stereo, weekends in luxury hotels, which we shall take up one day, valuable gift vouchers and 150 golf balls. He also got to the last eight in the Singapore open competition and won a prize in a raffle at the dance we went to last Saturday — Guess what? Another stereo! It is nice to have the World Service in three rooms now. The Chinese really believe in luxurious living.

15 June 1986

This will be my last letter before we leave as we arrive on 30 June at 6.25 a.m., to be met by Andrew, and I will ring you when I have got over my sleepless night. Very exciting. It is nearly a year since I was home and I am feeling in need of a break from tropical climes, though the time has gone incredibly quickly.

For the next two weeks we have lunches some days and dinners every day, including two given by us. I suppose I shall survive, but the thought of the two weeks ahead makes me feel quite exhausted.

25 August 1986

Our flight back was good and on time, and after about four days recovering from jet lag life has now returned to normal.

We had HMS *Illustrious* through. This is one of our three British air-craft carriers, which is on a naval exercise with Australia and other countries. We had dinner with the admiral in charge of the exercise and there was also a drinks party on the ship. This was quite an experience as it is so vast and the equipment so modern, complicated and powerful. Russia and the USA have ships three times the size — and the Russians lots of them — but we only have three and one of those is in dry dock. The do on the ship was very grand, with bands playing and officers and guests all looking very smart, except for our High Commissioner, who turned up in baggy black-and-white striped trousers and an open-necked black shirt.

22 September 1986

My friend and neighbour, Inge, the wife of Richard Louis, the German ambassador here, is sadly leaving soon. She is off to Paraguay, which is full of Nazi exiles, and is not looking forward to it one bit. They would far rather retire and have had quite enough diplomatic life — they have had a lot of difficult posts including Teheran and Libya — but are not allowed to until he is 60 without great damage to his pension rights.

21 October 1986

Alessandro Vattani, one of the guests at a dinner we were giving, brought along a visiting Italian musician to entertain us beforehand.

He was an extremely weird gentleman with flowing hair and flowing robes who played the double bass in the most modern and way-out fashion. He played the last piece of music (they were all his own compositions and rather difficult for us to comprehend) bent over on all fours with the instrument lying on the floor in front of him. He is very well known in Italy and he was playing in a very romantic setting — on the terrace in our garden under the full moon surrounded by hibiscus, orchids and bougainvillaea — to very smartly dressed guests, even though all they could see was his backside.

We celebrated Michael's birthday with some banking friends, and with John and Hilary Andrews who have recently arrived in Singapore where he is based as the *Economist*'s Far East correspondent. We started with champagne here followed by dinner at a good French restaurant. [Because of censorship in the Singaporean press, after a year or so the Andrews moved to Hong Kong.]

There was a wonderful phone call from Lucy during our champagne, which was good timing. She had put in 50p, just enough to say 'Happy Birthday Daddy', and something was wrong with the phone box and they went on and on and on talking for about half an hour until they finally decided to stop. Then Lucy pressed Button B and got her 50p back.

30 October 1986

This will be a very short letter as I am trying to learn to work my newly acquired computer — everyone in Singapore has a computer — and keep pressing the wrong keys; but I shall persevere.

The other day we were invited to the races and, after a luxurious lunch in the chairman's box, joined in the Chinese love of gambling. We have been once before. It is very grand and great fun and I join in very happily with the betting and the studying of form, though needless to say my stakes are tiny compared to theirs.

The Chinese gamble on everything. They even have dice on the tables at the golf club to see who will pay for the drinks — there is no question of the winner buying the first round — and of course they play every hole for money.

3 December 1986

Have you heard of gardiosis? I am sorry not to have written since 30 October, but that is the reason.

It all started on our return from Malacca, where we had spent a golfing weekend with a group of businessmen at the beginning of November. It went on and on, getting worse and worse, diarrhoea plus everything else, nothing helped.

Finally, on 21 November I went into hospital on a drip and had massive doses of Flagyl pumped into me. It is foul stuff, which makes you feel even worse. Gardiosis, probably caused by rats, is common in Malaysia and can last for months if not treated. After six days on a drip I came out, feeling pretty weak.

I had thought I would take you to Penang for a few days when you are with us in January, but after this illness I have gone off travel. I think we will all be better off in comparatively safe Singapore.

13 December 1986

Sorry my correspondence has been rather scanty recently, but I really was laid low with this rotten gardiosis. I am slowly, slowly beginning to feel better. The only good thing I can say is that I have lost over a stone and everyone tells me how thin and drawn I am looking.

Sadly this is a rather hectic time of year with lots of dinners. We have been to two dances in an official capacity and on these occasions it is very difficult to leave early and I have to give a large buffet dinner for some visiting MPs.

Lady Wright is at present accompanying her husband, Sir Patrick Wright, who is head of the Diplomatic Service, on an tour of overseas missions. Lady Wright is a charming person who, as president of the DSWA, is interested in learning more about the morale and happiness of wives and women working in the High Commission. Although Singapore is a very comfortable country it can be a boring posting for wives as it is almost impossible to get work here — thank heavens for TEFL — and the charm of heat, sunshine and swimming pools wears off quite quickly: wives are inclined to spend a lot of time away from Singapore and their husbands.

Hope you all have a very happy, jolly Christmas. We shall be thinking of you all as we shall be childless again and the two of us are going to have a completely non-Christmassy Buddhist time in Thailand.

17 December 1986

Have been prostrate again, with gastro-enteritis, probably not connected with my gardiosis. But I struggled around to organize the MP dinner yesterday, then vanished from the scene. Joys of diplomatic life!

27 February 1987

We are now rushing around in circles with all the preparations for leaving. Time is passing incredibly fast and we still have masses of things to do before we leave on 18 March.

But we still do not know what is going to happen next, where we are going to go, or what we are going to do!

In an hour's time I have the whole commercial section of the High Commission, approximately 40, in for a farewell curry lunch. So this letter may be rather disjointed.

We have had several friends to stay, which has been lovely as it has made us put off the evil hour of organizing the packing and farewells until the last ones left. Also, it was fun showing people around Singapore, being tourists ourselves and paying farewell visits to Chinatown, the Bird Park, mosques, temples and grand hotels.

I have just sent out 150 change of address cards for the thirteenth, but not last, time in our married life.

There are so many farewell parties, lunches, dinners and receptions being given for us that it is all utterly exhausting. We give a farewell cocktail for 200 here next Tuesday, which gives me Wednesday to sort out the kitchen and glasses and on Thursday the packers come in to do our heavy luggage.

Lita has just come in about the lunch. We do not seem to have enough plates so I must go next door and borrow some.

So we shall see you very soon now. Marvellous that we shall be back just in time for your golden wedding celebrations. I will ring you. It will be good to have a conversation without that wretched echo and a cost of £1 a minute.

7

Barbados

After Singapore we were told that we would have another overseas posting, though in the event it took five months to receive a firm and acceptable offer. This was as Deputy High Commissioner in Barbados, where Kevin Burns, whom we had been with in Ghana, was High Commissioner. Michael happily agreed.

As the post covered other islands in the Eastern Caribbean (Antigua, St Kitts and Nevis, St Lucia, St Vincent, Grenada and Dominica) and involved a fair amount of travelling, we decided to go for two years, enjoy the Caribbean, then leave the FCO early and settle back in London. Much as we enjoyed diplomatic life we agreed that we had had enough of being overseas and wanted to re-establish our life with our family and friends in the UK. Furthermore, Michael thought that he would more easily obtain another worthwhile job if he left the FCO well before retirement age.

With no revolutions and little violence for some 300 years, Barbados has the most stable history of all the Caribbean islands. It was a British colony until its independence in 1966. With its marvellous beaches, balmy weather and mostly good-natured inhabitants it was no wonder it was a popular international holiday resort. But it was less interesting politically and we were to take every opportunity to pay regular visits to other islands with more pressing problems, including drug trafficking and hurricanes destroying entire banana crops. We arrived in Barbados in August 1987.

24 August 1987
Last night Loretta from St Lucia, our part-time temporary maid, left me

alone in the house, Rosedale, at 6.30 p.m. bolted and barred as if to survive a major siege. Michael was on one of his frequent trips away, to Dominica this time. Loretta had earlier in the day told me that the apartment block over the road had been burgled the previous night when the security guards went off duty.

Michael's equivalent in the US Embassy came to dinner the other night with his wife and were very surprised we did not bolt our front gate at night. They described the security precautions behind which US diplomats have to live, from a direct radio link with Washington by their bedside to guards at their gates 24 hours a day.

Luckily our diplomatic service is a less high-risk occupation than theirs and personally I find Barbados life very relaxed. This is not another Accra, Georgetown or Ankara posting with all their attendant problems. There are burglaries, yes, but so far mostly of the non-violent type. The overriding feel of the country is of complete relaxation, freedom of movement and uncomplicated living in beautiful surroundings.

And here I come, as far as I am concerned, to the biggest attraction of life in Barbados. The setting of our very pleasant house up a quiet little lane at the end of which is a beautiful white coral beach with perfect swimming in the Caribbean, which I think must be the best sea in the world. It sparkles with indescribable changing colours and is free from any of the nasty things seas so often have, like dangerous currents, hungry sharks, painful jellyfish, sewage and oil slicks. Perfect!

Overall, everything works in Barbados given time. But the vital things of life like water, food and electricity are all here. In fact the water is the best I have tasted. It comes fresh from underground springs and beats recycled dubious London water any day.

There are shortages of odd things, for example milk at the moment, and vegetables and fruit are in surprisingly short supply — very little seems to be grown on the island apart from sugar. Luckily our garden has a lot of fruit trees in it and at the moment I am trying to decide what to do with vast quantities of guavas. The prices, which are about three times those of the UK, are the only drawback. In all ways this is an extremely expensive place in which to live.

I have now got a nice little Japanese Suzuki car and am beginning, even with my terrible sense of direction, to find my way around. It makes it much easier when the sea is always close at hand. Bajan drivers are so courteous; they always let people in from side roads, stop to let people cross the roads, or stop in the middle of the road to talk to a passing friend. Consequently the speed of travel is very slow.

There was a lovely introductory party given for us by Kevin Burns, our High Commissioner from Ghana days [whose wife Nan had been tragically killed in a car accident in Ghana after we had left the country]. There were 200 or so present and at the end I remembered precisely no names at all.

Since then there have been some pleasant dinners and drinks, but thankfully not every night. This week we are giving a dinner for 24 for a colleague who is sadly off to Bangladesh, but this will be our first big party and I will be glad when it is over.

Continued on 3 September 1987

And it *is* over and I really do not know why it has taken me nine days to finish this letter. But Barbados is a very laid-back place and things happen in their own time. The dinner was fine, two couples did not turn up and one couple turned up in the middle of the second course. This is apparently typical for Barbados, but we had forgotten what unreliability was after three years of Chinese efficiency in Singapore.

24 September 1987

Our official policy is now to be 'friendly with the Chinese', who have a surprisingly large presence here. We were invited to a very long evening of table tennis and supper at their Embassy, followed by a film of open heart surgery with acupuncture, in which the patient smiled happily and talked away as needles were plunged into his aorta. They are very good at table tennis, but not very good at English, and speaking through interpreters makes for very slow conversations. Nevertheless, everyone smiled at everyone throughout, even without the help of alcohol, and the food was delicious.

22 October 1987

The USA, the UK and many Caribbean governments are becoming increasingly worried about the growing trade in hard drugs in the region, particularly crack. Drugs are already a great problem in Barbados, with the beaches making very good selling places to the tourists.

The East Caribbean islands, indeed all the Caribbean islands (independent, French and Dutch) make handy staging posts for changing planes and boats and for switching shipments of drugs from Latin America — turn left for Miami or turn right for Europe.

The drug trade is carried out in a whole range of ways, from transferring baggage at international airports like Barbados to switching boats in the remote inlets of underpopulated islands, from bribing policemen and other guards to look the other way to nobbling politicians and influencing government elections and import policies. Trying to control all this is a major task in which the UK is extremely involved, especially in supplying experienced police and sniffer dogs.

We had a lovely few days in Grenada, which we last visited when in Guyana. It is as beautiful as ever, but politically still dodgy after the US invasion in October 1983. At all the dinners and parties we went to — it was a business trip — the talk was about the government, the economy and the future.

Compared with Barbados the poverty is noticeable. You just do not see people in Barbados without shoes — well, hardly ever. But as always these things are relative and Grenada is still a most lush island. But sadly for its economy, there have not been many tourists since the 'trouble', 'confrontation', 'war' — it goes under many names.

I am still not sure whether or not to keep my 'maid', Shirley. She is Guyanese and it is very difficult for her to get a work permit over here unless it is for diplomatic work. She has two children whom she has left with her mother in Guyana and a husband, also left in Guyana, who used to beat her up and from whom she wishes to escape for safety's sake.

But she has very little clue about anything useful like making a bed, ironing, or cleaning, though she is quite keen on cooking from time to time and eats vast quantities of food. She moves very slowly — she is very overweight — but smiles most of the time, which makes up for an awful lot and it is very useful to have someone around.

The alternative would be a local lady, who would come in daily for a few hours only, would cost an awful lot and would frequently not turn up. Lita, from Singapore, still wants to join us, but the air fares alone would cost us a fortune. Also, she would be very lonely and would certainly not be accepted by the local community.

31 October 1987
Here we are very out of touch with the goings-on in the world and, as

ever, rely on the World Service news, apart from information coming through from the FCO.

At 6.00 a.m. on Black Monday [the collapse of the stock exchange in London] we had a phone call from Jean-Pierre [my French brother-in-law] from Paris telling us (a) they could not come and stay for the time being and (b) to sell any shares we had.

We did not know what he was talking about and tried to phone London, but needless to say it was quite impossible at that stage to get through to anyone or do anything. I can imagine the chaos and confusion reigning in Singapore amongst all our friends in banking and finance.

Andrew has arrived on holiday. It is lovely having him here and he is being indoctrinated into diplomatic life with a series of cocktail parties and dinners.

28 November 1987

Once a week I go to the children's ward at the hospital to unlock the toy cupboards and hand round toys. Otherwise the children do not have anything to play with. It is very tempting to leave some of the toys out when I leave, but sadly I have to be very fierce and lock them all up again or everything vanishes.

The hospital is a lot better than, say, Ghana, but pretty basic, with very large wards, iron bedsteads and buckets to catch the rain from the leaking roofs. To visit Great Ormond Street Hospital would be like entering another world. There are two children in the ward with hydrocephalus and some other badly deformed ones, but some have normal childhood problems such as broken bones, tonsils and appendicitis.

But the worst case is a poor little girl from one of the islands whose parents have both died of Aids. She is HIV positive and no one knows what to do with her. She is imprisoned in a cot in a cell-like room with no windows; the nurses are too terrified to go near her and if they have to they put on masks and gloves. I think she is about seven, but she can hardly speak and is incontinent. If we hand her toys or books, within seconds she will have thrown them onto the floor. They are trying to move her out — but where to? Aids is only beginning to be a problem here, but no doubt it will spread rapidly.

It is also a problem to get helpers for the children's ward. Some people try and find it too depressing, but after the leper colony in Guyana and the starving children in Ghana I do not find it too bad, but am always glad to get home afterwards.

The country is full of 21st independence celebrations at the moment. There was a very colourful Trooping the Colour last weekend and this weekend we have all sorts of events to attend, including vast receptions, cathedral services and a fireworks spectacular. Things start reasonably punctually here, not quite like Singapore but an awful lot better than Ghana. Needless to say lots has been going on in the cricket and golf worlds as well. We watched one star-studded cricket match (with cricketers from Sir Garfield Sobers downwards) from the president's box and were given lots of rum to add to the pleasure.

11 January 1988

It is marvellous having Tim here. He is staying until 9 February, two days after his 28th birthday. This will be the first time he will have spent his birthday with us for 20 years.

Christmas was lovely too and having Tim around made a great change after three childless Christmasses in Singapore, though we missed Andrew and Lucy. Now we have Rozy and Jean-Pierre [my sister and brother-in-law] and Catherine and Sebastien [their children] here and Rosedale Hotel is really underway.

19 March 1988

We have been waiting for three weeks now for the stone in Michael's kidney to pass. He has been in almost continual agonizing pain and has been taking various pills and pethidine by the handful.

Needless to say the only treatment they have in this country is to cut you open. They have none of the modern blasting or wire claws they have in the UK, so I am continually wondering whether he should go home. But our doctor, a Bajan, has said that he should carry on and that it will eventually pass by itself. He had an IVP at the hospital yesterday and was told that the stone was still in exactly the same place. So all that agony has achieved nothing.

Anyway it has all been very difficult and one is never quite sure that the doctors know what they are doing. They do, however, have a lot of knowledge about kidney stones here, as they are apparently very common due to dehydration and the high calcium content of the water.

The weather has been beautiful — no rain for ages and lovely breezes. At this time of the year the gardener vanishes for three months to cut cane and the watering takes me hours every day, but if I don't do it everything dies.

26 March 1988

We have decided to fly home on the first available flight so that Michael can get some proper treatment. This is going against the local doctor's advice, but after four weeks he is as ill as ever with no sign of the stone passing, and the only possible treatment here is to cut him open. [We stayed in England for two weeks and, following successful treatment, returned to Barbados.]

19 May 1988

I have fallen in love with Dominica. It is unspoilt and beautiful and the Minister of State, Mrs Eugenia Charles, is a very impressive and charming lady who manages to get more aid and help for her country than any other in the region. She is a great admirer of Maggie Thatcher, but manages better than Maggie because both men and women like her.

We were there to present the Caribs, who are rather backward and scarcely assimilated into Dominican life, with a health centre in the middle of the country, or bush. The 'Callinogos', who were renamed 'Carib' by the Europeans, were a nomadic warlike race from South America who replaced the Arawaks in the Caribbean around AD 1000. There are very few of them left and, apart from the organizers, did not appear to be very interested in their new health centre. However, as the ceremony progressed and the Prime Minister, Michael and others made their speeches, more and more of them came — literally out of the jungle and trees — and, with some amazement, watched the goings on. To judge from their reactions, it seems unlikely that much use will be made of the new health centre in the immediate future.

We then went on to open an agricultural health centre and were given a large box of the most delicious grapefruit I have ever tasted.

Back in Barbados life continues as usual. We are busy every night for ten days, including two large dinners here.

6 June 1988

It is very hot now, 89 to 90 degrees, but at last we have air conditioning installed, which is lovely — except now when we have an electricity cut. The garden is parched with the drought and we are not allowed to water, so everything is dying and it all reminds me of Africa.

Michael is much better and is playing quite a lot of tennis in the evenings for his club, Summerhayes. It is a small club, mainly for Bajans, with two tennis courts and a small shed to provide shade and a bar for gentle relaxation. This is where the members, who include some leading civil servants, lawyers and businessmen, play cards and engage in insider chat about the political scene and idle or serious (though discreet) gossip about everything from the shortage of X-ray films at the hospitals to cricket and more cricket. Rather like a well-behaved club anywhere, it is an enjoyable place in which to relax and learn, but it is considered bad form to be seen to be striving too officiously to pick up information for professional purposes.

The FCO inspection team is here from London. This is an extremely unpopular group of five or six people who visit each post every four years or so to see what is going on and to decide what should be going on. Wherever we have been, on their departure they have invariably announced that staff and allowances are going to be cut. They have to compare costs of living here with costs of living in Bromley and ensure that we are not one penny better off than we would be if we were living in Bromley and working in Whitehall on a home posting. It is depressing and demoralizing. I am on a committee that deals with expenses and have to itemize every cent I spend on living and entertainment — on meat, vegetables, fruit, salt, bread, pepper, domestic help, candles, soap powder, garden, electricity and water. I have done it so often now that I am quite experienced, but it still gets worse every time.

I will ring you when I arrive home in two weeks.

7 October 1988
I had a very comfortable flight back and Michael met me on arrival with the news that Hurricane Helene was probably on its way. You will have heard about devastating Hurricane Gilbert. I said I would get the next plane back, but didn't. Instead I stacked up on candles, water and tinned food and checked the fastenings on all the doors and windows. Thankfully Hurricane Helene missed us, but it was a dicey weekend with very strong winds.

Rosedale Hotel should be closed in October and November. Here it has been raining since friends arrived four days ago. And today it is raining so much that the schools are closed and the roads flooded. Our guests have really had bad luck so far. The BWIA flight they came in on was 48 hours late and they had to spend two nights in a Heathrow hotel.

I am just about to set off for my hospital visit through the torrential rain. But on second thoughts, since all the schools are closed and people are advised to stay at home if they can, and the children's ward will be so depressing with the leaking roofs and not enough buckets to go around to catch all the rain, I may miss it this week.

25 October 1988

Now that I have become the DSWA's liaison officer I am getting organized with wives' coffee mornings and tea parties.

The DSWA, which is effectively our union, is important in many ways, from trying to lift morale generally to putting pressure on the FCO to fly children out for every school holiday and to settle other family matters.

It is surprising how many people are unhappy, even in a posting like Barbados, but then the wives suffer from boredom because it is virtually impossible to get a job here.

I had lunch with a Canadian friend this week and she says she does the same sort of work for her High Commission and is paid for it.

22 November 1988

You should be getting, or have got, depending on Caribbean mail services, a postcard from Martinique. We had a lovely few days there and thoroughly enjoyed the place with its mixture of France and the Caribbean. In lots of ways it is very different from the Caribbean we know; it is still a French department and you see bits of France everywhere.

I also discovered how nice the Caribbean is for a real holiday. It was lovely not to have to go anywhere, to do what we wanted and not to have to make polite conversation with everybody. The only official thing we did was to meet an English girl married to a white Martinican Frenchman who is going to be appointed as our honorary consul. She will be paid approximately £1000 a year and will be able to help in emergencies and help businessmen with enquiries.

It is amazing how popular we are now; we have guests to stay until the end of February.

29 November 1988

This is a rushed letter to catch the post before our Independence Day holiday tomorrow. This is a bad week. Yesterday I chaired a meeting of our wives' union. Today there is a farewell lunch for a leaving member of staff, cooked by me. Then there are independence celebrations and functions all day, starting at 7.30 a.m. On Thursday there is an official lunch here for 12, cooked by me for people I do not know. On Friday there is the hospital all morning and cocktails and dinner in the evening. On Saturday there is another dinner, and then preparations for cocktails for 150 people here next week.

Shirley is sweet, but has not a clue about entertaining. She often vanishes in the middle of a dinner when it is time to clear away and serve the pudding; I then find her up in her room and have to persuade her to come and help. This can be very difficult when I am trying to have an intelligent conversation with some government minister or whoever. She then vanishes again and I have to find her once more to give me a hand with the coffee.

10 January 1989

Just recovering from Christmas and New Year and exhaustion. We were so lucky to have Tim and Andrew with us, and we spoke to Lucy on the phone.

The Caribbean goes wild at this time and there are endless visitors passing through. Over three weeks we have had more than 200 people to the house, so my long list of people to whom we owe hospitality is now much shorter. There is far too much to do, especially as I now seem to end up doing all the cooking myself and really do not mind if I never see 90 per cent of the guests again.

One of the dinners I did really enjoy though was with Ted and Sue Dexter. He was over here on a golf tournament and we all met up for the first time in 30 years. He is now a born-again Christian and much mellowed since Michael and he played cricket together for three years at Cambridge. [Shortly afterwards Dexter became chairman of the test selectors.] Sue, his wife, who was an extremely glamorous model, and I used to watch our boyfriends playing cricket together and on one occasion we followed the team on tour, which in the 1950s was a rather *risqué* thing to do. Also present was Henry Cooper, the very famous retired heavyweight professional boxer, who has been a company director since 1972 and whose hobby now is golf. He is very sweet, natural and charming, and he has a lively Italian wife whom he met years ago working in the café in London where he used to eat.

Last Saturday evening Michael and I flew over to St Vincent, spent the night there with our representative, then next morning flew to a little island in the Grenadines which had just opened an airstrip with British aid. The ceremony lasted for two hours, in the blazing sun, with no shade or anywhere to sit, and the longest speech was 40 minutes' long. There were further functions on the Sunday afternoon, then we had great problems getting on the six-seater from the island to St Vincent to catch up with the Liat flight and were finally home at midnight. I rather wished I had missed that trip!

Tonight I give a dinner for ten, only two of whom I know, and the rest I shall never see again. I have another very useful recipe from a friend of chicken and broccoli in a mayonnaise sauce. I churn it out frequently nowadays as it seems to feed a lot of people and, most important, we can always get local chickens here.

11 March 1989

Yesterday we met the Queen at Government House; she is lovely — tiny, pretty, charming, so natural and I was very, very impressed by her. She takes such an interest in the people she talks to and really wants to hear all about you. The Duke has behaved very well on this trip and has not lost his temper once. She is a guest of the government and certainly has a busy schedule. There is no swimming pool at Government House, where they stayed, so I doubt if she even had one swim.

The winter visitors have continued. Michael had three days in Grenada with Baroness Trumpington, who is the Junior Minister of Agriculture. I met her at lunch before they went off together. She is a larger than life ebullient lady with no side and the West Indians can identify well with her. Michael found her a great travelling companion.

Look forward to seeing you in a few weeks' time.

26 May 1989

I could not believe how hot it was here. A blanket of dampness greeted me when I got off the plane from Heathrow. It really knocked me out for the first week. It was 30 to 31 degrees and very humid.

But nothing had changed in the five weeks I was away. When I left the main topic of conversation was whether or not Macdonalds should be allowed to open in Barbados and when I returned the main topic of conversation was whether or not Macdonalds should be allowed to open in Barbados!

If I look very hard on the inside pages of the *Advocate* I might find a small item on the Beijing Tiananmen Square massacre two days ago.

There was an amateur production of *Run for Your Wife*, and the best thing about it was the audience participation. The Bajans, who are normally staid, reserved and sometimes rather sullen, really got involved with the plot, and their laughter, stamping and cheering and literally rolling in the aisles made it a memorable evening.

I am now having to think about packing up. The date is fixed for 3 September. I am hoping to go to Antigua, St Kitts and Nevis, as these are the only islands we cover I have not visited. These will no doubt be the last occasions on which we shall have casual lunches with Prime Ministers.

15 June 1989

US vice-president Dan Quayle has just cancelled his trip to Barbados because the authorities here seem incapable of organizing beds in two hotels for the vice-presidential party of 120 people. They had assured John Clark, who is the chargé at the US Embassy here, that reservations would be made for the party, but on checking the situation the Embassy found not nearly enough bookings had been made and were told by the authorities in charge that they had other things to do and other visitors to organize for the forthcoming celebrations of 350 years of Parliament in Barbados.

Shirley, our Guyanese maid, was stopped in the street in Bridgetown by plain clothes immigration chaps and questioned. They did not believe her account of working for us with a work permit and took her down to the police station where she underwent further roughish, rude questioning. They finally let her go when she told them to contact our High Commissioner for verification.

Since the massacre at Beijing there has been no sign of any Chinese Embassy staff on the beach where they are allowed to come and swim *en masse* at a routine time each evening. They are definitely keeping a very low profile after Tiananmen Square. I miss my swim with the wife of the Chinese No. 2. She is very friendly and we often swim up and

down together, during which I learn about life in China and she prac-
tises her English, which is getting a lot better.

When her husband was appointed here she had to leave their six-
year-old child behind in China with his grandparents. She has not seen
him for over three years and has no idea when they will be going back
to Beijing. When she does return she will have no alternative but to go
back to her original job of working endless hours each day in a factory
one and a half hours away from home. She would love to have more
children, but seems to accept very calmly that one is the limit. Apparently this limit is imposed far less strictly on people living in the countryside, where there is less supervision.

24 June 1989

We went to a reception on an enormous British ship, HMS *Intrepid*,
and saw the Chinese ambassador walking around looking lost. He came
up to talk to the High Commissioner and me and was full of smiles. He
does not use an interpreter and his English is quite good. He was very
anxious to explain to us that what had happened in China recently made
no difference to the country's relations with the outside world and that
the sit-in at Tiananmen Square had involved only a tiny proportion of
the population. This was obviously the official explanation.

So I asked him why the action of such a tiny proportion needed such
massive and violent action against it? He looked embarrassed and waf-
fled away confusedly about the lack of any real violence and about how
very few people had been killed.

He told me that the husband of the lady I used to swim with had now
been posted back to Beijing and that she is now working in the factory
she left three years ago. But he said she is quite happy and accepts it.
What was the point of all her efforts to learn English? I wish I had been
able to say goodbye to her.

The ambassador had always seemed so civilized and friendly, but I
doubt we shall be having any more table tennis tournaments between
the Chinese Embassy and the British High Commission, with snacks
and soft drinks to follow, for some time.

27 June 1989

We went to another naval reception, this time on an enormous US naval
ship, USS *Wainwright*. At the bottom of the gangway we were asked

for our name and position. An officer with a radio sent a message to the top of the gangway. As we started our ascent, not too wobbly but the steps needed concentrated effort to avoid embarrassing stumbling, a large brass bell was tolled loudly for us over the very effective Tannoy system. Mr and Mrs James were announced and 20 sailors on deck stood extremely smartly to attention and we marched to the receiving line in honour and glory.

US ideas of food are certainly original. For a reception at 7.00 p.m. the tables were laden with popcorn, smarties, ginger cookies with cheese dips, prawns, very small slices of tinned ham and processed cheese. But fortunately on this occasion the teetotal US Navy provided beer and wine for those like us who cannot survive such occasions without alcoholic help.

28 June 1989

We went to an interesting dinner with colleagues at which all the other guests were middle-aged to elderly white Bajans. Their conversation so often dwells on their future in Barbados and the threat of black take-overs on all fronts. They are frightened too, and often carry guns in their cars for self-protection. This is the most colour-conscious country we have lived in. There is mixing of black and white on official occasions, but their private lives are kept separate and rarely do they enter each other's houses.

Our American neighbour told me today that her white Bajan brother-in-law and his wife who live opposite us are so nervous that at dusk each evening they lock up their house, close the shutters and do not venture out again till the morning.

There is a Caribbean crisis on at the moment. During meetings at the police headquarters in Grenada, a policeman on loan to the Grenada Police Force from St Vincent went wild and killed the Grenadian commissioner and deputy commissioner and a US diplomat, and injured two other policemen. He then either killed himself or was killed by another policeman. The Vincentian was unpopular and the Grenadians had reportedly been asking him to return to St Vincent. There are talks of drug involvement.

The CARICOM conference next week is due to take place in Grenada. The Prime Minister of St Vincent has said it should now take place somewhere else. The Prime Minister of Antigua, Mr Bird, who is a member of the rather suspect Bird family, also seems unhappy about the venue. The Prime Minister of St Lucia, sensible John Compton, says it should continue as planned. This shows the frailty and lack of friendship between the Eastern Caribbean islands and the necessity for Britain, America and Canada to continue to look after these islands as an awful lot can still go wrong.

6 July 1989

We have had two farewell trips to our resident representatives. The first was to Antigua, St Kitts and Nevis — the latter was unspoilt and peaceful and we adored it — and the second was to St Vincent and St Lucia. They were very busy trips as they averaged only 36 hours each, and flying by Liat is always awful. We had one good flight on Air Martinique. It left ten minutes early and we were the only passengers, but sadly that does not happen often. There were farewell parties and farewell calls to be made. I caught heat stroke one day in St Lucia after having spent two hours on a beach; I felt terrible, but had to recover for a dinner in our honour that night. I just cannot take heat or sun like I used to.

The news has now broken that we are off on 3 September, which makes life much easier. Now the preparations start.

20 August 1989

Now there is the usual rush of farewell parties. We shall give one large party the night before the packers come in.

My main problem is the piano. It is far too large to take home as we would never get it up the stairs in Highgate. I have two Bajans who say they would like to buy it, but though I am constantly chasing them the money is never forthcoming and there are always hitches. If I have to bring it home all our effects will have to come by sea; if I don't they will be flown back. I can now see how difficult it is to do business in the Caribbean; nothing ever happens when it should and even efficient-looking Bajans are extremely inefficient when action is needed.

But it is a lovely place for holidaying and relaxing. I enclose our change of address card. It is the fourteenth I have sent out since we were married and this time, hopefully, it will really be the final one.

8

Back Home

And it was the final one. We returned to live in London, Michael
started work with the Timber Trade Federation and as director
of the Forest Forever Campaign and the adjustment to
permanent living in England began. It took a while. For a long time I
would go walking on Parliament Hill, with its views over London,
filled with happiness but not really able to believe that we were here to
stay.

Every two or three years during our Foreign Service life when a
move was on the cards I would feel a restlessness or 'itchy feet' and
begin to wonder where we would go next. But since returning from
Barbados, although we have now been home for five years, which is the
longest we have lived anywhere since our marriage in 1959, this has
not happened. I think now we are well and truly settled and the urge for
travel is completely satisfied.

Index